D1500968

BASIC SKILLS FOR THE
WORKPLACE

READING FOR INFORMATION ▪ APPLIED MATHEMATICS ▪ LOCATING INFORMATION

Career Readiness Preparation

McGraw Hill Education

Bothell, WA • Chicago, IL • Columbus, OH • New York, NY

Cover Photo: (l)Christine Balderas/Photodisc/Getty Images;
(r)Michael Hitoshi/Stockbyte/Getty Images

www.mheonline.com

 **Education**

Send all inquiries to:
Contemporary/McGraw-Hill
130 East Randolph St., Suite 400
Chicago, IL 60601

ISBN 978-0-07-661062-4
MHID 0-07-661062-4

Printed in the United States of America.

8 9 10 11 12 LHS 22 21 20 19 18 17

The *McGraw-Hill* Companies

Contents ...

Introduction ...

You need certain basic skills in order to be competitive in the workplace and in society. *Basic Skills for the Workplace* is designed to help you strengthen the basic skills that you already have. It will also help you gain new skills. By completing this program, you will be better prepared for everyday living and workplace functions. This will allow for greater confidence, career success, and mobility.

Basic Skills for the Workplace is the beginning program in the *Workplace Skills: Career Readiness Preparation* series. This book provides instruction and practice in three key subject areas: Reading for Information, Applied Mathematics, and Locating Information. Each subject area is in a separate section. The lessons in the book will guide you through two skill levels for each subject area. The skills you build in these levels will help you succeed as you pursue further education and training.

All the scenarios are taken from real workplace situations. You may have experienced similar situations. They are designed to help you to identify, understand, and solve basic workplace problems. The problems refer to industry-specific careers in a wide range of career clusters, such as information technology, manufacturing, health science, marketing, government and public administration, and architecture and construction.

Each lesson contains explanations of the skills and gives step-by-step examples to illustrate them. *Skill Practice* problems provide support as you practice the skills. This prepares you for the *On Your Own* problems at the end of each lesson.

Photo: Image Source/Getty Images

Basic Skills for the Workplace

When working through the lessons, look for useful information in the *Remember!* and *Skill Support* sidebar notes. These assist you in building your skills. The *Remember!* notes remind you of basic skills. The *Skill Support* notes help you strengthen your skills so you can better answer the questions.

There are *Performance Assessments* at the end of each level of each subject area. These assessments allow you to practice what you have learned. Check your answers at the back of the book. Your teacher will give you *Performance Assessment Tracking Charts* and a *Performance Assessment Student Self-Monitoring* chart for each level of each subject. These charts will signal the areas that you may need to review.

The answers to all the *Skill Practice, On Your Own,* and *Performance Assessment* questions are in the Answer Key at the end of the book. There is also a Glossary of all the Key Words from all the lessons.

After you have completed *Basic Skills for the Workplace,* you will be ready to move on to higher levels in the individual books in the series: *Reading for Information, Applied Mathematics,* and *Locating Information.*

Two-Step Approach

Different problems require the use of different skills. However, you can solve all problems using the two-step approach. The two-step approach to problem solving is an easy-to-follow model. You can use it to solve problems you come across in the workplace and on a career readiness certificate test. This will help you be more confident and reduce errors. The *Try It Out!* section of each lesson models the two-step approach using the lesson skill.

 ## Understand the Problem

The first step is Understand the Problem. Before approaching any problem, you must be sure you understand what you are being asked to do. You must identify important information and key words or symbols. Use the *Plan for Successful Solving.* Ask yourself three questions: *What am I asked to do? What are the facts? How do I find the answer?* This is a way to organize the information and solve the problem.

 ## Find (and Check) Your Answer

The second step is Find Your Answer in Reading for Information and Locating Information. In Applied Mathematics, this step is Find and Check Your Answer. Sometimes finding the right answer may require you to change your first plan. You must solve the problem and then review it to see if you are correct. First pick the best answer choice. Then take another look at the original problem. Be sure your answer makes sense.

Reading for Information …

R eading for information is an essential workplace skill. Written materials are everywhere. You read signs and directions on the road. You read notices, e-mails, and memos at work. You are expected to communicate through written text. You must understand information in these materials.

The level of reading you need is often basic. For example, you might need to identify the main idea in an e-mail. You might have to figure out what a word means in a memo. At other times you may need to read more complex documents.

Workplace Skills: Basic Skills for the Workplace contains lessons that help you develop and improve your reading skills. It will also help you apply them in the workplace. All examples in this book are based on real workplace documents. Each lesson has step-by-step examples of how to perform a skill. You are given the opportunity to try the skill on your own. You will also learn to use the two-step approach to problem solving.

Level 1

Level 2

Photo: SelectStock/Getty Images

Two-Step Approach ...

It is important to learn how to approach reading for information questions. You can answer them using two steps. First you must be sure you understand the question. You must identify important information and key words. Then you need to find and check your answer. The two-step approach to problem solving is an easy-to-follow model. It can also be used on a career readiness certificate test.

Here is an example. You work as a cook. You receive the following e-mail message. What is the main idea of the e-mail?

From:	Supervisor
To:	Employees
Subject:	Vacation Days

Ask your supervisor in advance if you need to take vacation days. We are very busy this time of year. Give three-weeks notice for any time off in the next month. This is longer than the normal two-week notice.

Step 1 Understand the Question ▪ ▪ ▪

Complete the *Plan for Successful Solving.*

Plan for Successful Solving

What am I asked to do?	What are the facts?	How do I find the answer?
Determine what information you are being asked to find. This is usually found in the question. You need to find the main idea.	Identify what information is shown in the document. This will help you determine the passage's purpose. The topic of the e-mail is vacation days.	Determine where in the document the answer can be found. Context clues can help. Find the most important idea about vacation days.

Step 2 Find Your Answer ▪ ▪ ▪

- Review the facts. You need to find the main idea. Use the topic to help figure out the main idea.

- The topic of the e-mail is vacation days.

The main idea of the e-mail is to ask employees to give advance notice if they need to take vacation days.

Skill Support

The **main idea** is
the most important
idea in a passage or
document. It might be
in the subject line or
the title. The main idea
may also be stated in
a sentence. This is the
topic sentence. Other
sentences in a passage
give details. The main
idea is general enough
to relate to all the
details in the passage.
The details may include
facts and examples.
They may tell more
about the main idea.

Remember!

There may be several
ideas in a document.
The main idea is the
most important one.
The other ideas help to
support the main idea.
They may also explain
the main idea.

Lesson 1 ...
Identify Main Idea

Skill: Identify main ideas in workplace documents

You see many kinds of documents at work. Training manuals help explain
procedures. Memos are used to send information. Coworkers share
messages in e-mails. To understand these documents, you must read
them carefully. Look for the main idea. The main idea is what the passage
or document is about. It is the most important idea in the passage or
document. It is often located in the subject line or the first sentence of a
paragraph. It may also be located elsewhere in a paragraph.

In order to identify the main idea of a passage or paragraph, you must be
able to do the following:

- Identify stated ideas.
- Identify the location of main ideas.

Skill Examples ■ ■ ■

EXAMPLE 1   Identify the stated main idea in a workplace document.
The main idea is what the document is about. What is the main idea of
this e-mail and where is it?

E-mail Message

From: Store Manager
To: Stock Clerks
Subject: Pay Attention to Expiration Dates

Stock Clerks,

Most grocery items are stamped with a date. This is the expiration date.
It is the last day the product can be sold. Place newer items at the back
of the shelf. Move older items to the front. This helps to sell items before
the expiration date. Look for items with expiration dates that have passed.
Remove those items.

Thank you.

- Read the e-mail. The location of the main idea can vary.
- The first sentence of a paragraph is often the main idea. The main
  idea might come at the end of a document, though. Or it could be
  somewhere in the middle.
- The subject line is often the main idea.

The main idea in this e-mail is "pay attention to expiration dates." This is
the subject line.

EXAMPLE 2 Recognize the main idea at the beginning of a paragraph.
What is the main idea of this e-mail and where is it?

E-mail Message

From: Human Resources

To: New Employees

Subject: Welcome

New Employees,

Our employees have a dress code. According to the dress code, you must wear black pants. You must also wear a white button-down shirt. If you have questions about the dress code, please e-mail me. I am happy to answer them. Welcome to the company.

Thank you.

- Read the e-mail. Many documents have the main idea at the beginning. This helps readers understand the document.
- The rest of the paragraph has details that support the main idea.
- This message explains what employees should wear to work.

This e-mail is about the dress code. The first sentence is the main idea of the e-mail.

EXAMPLE 3 Recognize the main idea elsewhere in a paragraph.
What is the main idea of this memo and where is it?

MEMO

Company Smoking Policy

Attention all employees: Previously, smoking was permitted on the sidewalk next to the building. Last week the employee health committee held a meeting. At the meeting, they changed this policy. Smoking is no longer permitted on the sidewalk next to the building. This policy begins on Monday. If you have any questions about this policy, contact health@workplace.com.

Thank you.

- Read the memo. Often the main idea is in the subject line of a message. Sometimes it is in the first sentence. The main idea may also be in the middle of the paragraph. It may be at the end of the paragraph.
- To find the main idea, find the topic sentence. This is what the document is about.
- Find the most important idea.

The main idea is that smoking is no longer permitted on the sidewalk next to the building. It is the fourth sentence.

Remember!
To understand a document, look for the main idea. To find the main idea, look for the topic first. The topic is the subject of the document. Then ask yourself what the most important point about the topic is. This will help you find the main idea. Sometimes the main idea is not stated directly. You must figure it out from the details.

Skill Support
To find the main idea, use these tips:
- Think about how the details relate to one another.
- Think about what unites the details.
- Identify the main idea. Then reread the document to confirm your choice.

Skill Practice ...■■

Read the workplace documents. Then answer the questions.

From:	Project Manager
To:	Site Foreperson
Subject:	Remember to Complete the Daily Report

Before leaving the construction site each day, be sure to complete the daily report.
1. List all workers who come to the site. Include information about the work they complete.
2. Describe any problems you have on the site. This includes problems with equipment.
3. Provide information about all phone calls.
4. Describe the work completed during the day.

1. You are the site foreperson. You received this e-mail from your manager. What is the main idea of the e-mail?

   A. Remember to complete the daily report.

   B. List all workers who come to the site.

   C. Describe any problems you have on the site.

   D. Provide information about all phone calls.

   E. Describe the work completed during the day.

   HINT: The main idea is the main point of the document.

From:	Laura Parnel, Director
To:	All Preschool Teachers
Subject:	Attention

Please help prevent the spread of pink eye in the school. A child in the 3-year-old class has conjunctivitis. *Conjunctivitis* is known as "pink eye." It is not dangerous, but it is very contagious. Children share toys. They can pass the disease on the toys. If a child in your class has itchy, red eyes, please ask a parent to take the child to the doctor. The doctor will order eyedrops. If you have questions, please call me.

2. You are a teacher at a preschool. All the teachers in your school received this e-mail. Where is the main idea in the notice?

   F. in the subject line

   G. in the first sentence

   H. in the subject line and the first sentence

   J. in the third sentence

   K. in the eighth sentence

   HINT: Sometimes the main idea is at the beginning of the document.

Try It Out! ▪▪▪

Construction Worker You are roofing a building. The site manager wrote a memo. Your coworker is out sick. He asks you about the memo. You want to tell him the most important point. What is the main idea of the memo?

| From: | Site Manager |
| To: | All Site Workers |

I have an important issue to discuss. We need to prioritize workplace safety. All workers must wear hard hats at all times. Wear proper footwear while at the work site. There are three fire extinguishers at the site. Please learn their locations. Finally watch for construction debris.

A. There are three fire extinguishers at the site.

B. I have an important issue to discuss.

C. We need to prioritize workplace safety.

D. All workers must wear hard hats at all times.

E. Watch for construction debris.

 Step 1 ## Understand the Question ▪▪▪

Complete the *Plan for Successful Solving.*

Plan for Successful Solving

What am I asked to do?	What are the facts?	How do I find the answer?
Find the main idea.	The topic is workplace safety.	Find the most important idea about workplace safety.

 Step 2 ## Find Your Answer ▪▪▪

- Review the facts. You need to find the main idea. Use the topic to help.

- The topic of the memo is workplace safety. The memo asks workers to prioritize workplace safety. This is the main idea.

- Before selecting an answer to the problem, read the question again. Be sure your answer makes sense.

- **Select the correct answer:** C. We need to prioritize workplace safety. You read the memo carefully. You identified the topic. Then you identified the most important idea about the topic. This is the main idea.

Remember!
Be sure to read the passage carefully. Study each sentence and look for details. Think about the main idea of the message.

Skill Support
Some documents state a topic or subject. The topic or subject is usually given at the beginning of the document. Documents may also contain titles and headings. They can help you find the main idea. For example, a topic may be "shift change." Look for ideas about a shift change. The main idea will be the most important idea about the topic.

On Your Own ■ ■ ■

Read the workplace documents and answer the questions.

MEMO

From: Building Supervisor

To: All Employees

Closing the Office

This is to remind everyone of the procedures for closing. If you are the last to leave, secure the office for the night. Follow these steps:

First turn off all daytime equipment. Shut down the computers. Next switch the phones to voice mail. Turn on the office alarm. Turn off the office lights. Turn off the hallway lights. Finally lock the office door.

The evening security guard will escort you to your parked car, if needed.

---

1. **Medical Transcriptionist** You are the last worker to leave the office. What is the main idea of the memo?

   A. building supervisor

   B. office closing

   C. office equipment

   D. evening security guard

   E. parked cars

2. **Travel Agent** You prepare to close the office. What is the main idea of the second paragraph?

   F. equipment needing to be turned on

   G. shutting down the computers

   H. an escort to the car

   J. steps to follow

   K. ways to lock up

> **MEMO**
>
> From: Supervisor
> To: Employees
>
> ### Holiday Hours
>
> Our hours are longer during the holidays. We are also open on all holidays.
>
> Ask your manager in advance if you need days off. Give three weeks' notice for holidays. This is longer than the normal two weeks' notice.
>
> Make your requests for overtime now. This is a great opportunity to make extra money. Tell your manager if you want to work overtime.

3. **Cook** You want to work more hours. What is the main idea of this memo?

   A. vacation days

   B. the holiday party

   C. holiday hours

   D. the new schedule

   E. overtime hours

4. **Waiter** You want some days off over the holidays. What is the main idea of the second paragraph?

   F. working longer hours

   G. giving two weeks' notice

   H. making overtime requests

   J. asking for days off

   K. making extra money

5. **Bus Person** You want to work some extra hours. What is the main idea of the last paragraph?

   A. working holiday hours

   B. asking for days off

   C. requesting overtime

   D. making more money

   E. asking for a raise

E-mail Message

From: United Farm Laborers (UFL)

To: Local Farmers

Subject: Grant Money Available

Local farmers can now apply for grants. Read on to learn more.

The grants offer between $500 and $15,000. The amount depends on the size of the farm.

Your application must show how the farm meets local needs. Your project should address a specific problem and attain measurable goals. Experts should support your project. You should get recommendations from the local farm bureau.

Send grant applications to UFL. Contact UFL to learn more about sending applications.

---

6. **Farm Labor Contractor** You discuss this e-mail with another contractor. What is its main idea?

    F. local farms

    G. the UFL

    H. available grants

    J. local needs

    K. measurable goals

7. **Farm Manager** You want to apply for a grant. What is the main idea in the last paragraph?

    A. Local farmers can apply for grants.

    B. Applications should go to UFL.

    C. Grants must meet local needs.

    D. Grants must address a specific problem.

    E. All farmers must contact UFL.

```
┌─────────────────────────────────────────────────┐
│              RELEASE FORM                         │
│           Best Shot Photography                   │
│                                                   │
│ I give Best Shot all rights to the photos they    │
│ take of me. I agree to all of the following:      │
│                                                   │
│ The photos may be used for any purpose. I have    │
│ no say in what they are used for.                 │
│                                                   │
│ The photos may be changed. The photographer has   │
│ the right to alter or change any photo.           │
│                                                   │
│ I will not make legal claims to the photos. I     │
│ waive all legal rights to these images.           │
│                                                   │
│ I agree to these terms.                           │
│                                                   │
│ Name (Print) _____ Date _____    │
│                                                   │
│ Signature _____   │
└─────────────────────────────────────────────────┘
```

8. **Photographer** You take a photo of a person at a news event. You want to keep the photo. You ask your subject to sign this form. What is the main idea of the form?

    F. to release all rights to the photo

    G. to use the photo for any purpose

    H. to change the photo

    J. to make no legal claims to the photo

    K. to agree to any changes to the photo

9. **Photographer's Assistant** You do a photo shoot with a model. The model has a question about the fourth paragraph. What is the main idea of this paragraph?

    A. The model can keep the photos.

    B. The model can make legal claims to the photos.

    C. The model gives up legal claims to the photos.

    D. The photographer gives up legal claims to the photos.

    E. The photographer agrees to the terms.

10. **Reporter** A photographer takes your picture. She asks you to sign the form. What is the main idea of the last sentence?

    F. You have read the form.

    G. You agree with everything on the form.

    H. You had your photo taken.

    J. You work for Best Shot Photography.

    K. You do not want photos of you used anywhere.

Skill Support

Details are individual facts or features. They help to support the main idea. They answer questions you may have about the main idea.

Remember!

Details help you better understand a document. You need to read them closely. You can connect details to help you identify the main idea.

Lesson 2 ...
Recognize Details

Skill: Recognize details in workplace documents

Details show you more about the topic of a document. They support a main idea. Details can be examples. They can be facts. They can be statistics. For example, schedules provide details about dates.

Details can also provide reasons for doing something. For example, details can be used to explain a procedure. It is important to identify details in workplace documents. These details can help you understand a task or message.

In order to recognize details in a document, you must be able to do the following:

- Identify the main idea.
- Identify connections among ideas.

Skill Examples ▪ ▪ ▪

EXAMPLE 1 Use details to learn more about the main idea.

This memo is about a new policy. It is addressed to all the delivery drivers. What are some details about the policy?

From:	Reggie Ling, Trucking Manager
To:	All Delivery Drivers
Subject:	New Policy during Construction

Attention Delivery Drivers:

There is construction on Highway 12. The construction causes traffic delays. Many deliveries were late last week. Please observe our new policy.

Delivery truck drivers must arrive 30 minutes early starting on Monday. On Monday you will get a map. The map will tell you a new route to use. There are tolls on the new route. You will also receive some petty cash. The petty cash is for tolls.

Call me with any questions.

- This memo contains details about the main idea—a new policy during construction. The subject tells you the main idea. The details follow the main idea.
- The details tell you many things. They explain the new policy. They tell you when you need to arrive at work. They explain how to get to each delivery. They also say how to pay for tolls.

You need to get to work 30 minutes early. You will receive a map with new routes. You will receive money to pay for tolls.

EXAMPLE 2 Find details that give facts and figures.

This is an e-mail about your September bill. Details help explain the bill. What is the total payment due?

From:	Billing Department
To:	Felix Mondstein
Subject:	Credit Card Payment

We are contacting you about your late payment. We did not receive your payment last month. It was due October 5. Your total charge was $65. This includes charges from August 20 to September 30. A $10 late fee has been added. The new charge is $75. Please submit payment as soon as possible.

- The e-mail states when the charges were made. It states the total of the bill. It states when payment was due. It explains the $10 late fee.
- The details give you facts and figures. The charges were made between August 20 and September 30. The bill was for $65. There was a $10 fee for a late payment. The new total is $75.

The total due is $75.

EXAMPLE 3 Find details that include reasons for doing something.

This is a memo to employees at a store. The first sentence tells you the main idea. What are some details about this idea?

From:	Patrice Nubson, Manager
To:	All Employees
Subject:	Next Week

We will have a new store schedule next week because of the holiday season.

Next week staff must arrive by 8 a.m. The store must be open by 8:30 a.m. You can help business run smoothly next week. To do so, please:

- Be on time.
- Check new orders when you arrive.
- Ask your supervisor where you can help.

This will help us prepare orders for pickup. They should be ready by noon.

- In the second paragraph, the first sentence tells you when you must be at the store. The second sentence tells you why.
- The list contains additional details. Each point describes one task. The last paragraph tells you why you need to do the tasks.
- This memo explains what will happen next week. You also know why. The store will open early for holiday hours.

The store opens at 8:30 a.m. You need to be there before the store opens. You will help prepare orders for pickup.

Skill Support

Writers use **supporting evidence** to help make their points. There are various types of supporting evidence. Writers use statistics, facts, examples, or reasons. The type of supporting evidence depends on the topic and the point they want to make.

Remember!

Details help you understand the reasons for doing something. They can help you answer the following questions:

- What is the main idea?
- How do I do something?
- What order should I do things in?
- How can I understand the reason for something?

Remember!

Use your prior knowledge to understand details. This is useful for details that are not clearly stated. Recall what you know about a subject when reading. Apply that knowledge to the text.

Skill Support

Keep track of details by marking them. You can underline the details. You can also highlight the details. You may want to label things like the main idea. These marks can assist you with understanding a document.

Skill Practice ...

Read the workplace documents. Then answer the questions.

From:	Manager
To:	Employees

Mr. Ramirez's Order

Mr. Ramirez placed an order yesterday. It must be ready Friday. He ordered two dozen red roses. If we don't have enough red roses, give him white ones. That will be all right with him.

Next week he will order daisies, yellow carnations, and pink tulips. Please make sure we have these.

1. You work as a florist. You must put together orders for customers. What did Mr. Ramirez order this week?

   A. pink tulips   **D.** daisies

   B. red roses   **E.** white roses

   C. yellow carnations

   HINT: *The note contains many details. You are looking for what Mr. Ramirez ordered yesterday.*

From:	Ward 6 Head Supervisor
To:	Staff
Subject:	Visitors

The patients in Ward 6 may have visitors. Visiting hours are limited. Please make sure that visiting rules are followed.

Visitors may not bring food or drinks into the ward. All visitors must sign in. Write down the time they arrive. Each visitor may stay for only one hour. If you notice that visitors have stayed too long, knock on the patient's door. Explain that visiting time is up. Patients may get agitated easily. Explain that visitors can come back tomorrow. If the patient is upset, you can call a supervisor for help. The supervisor will relieve you.

2. Which detail explains when to call a supervisor?

   F. Visitors may not bring food or drinks into the ward.

   G. Each visitor may stay for only one hour.

   H. If you notice that visitors have stayed too long, knock on the patient's door.

   J. If the patient is upset, you can call a supervisor for help.

   K. The supervisor will relieve you.

   HINT: *What situation would need a supervisor's help?*

Try It Out! ■ ■ ■

Child Care Provider You have just been hired at a day care center. Your coworker has left a note with instructions. You review the note. What should you do if Kimberly and Joseph are late?

Eva,

I hope you enjoy working here. I will go over some quick rules. Some children might need to lie down during the day. They can take naps on their mats. The other children can play in another room.

Kimberly and Joseph are sister and brother. Their mom said they might be late today. If they are late, they will be hungry. Make sure they get a snack if they are hungry. If everyone has arrived and had a snack, you can take the children to the park. If it is too cold, stay inside and play games.

Yolanda

A. Have them lie down.

B. Stay inside and play games.

C. Have the other children play in another room.

D. Make sure they get a snack.

E. Go to the park.

 Step 1 Understand the Question ■ ■ ■

Complete the *Plan for Successful Solving.*

Plan for Successful Solving

What am I asked to do?	What are the facts?	How do I find the answer?
Find what the coworker tells you to do if Kimberly and Joseph are late.	Joseph and Kimberly may be late. They will be hungry if they are late. If they are hungry, they should eat a snack.	Look for the sentence that explains what to do if they are late.

 Step 2 Find Your Answer ■ ■ ■

- Details in the document tell what to do if the children are late.
- Before selecting an answer to the question, read the question again. Be sure your answer makes sense.
- **Select the correct answer: D.** Make sure they get a snack.
  You found details about the children being late. All of the other details are about different things. You found the correct detail.

Remember!

Study each sentence. Look for details. Read carefully to understand any details that are not stated clearly. Connect the details to the main idea.

Skill Support

The information you need may not be the main idea. Recognize all details. Know what information you are looking for. It may be anywhere in the document.

On Your Own ▪ ▪ ▪

Read the workplace documents and answer the questions.

MEMO

From: Building Supervisor

To: Custodians

Extra Cleaning

The building has only one staff break room. It needs extra cleaning. Please note these changes.

Empty the two trash cans twice a day. Clean the microwave once a week. Wash the coffeemaker daily. Check the refrigerator daily. Clean it as needed.

Arrange the furniture every night. There should be three tables. Set four chairs at each table. Set the five cushioned chairs under the windows.

---

1. **Janitor** You clean the break room. How often will you have to clean the refrigerator?

   A. twice a day

   B. once a week

   C. daily

   D. as needed

   E. every night

2. **Custodian** It is your job to arrange the furniture. What should you do with the cushioned chairs?

   F. Make them extra clean.

   G. Empty them.

   H. Set them at each table.

   J. Set them under the windows.

   K. Arrange them every night.

New Smoking Rule

Smoking is no longer allowed outside on Jackson Plaza. Smoking caused many problems. People complained about the litter. People complained about the smoke.

The building operator has removed all ash cans. Temporary notices are posted. Permanent metal signs will be installed soon.

Security officers will enforce this policy. They will ask you to stop smoking.

---

3. **Corporate Trainer** You arrive at Jackson Plaza. You read this notice. What has happened to the ash cans?

   A. They were causing smoke.

   B. They made people complain.

   C. They were placed in a new location.

   D. They were temporary.

   E. They have been removed.

4. **Building Manager** You have to make sure everyone follows this new policy. What will security officers do if they see someone breaking this rule?

   F. They will allow the smoker to finish smoking.

   G. They will ask the smoker to stop smoking.

   H. They will pick up the litter.

   J. They will complain about the smoke.

   K. They will install metal signs.

5. **Security Officer** A smoker asks you why smoking is no longer permitted. Why is it no longer allowed outside Jackson Plaza?

   A. People complained about the litter.

   B. Security officers complained about the smoke.

   C. All the ash cans were removed.

   D. Temporary notices were posted.

   E. Smoking caused many problems.

6. **Audio and Video Equipment Technician** You check the IC cameras to see if this notice applies to them. What problem should you look for?

   F. broken screen

   G. broken flash

   H. distorted images

   K. humid weather

   J. high repair costs

7. **Media and Communication Equipment Worker** Your company owns a few IC cameras. You take them to the dealer for maintenance. The technician shows you the notice from the company. What should you do with the cameras?

   A. Throw them away.

   B. Pay to repair them.

   C. Complain to the dealer.

   D. Exchange them for new ones.

   E. Have them repaired at no charge.

E-mail Message

From: President, National Locksmith Association

To: Members of National Locksmith Association

Subject: Locksmith Best Practices

Our profession is in danger. People are pretending to be locksmiths. They are unskilled. Customers are paying too much. The quality of the work is bad.

We want our customers to trust us. Let's all do the following:

- Always carry your locksmith license. This proves you are a locksmith.
- Always carry your state ID card.
- Always carry your company's business cards.

Also, we have standard rates. A service call should be $50 an hour. Fixing door locks should cost $5–$25 per lock cylinder. Installing new door locks should cost $20 to $30 per lock. Copying keys should only cost $1.50–$4 per key.

8. **Locksmith** You are concerned by this notice. Why is your profession in danger?

   F. People are pretending to be locksmiths.

   G. People are carrying their ID cards.

   H. Customers are paying lower prices.

   J. Customers don't trust locksmiths.

   K. Locksmiths don't carry business cards.

9. **Lock Technician** You always carry your license with you to jobs. Why do you do this?

   A. to get a state ID

   B. to make a service call

   C. to pretend to be a locksmith

   D. to charge standard rates

   E. to prove you are a locksmith

10. **Bookkeeper** The locksmith installed a new door lock. You write an invoice for his bill. How much should he charge?

    F. $1.50 to $4   J. $20 to $30

    G. $5   K. $50

    H. $25

Skill Support

Synonyms are words that have the same meaning. The words *cheerful* and *jolly* are synonyms. They both mean "happy."

Antonyms are words that have opposite meanings. The words *fast* and *slow* are antonyms.

Abbreviations are shortened forms of words. They are not whole words. They are sometimes parts of a word. *Ave.* is an abbreviation for *Avenue*. Other times they are the first letters of several words. An abbreviation made from the first letters of several words is called an **acronym**. *FAQ* is an acronym for "frequently asked question."

Remember!

If you are unsure of what a word means, try reading the sentence twice. This may help you determine the meaning.

Lesson 3 ...
Determine Word Meaning

Skill: Recognize synonyms, antonyms, and abbreviations

Knowing the meanings of words helps you understand documents. Some words have the same or almost the same meanings. These are called *synonyms*. For example, *strong* and *powerful* are synonyms. They have the same meaning.

Some words have opposite or nearly opposite meanings. These are called *antonyms*. For example, *strong* and *weak* are antonyms. They have opposite meanings.

Abbreviations are shortened forms of words. For example, *Mon.* is an abbreviation of *Monday*.

In order to determine word meaning, you must be able to do the following:

- Understand context meaning.

- Understand sentence structure.

Skill Examples ...

EXAMPLE 1 Recognize synonyms in workplace documents.
You are a server in a restaurant. You use these instructions to serve soup. Which word is a synonym for *small*?

Instructions for Serving Soup for Dine-in or Takeout

Dine-in
Pour soup into a bowl. Put a small plate under the bowl. Place two crackers on the plate. Sprinkle garnish on the soup. Put a spoon next to the crackers.

Takeout
Ladle soup into a plastic container. Sprinkle garnish on the soup. Place a lid on the container. Put the container in a little paper bag. Place two crackers in the bag. Place a spoon in the bag.

- Synonyms are words that have the same meaning. There are synonyms in this document. These instructions have different words that mean the same thing.

- You know what *put* means. The "Dine-in" paragraph says to *put* a spoon next to the crackers. The "Takeout" paragraph says to *place* a spoon in the bag. *Place* and *put* are synonyms.

- There are other synonyms in the document. *Small* is in the second sentence of the first paragraph. *Little* is in the fourth sentence of the second paragraph.

Little is a synonym for *small*.

EXAMPLE 2 Recognize antonyms in workplace documents.

You are a shipping clerk. You follow this safety policy. Which word is an antonym of *safe*?

Shipping Department Safety Policies

The following guidelines help maintain a safe workplace:

1) Report any spills to the supervisor immediately. Delayed reporting can lead to dangerous conditions.

2) Lift only one crate at a time. Some crates may be heavy. Others may be light. They should also be carried one at a time.

3) Hard hats must be worn at all times. Protect yourself with proper headwear.

- Antonyms are words with opposite meanings.

- *Safe* is in the first sentence. It means "free from danger." *Dangerous* is in the last sentence of point 1. It means "unsafe."

Dangerous is an antonym of *safe*.

EXAMPLE 3 Recognize and understand abbreviations in workplace documents.

You are a teacher. You receive an e-mail. It contains abbreviations. Which one is an abbreviation for *as soon as possible*?

From: Madison Starbright, Gym Instructor
To: Classroom Staff
CC: Principal Sanchez
Subject: Re: Field Day

Hi all,

Thanks for your help in organizing Field Day. We have plans for races, games, and team sports. We will pick up equipment on Tues. We could use help bringing it into the building. Then we can set it up in the gym. It will be cold, so most games will be inside. Please let me know if you can help with load-in. Let me know ASAP. If there is not enough staff, I will ask parents to help.

Thanks again,
Madison

- Abbreviations are shortened forms of words or phrases. They are not whole words. They are sometimes part of a word. Other times they are the first letters of several words.

- Re: is short for *Regarding.* This is an abbreviation. It is part of a word. It is a common abbreviation. *Tues.* is short for *Tuesday.* Days of the week are often abbreviated.

- Some abbreviations, called acronyms, use the first letters of several words. For example, *CC* is an acronym for *carbon copy.* A carbon copy is the same as the original. The document also contains *ASAP.*

ASAP is an abbreviation or acronym for *as soon as possible.*

Remember!
A word's meaning may not always be stated. This is true if the word is common to a task. You can identify the meaning by looking for clues. These clues may include synonyms. They may also include antonyms.

Skill Support
Abbreviations are commonly used in the workplace. Below is a list of abbreviations. They can be found in many work documents:

- Attn.—attention
- Dec.—December
- EOD—end of day
- ETA—expected time of arrival
- in.—inches
- Mr.—Mister
- N/A—not available or not applicable

Skill Practice ▪ ▪ ▪

Read the workplace documents. Then answer the questions.

Dear Armand,

Thank you for maintaining our yard while we are away. Please trim the bushes in the front. Mow the grass. Mulch the garden beds. If it hasn't rained in a week, water the lawn. The hose is near the garage. Rake any debris and put it in bags. We will take them to the dump when we return. Let us know if you have any questions.

Thanks again,
Lucilla, 301-555-0165

1. You work for a landscaping company. You maintain yards and gardens for clients. You need to understand the whole document. Which word is a synonym of **lawn**?

   A. hose   **D.** bushes

   B. grass   **E.** beds

   C. debris

   HINT: The note tells you to water the lawn if it does not rain in a week. Look for another word that means "lawn."

From:	Dr. Oswald
To:	Fatima

Instructions for Puppy Care

Cages need to be tidy. Clean the puppy cages Mon.–Sun. Replace newspaper in the mornings. After you replace newspaper, make sure cage is latched. Puppies will be hungry. Feed puppies at 9 a.m. After feeding, let puppies into play area for 15 minutes. Some puppies are very energetic. They might try to escape. Some puppies are very sleepy. They like to nap all day.

2. You work as a veterinary assistant. You need to make sure you understand these instructions. Which word is an antonym of **energetic**?

   F. important   **J.** sleepy

   G. latched   **K.** hungry

   H. tidy

   HINT: Energetic puppies will be very active. Identify how puppies act if they are not active.

Try It Out! ■ ■ ■

Baker You are the baker at Patty's Bakery. You try a new muffin recipe. How much flour goes in the muffin batter?

A. 3 cups

B. 1 tablespoon

C. 3 teaspoons

D. 2 cups

E. 1 pound

New Muffin Recipe

Ingredients
4 eggs
1 T. vanilla extract
2 c. milk
1 lb. butter
3 tsp. baking powder
3 c. flour

Preheat oven to 375 degrees. Cream butter. Add eggs. Mix together dry ingredients. Slowly fold in. Add milk and vanilla. Blend until smooth. Pour into lined cupcake tins. Bake for 25–30 min.

Remember!
Think about when you have seen an abbreviation before. Apply that knowledge to the recipe.

 Understand the Question ■ ■ ■

Complete the *Plan for Successful Solving.*

Plan for Successful Solving

What am I asked to do?	What are the facts?	How do I find the answer?
Find how much flour goes in the batter.	The abbreviation for the flour measurement is 3 c.	Determine what *c.* stands for in a recipe.

 Find Your Answer ■ ■ ■

- First remember to answer the question. You need to identify how much flour goes in the recipe.

- The recipe measures ingredients by quantity, weight, and volume. *T.* stands for *tablespoon*. *Tsp.* stands for *teaspoon*. Flour is also measured by volume. *C.* must stand for a measure of volume.

- Flour is usually measured in cups. The abbreviation *c.* stands for cups.

- **Select the correct answer: A.** 3 cups
  You read the question. You looked at the recipe. You used the clues in the recipe to find the meaning. You determined the abbreviation *c.* stands for *cups*.

Skill Support
You may need help to determine a word's meaning. A dictionary and a thesaurus are resources you can use.

A dictionary gives the meanings of words. Some dictionaries also have a list of abbreviations. They will list common abbreviations with their meanings.

A thesaurus gives synonyms of words. It may list antonyms, too.

Look for words in alphabetical order.

On Your Own ▪ ■ ▫

Read the workplace documents and answer the questions.

> **Lawn and Garden Crew Guidelines**
>
> Let's have a great season providing esp. outstanding services.
>
> Lawn crews: Maintain your equipment. Service your tools so they always work. Clean up yard waste. Place grass clippings in compost bins.
>
> Garden crews: Always ask clients for instructions. Make sure you plant in the right places. Always water after you plant. Pull up weeds only.

1. **Gardener** It is your first day of work. You receive these guidelines. What does the abbreviation **esp.** stand for?

   A. extrasensory perception

   B. exceptional

   C. etcetera

   D. extra

   E. especially

2. **Lawn Care Worker** You want your equipment to be ready. You read these guidelines. What word means the same as **maintain**?

   F. service

   G. ask

   H. plant

   J. provide

   K. water

Customer Service Tips

Always be polite and professional. You represent our company.

The way you speak is very important. You need to give customers information. Prepare in advance what you will say. Plan carefully. Don't speak rapidly or mumble. Speak slowly. Be clear and direct. Avoid slang and misc. items a customer might not understand. Your tone of voice should be pleasant and cheerful.

How do you like to be treated? That's how you should treat customers.

3. **Hotel Desk Clerk** You start a new job at a hotel. You read these customer service tips. What does the abbreviation **misc.** mean?

   A. miniscule

   B. microscopic

   C. militaristic

   D. missing

   E. miscellaneous

4. **Restaurant Server** You go to a training session on customer service. You receive this sheet of tips. What word means the opposite of **rapidly**?

   F. quickly

   G. slowly

   H. moderately

   J. suddenly

   K. promptly

5. **Events Coordinator** You are coordinating an event at the hotel. What word in the tips means the same as **prepare**?

   A. use

   B. enable

   C. teach

   D. plan

   E. try

> **MEMO**
>
> From: Weatherization Supervisor
>
> To: Weatherization Team
>
> ### Home Weatherization Plan
>
> Please follow these instructions:
>
> Add 10 in. of insulation to the attic. This will keep the house warmer.
>
> Seal the openings on exterior walls. Set up a ladder outside for high openings.
>
> Check any cracked windows. Replace the windows that are completely broken. Keep the windows that can be repaired.

6. **Weatherization Installer** You get ready to go to a job site. You read the plan. What word means the same as **exterior**?

    F. outside

    G. inside

    H. between

    J. overhead

    K. open

7. **Weatherization Technician** Review the list of what needs to be done. What word in the plan means the opposite of **replace**?

    A. seal

    B. instruct

    C. switch

    D. keep

    E. exchange

E-mail Message

From: Emergency Management Director

To: Road Crews and Managers

Subject: Car Accident Emergency Plan

While you are doing your jobs, you will witness car accidents. Be prepared. If you see an accident, follow these straightfoward steps.

Notify the police immediately. Say where the accident is. Give details. For example, "Two cars had an accident in front of 112 Elm St."

Decide if it is dangerous to go near the accident. If it is safe, try to assist the people involved. Don't make the situation worse. Don't move someone who is seriously hurt.

Tell people not to leave. The police need to talk to them. Don't stop someone who tries to leave. Write down his or her license plate number.

Stay until the police arrive. Be ready to tell them what happened.

8. **Emergency Management Director** Road crews often witness car accidents. Crews and managers need to know what to do. You write this plan. What word means the same as **prepared**?

F. ready   J. unqualified

G. scheduled   K. late

H. done

9. **Transportation Manager** Before you give this plan to your workers, you review the second paragraph. What does the abbreviation **St.** mean?

A. state   D. statue

B. street   E. start

C. saint

10. **Regional Planning Aide** You read this emergency plan for road crews. What word means the opposite of **safe**?

F. prepared   J. straightforward

G. worse   K. hurt

H. dangerous

Skill Support

Context can help you understand the meaning of a new word. **Context clues** are hints that help you guess the word's meaning. Context clues are found in the words that surround a word. They are also found in sentences and paragraphs.

Sometimes a sentence does not give enough context clues for the unknown word. You need to look at the whole paragraph. The paragraph may contain clues to the new word's meaning.

Remember!

You can look up words in a dictionary. However, you may not always have a dictionary with you. Sometimes you must rely on context clues.

Lesson 4 ...
Determine Word Meanings from Context Clues

Skill: Use sentences and paragraphs to determine word meanings

People often learn new words at work. A handbook may use new words. A coworker may call something by a new name. Sometimes you can figure out the meaning of the word from its context. To do that, look for words and sentences near the unknown word. They may give you clues to its meaning. Context might be a synonym that will help you. It may also be an antonym. Context can be a sentence. It can also be a paragraph.

In order to use context to determine word meanings, you must be able to do the following:

- Understand context meaning.

- Understand sentence structure.

- Identify main idea and details.

- Recognize synonyms and antonyms.

Skill Examples ■ ■ ■

EXAMPLE 1 Use a paragraph to determine word meanings.
The main idea of this paragraph is that workers must be on time. *Punctual* is a new word. What does **punctual** mean?

Clocking In and Out

Workers must be on time for work. As soon as you arrive, clock in. Time cards are in the hallway. They hang on the wall near the break room. It is your responsibility to clock in and out. Shifts can be very busy. It is important that everyone be punctual. If you are late, someone else has to cover for you. Time cards are reviewed every week. If you are late twice in one week, you will receive a warning.

- Read the notice. The first sentence says workers must be on time. Details in the paragraph support this idea.

- One detail explains why you must be on time. One detail explains what will happen if you are late.

- One sentence says it is important to be *punctual*. The paragraph is about being on time. It tells you why and what will happen if you are late.

Punctual must mean "on time."

EXAMPLE 2 Use a sentence to determine word meanings.
This e-mail is from the manager. It tells you to follow cleaning procedures. What does the word **immaculate** mean?

From: GeneralManager@Hotel.com

To: HousekeepingStaff@Hotel.com

Subject: Bathroom cleaning

Hello, everyone.

I want to remind everyone of the procedures for cleaning bathrooms. Some guests have complained of dirty bathrooms. Please follow the handbook procedures. Collect and replace used towels. Sweep and mop the floor tile. Scrub down bathtubs and counters when dirty. Also scrub them after guests check out. Wipe mirrors with glass cleaner. Always empty trash cans. If you follow the handbook procedures for cleaning, the bathroom should look immaculate. This will impress the guests. It will reflect well on the whole hotel.

Thanks for your hard work. Keep it up.

Stephanie Abu
General Manager

- Read the e-mail. It tells you to follow the handbook procedures for cleaning. The main idea is that the bathrooms need to be clean.

- The message tells you to follow the handbook procedures for cleaning. If you do, the bathroom will look immaculate.

Immaculate must mean "very clean."

EXAMPLE 3 Use a sentence to determine word meanings.
These instructions tell you how to deliver files. What does the word **recipient** mean?

From: Ms. Ramirez

To: Sandra

File Delivery

Please print all files when they are to be delivered. Take the printed files to the main office on Jackson Avenue. Make sure the proper person receives the file, and ask the recipient to sign for the file. Bring the signature back to this office to prove that the file was received.

- Read the notice. The main idea is to deliver files to the right person.

- The third sentence tells you to make sure the proper person receives the file and to ask the *recipient* to sign for the file.

Recipient must mean "a person who receives something."

Skill Support

Sometimes the meaning of words may be unclear. When you don't understand a word, ask yourself the following questions:

- Do I understand the rest of the sentence?
- Does the sentence have clues I can use to understand this word?
- What are the clues?

When you think you know what a new word means, reread the document. Imagine what the new word means. Think of a similar word. Substitute it into the sentence. Does the whole document make sense? If so, you have probably guessed correctly.

Remember!

The subject line of a memo tells you about the main idea. This may help you figure out the meaning of an unfamiliar word.

Skill Practice ■ ■ ■

Read the workplace documents. Then answer the questions.

From:	Management
To:	Cashiers

Accepting Checks

We now accept checks. This is a new policy. Please make sure to check IDs when a customer pays by check. Customers have reported cashiers not checking IDs. Using someone else's checks is a crime. That infraction can result in a large fine. The checkbook may have been stolen.

Take the time to look at each ID closely. Make sure the names match, and make sure the picture resembles the customer. If an ID is from another state, scan it. If you are unsure, ask for a second form of ID. We don't want to take bad checks. Be careful not to do so.

1. You are a cashier. You understand most of the document. Some words are new. What does **resembles** mean?

   A. accepts   **B.** reports   **C.** looks like   **D.** scans   **E.** asks for

   HINT: Look at the sentence that includes the word resembles. *The sentence is about the customer's ID. It says the name on the ID must match the name on the check. It says the picture must resemble the customer. Think about how these ideas relate.*

From:	KendrickHolmes@JumpRightShoes.com
To:	Shoemakers@JumpRightShoes.com
Subject:	Machinery Maintenance

Next week there will be scheduled machine maintenance. Every machine on the floor will be serviced. We do not expect this to slow production. You will have a replacement machine to work with. The replacements are older machines, but they work well. They should suffice for a few hours. After a few hours, you will have your usual machine back. To reiterate, we do not expect production to slow down. It is important to service the machines. It is also important to make our quotas for the week. If you have any questions, please let me know.

Kendrick Holmes
Jump Right Shoes

2. What does **reiterate** mean?

   F. service machines   **J.** replace
   G. ask a question   **K.** say something again
   H. work well

   HINT: Look for clues in the whole paragraph. The supervisor repeats important information at the end of the message.

Try It Out! ▪ ▪ ■

Membership Coordinator at a Fitness Center You answer questions about fitness center membership. A guest has written an e-mail to the membership department. What does **complimentary** mean?

From:	Dolores Csyrensky
To:	Membership@BodyTimeFitness.com
Subject:	Guest Passes

I have been a member of Body Time Fitness for three years. I always recommend your gym to my friends. Many of my friends are interested in joining. They want to try a gym before joining. I understand that is not your policy. However, if my friends could visit the gym, they would be more likely to join. Is it possible to get a few complimentary guest passes? Many gyms offer free trial periods. Perhaps this could be a benefit to membership.

A. healthy   D. clean

B. free of charge   E. interested

C. comfortable

 ## Understand the Question ▪ ■ ■

Complete the *Plan for Successful Solving*.

Plan for Successful Solving

What am I asked to do?	What are the facts?	How do I find the answer?
Determine the meaning of the word *complimentary*.	There are context clues within the sentence. There are context clues in the paragraph.	Read the memo. Find words surrounding *complimentary* that mean the same thing.

 ## Find Your Answer ▪ ■ ■

- Look at clues in the paragraph. Read the sentence with *complimentary*. Read the sentences before and after it.

- The next sentence talks about free trial periods. *Complimentary* must mean "free of charge."

- **Select the correct answer: B.** free of charge
  You read the e-mail carefully. You needed to determine the meaning of *complimentary*. You found details that you used as clues. Then you determined the meaning.

On Your Own ▪ ▪ ▪

Read the workplace documents and answer the questions.

E-mail Message

From: Supervisor

To: Staff

Subject: Good Communication

We all must keep customers happy. When a customer calls, be polite. Never be rude. Don't raise your voice. Don't insult the customer. Even if the customer is rude, you must remain friendly and courteous.

If callers are angry, be patient. Stay calm. Speak to them with respect. Use good communication skills to help resolve all problems.

---

1. **Call Center Representative** Your manager wants to talk with you about a difficult call you had. What does **courteous** mean in the message?

    A. clear

    B. quiet

    C. polite

    D. patient

    E. natural

2. **Customer Service Representative** The e-mail explains how to treat callers. What does **rude** mean?

    F. impolite

    G. respectful

    H. honest

    J. gentle

    K. loud

MEMO

From: Human Resources
To: All Staff

Inclement Weather Procedures

It is winter. That means snow season. This memorandum will address inclement weather.

In general, the office will try to stay open in bad weather. When possible, report to work at your normal time.

In severe weather, the office will close. Do not drive on hazardous roads. Please stay home when conditions are dangerous.

We suggest you take a copy of this note home with you.

---

3. **Human Resources Assistant** You give this message to all staff. What does **memorandum** mean?

   A. procedure

   B. note

   C. weather

   D. condition

   E. storm

4. **Project Manager** You have a deadline. You need to get to work on time. You check the weather report. What does **inclement** mean?

   F. bad

   G. wet

   H. mild

   J. heavy

   K. normal

5. **Executive Assistant** Before going to work, you check the road conditions. What does **hazardous** mean in the memo?

   A. clear

   B. closed

   C. helpful

   D. blocked

   E. dangerous

Dear Dr. DeFillipo:

Last month, your patient came to us for therapy. She fell on her left elbow. This caused her bone to break. Because of the fracture, she could not lift anything.

Due to the severity of her injury, she had to get therapy every day. We created a comprehensive program. This total plan included exercises, medicine, and special bandages.

She now has more strength in her arm. Thank you for sending this patient to us.

Sincerely,
Physical Therapist

6. **Physical Trainer** You helped this patient get better. What does **severity** mean?

    F. fracture

    G. cause

    H. location

    J. program

    K. seriousness

7. **Physical Therapist** You helped create the treatment plan. What do you mean by **comprehensive** in your letter?

    A. long

    B. complete

    C. strong

    D. fractured

    E. difficult

> ### Juvenile Institution
> ### Mission Statement
>
> This is a respectful institution. Here minors are treated with respect. The organization offers safe programs.
>
> Minors must follow regulations. They are accountable for their actions. They need to be responsible for following the rules.
>
> The staff will model good behavior. The staff expects good behavior.

8. Probation Officer You need to visit a juvenile client. What does **institution** mean in the mission statement?

    F. city

    G. statement

    H. program

    J. committee

    K. organization

9. Correctional Officer You work with a minor. You review the mission statement. What does **regulations** mean?

    A. chores

    B. dreams

    C. rules

    D. dialogues

    E. behaviors

10. Treatment Specialist You talk with a juvenile about his actions. What does **accountable** mean in the mission statement?

    F. clear

    G. reliable

    H. financial

    J. responsible

    K. independent

Skill Support

Time order states the order in which things happen. It may also be called **sequence**. Look for time-order words in instructions.

- *First* is used to show which events happen first. *Finally* is used to show what happens last.
- *Then* and *next* are used in the middle of the order. They show that another action is happening.
- *Before* and *after* also show time order. They are more exact than *then* and *next*.
- *Second, third,* and so on can also be used. They tell you the precise order to do things.

Remember!

Time order can be written in many ways. One way is a numbered list. It uses numbers to show time order. The list moves from the lowest to highest number. Another way is a bulleted list. It uses bullets to show time order. Each bullet separates a step.

Lesson 5 ...
Understand Time Order

Skill: Identify and use time order

Time order is the order in which things are connected. It can also be the order in which events take place. This is also called *sequence*. It is important to understand time-order words. Instructions may be written with time-order words. Instructions tell you how to do something correctly. Time-order words help make instructions clearer. Understanding these words helps you do a task in the right way.

To understand time order, you must be able to do the following:

- Understand sequence.
- Understand steps in a process.

Skill Examples ■ ■ ■

EXAMPLE 1 Identify time-order signal words.
This is an e-mail from a nurse in a hospital. The message tells nurses' aides what to do. What are the time-order words?

From:	Mr. Rodriguez, Supervising Nurse
To:	All Nurses' Aides
Subject:	Patients' Files

Patient files must be sorted. Check the files when you first get to work. All files should be in their right slots. Put loose files in their slots. Then sort the remaining files at the end of the day. The last thing to do is double-check the files. Make sure all files are in their correct slots. No files should be left unsorted.

- The word *first* is in the second sentence. *First* means "number one in a process."
- The word *then* also indicates time order. It tells you what to do next.
- The word *last* is in the sixth sentence. *Last* means "to be done at the end." You do this after everything else.

The time-order words are *first, then,* and *last.*

EXAMPLE 2 Identify the steps in the instructions.
You are a painter. You follow the instructions on p. 37 to paint a room. Which words tell you the order of the steps?

- The word *before* is in the first step. *Before* tells you what to do first. The first thing you must do is make sure there is nothing hanging on the walls.
- The word *then* is in the fourth step. *Then* tells you what you do after the step before.

- The word *after* is in the fifth step. *After* tells you what to do when you have done the earlier step. Put the furniture in the middle of the room. After that, cover it with a sheet.

- This list also contains numbers for each step. The numbers can help you identify the order of the steps.

Instructions for Painting a Room

1. Make sure nothing is hanging on the walls. Do this before you begin painting.
2. Ask the owner to remove pictures and other things hanging on the walls.
3. The owner may not be home. You may carefully remove wall objects.
4. Then move all furniture to the middle of the room.
5. After all the furniture is moved, cover it with a sheet.
6. All objects must be completely covered. They must be safe from paint drips.

The words *before, then,* and *after* help you identify the order of the steps.

EXAMPLE 3 Identify the day and time order that things happen.
You are a customer service representative. You receive this memo. It says you will get a new computer. It says you will get training. Which will happen first?

From: Management
To: All Employees

Update on Office Repair

Review the schedule below regarding office repairs.

Thursday: 10:15 a.m. Please put your items in a carton.
                      4:30 p.m. Leave the office.

Friday: Work at your desk or in the large meeting room.

Monday: 11:00 a.m. Repairs should be complete.

Tuesday: Everyone will get a new computer.
                      You should get your new computer by 3:00 p.m.

Wednesday: You will get a memo about computer training.
                      All training should be done by 5:00 p.m.

- The memo gives the days of the workweek. The first two days listed are Thursday and Friday. Then the following Monday, Tuesday, and Wednesday are listed. Saturday and Sunday are not listed. They are not workdays, so the office is closed.

- The memo tells workers the time things will happen. You put your items in a carton at 10:15 a.m. You leave the office at 4:30 p.m. 10:15 a.m. comes before 4:30 p.m.

- The memo says you should get a new computer by 3:00 p.m. on Tuesday. It says you should be trained by 5:00 p.m. on Wednesday. 3:00 p.m. on Tuesday comes before 5:00 p.m. on Wednesday.

You will get a new computer before you get training.

Skill Support

Documents may put things in a sequence for many purposes. They may explain how something works. They may explain the steps in a process. They may describe a routine. They may also tell about the time order in an event or an experience.

Remember!

Instructions often include dates and times of events. Look for dates and times when you read instructions. They will help you identify the order to perform tasks.

Remember!

Putting things in order is something you do every day. You may give someone instructions for using the printer. You are putting events in order. You may tell somebody how you organized a report. That is also showing order.

Skill Support

Writers tell stories using time order to describe the sequence of events. Whether you are reading a story or following directions, picturing the events in your mind can help you understand the time order.

Skill Practice ▪ ▪ ▪

Read the workplace documents. Then answer the questions.

From:	Don Ford, Personnel
To:	All Employees
Subject:	Personal Time Off

Hello everyone.

Please follow this plan when asking for days off.

First give advance notice. Try to tell your boss at least two weeks in advance.

Then your boss will give your request to our department.

Within three working days, we will tell your boss our decision.

Before making a decision, your boss will review our comments.

After reviewing our comments, your boss will approve or deny your request.

Finally your boss will give you the decision.

Thank you for understanding.

Don

1. You work in this office. You need to take two days off. What is the first step in the process?

   A. Your boss gives your request to the personnel department.

   B. You give advance notice to your boss.

   C. The personnel department reviews your request.

   D. Your boss reviews the personnel department's comments.

   E. Your boss gives you the decision.

   HINT: Find the word first. *It tells you what to do at the beginning of this process.*

Fire Safety Procedure

In case of a fire, follow these safety steps.
- First leave your desk.
- Second walk quickly but calmly to the nearest EXIT.
- Leave the building by walking down the STAIRS.

DO NOT TAKE THE ELEVATOR
- Exit the building. Walk to the end of the block.
- If firefighters give you other instructions, follow them.

---

2. You work in an office building. Where should you go after leaving the building?

   F. to the elevators

   G. to the end of the block

   H. to the stairwell

   J. to the fire department

   K. to the security office

   HINT: Read the message again. Read the sentence after "Exit the building."

Try It Out! ■ ■ ■

Office Worker You see more than one foot of snow on the ground in the morning. You follow these instructions. The office is open, and you have phoned in to say you are going to work. What should you do next?

From:	Management
To:	All Workers

1. Start by calling 555-0175. A recording will tell you if the office is open or closed. If the office is open, go to Step 2.

2. If there is less than one foot of snow, you should come to work. You may be up to one hour late. If there is more than one foot of snow, go to Step 3.

3. Phone the office to say if you are coming to work. Then go to the pickup area near your home. (See the map.) Wait for the office van to pick you up.

A. Call 555-0175.

B. Come in one hour late.

C. Phone the office to say you are coming to work.

D. Go to the pickup area near your home.

E. Wait for the office van to pick you up.

 Understand the Question ■ ■ ■

Complete the *Plan for Successful Solving*.

Plan for Successful Solving

What am I asked to do?	What are the facts?	How do I find the answer?
Find the next step after phoning to say you are coming to work.	Phone the office to say if you are coming to work. Then go to the pickup area near your home.	Find the sequence word that tells you the next step.

 Find Your Answer ■ ■ ■

- Remember that you are trying to find the next step. There is more than one foot of snow. You are going to work. You already phoned the office.

- The key word *then* tells you that going to the pickup area near your home is the next step.

- **Select the correct answer: D.** Go to the pickup area near your home. Each step explains what to do. The steps tell the order. After phoning the office, the next step is to go to the pickup area.

Remember!

Instructions give you steps in order. The first step is described first, the second step is described second, and so on. Look for time-order words. These words help you follow the instructions.

Skill Support

You don't need only key words and times to understand order. You can also use your common sense. Think about how things fit together—how they connect. For example, you work as a dog groomer. You are learning to wash a dog. Your common sense tells you that you must get the dog wet before you dry it. Use common sense to guide your understanding. Confirm your thoughts with facts from the text.

On Your Own ▪ ▪ ▪

Read the workplace documents and answer the questions.

E-mail Message

From: Company President

To: All Employees

Subject: Company Photos

Hello everyone,

On Thursday, a photographer will be in our office. She will take photos for the company website. She will take an individual photo of everyone. These photo shoots will begin at 10 a.m. They will end at 12 p.m. Then she will take small-group photos. These will go from 1 p.m. to 2 p.m. At 3 p.m., she will take a photo of the entire staff. Please be sure to dress well. Let me know if you have questions. Thanks!

---

1. **Editor** You receive this e-mail. You check when the full–staff photo will be. What time is the full-staff photo?

   A. 10 a.m.

   B. 12 p.m.

   C. 1 p.m.

   D. 2 p.m.

   E. 3 p.m.

2. **Desktop Publisher** You are scheduling a meeting. You do not want it to conflict with your individual photo shoot. What time do the individual photo shoots end?

   F. 10 a.m.

   G. 12 p.m.

   H. 1 p.m.

   J. 2 p.m.

   K. 3 p.m.

Instructions for Electronic Time Sheets

Begin by opening the time sheet file on your computer. Next choose the pay period date. After this, fill in your personal information. Then enter your hours for the week. Press Update Time Sheet and then Submit. Finally print out the time sheet and sign it. This gives you a hardcopy backup.

---

3. **Telephone Operator** Your company now uses electronic time sheets. You just set the pay period date. What is the next step?

   A. Sign the time sheet.

   B. Print out the time sheet.

   C. Fill in your personal information.

   D. Open the time sheet file.

   E. Enter your hours for the week.

4. **Supply Chain Manager** You need to help some new workers understand these instructions. Which word indicates the last step?

   F. finally

   G. then

   H. after

   J. begin

   K. next

5. **Financial Analyst** A client asks you to fill out an electronic time sheet. What should you do first?

   A. Print the time sheet.

   B. Enter your hours.

   C. Sign the time sheet.

   D. Open the time sheet file.

   E. Enter your personal information.

MEMO

From: Commissioner

To: Conservationists

Commissioners' Meeting of April 15

The commissioners approved the cleanup plan. The plan deals with a pollution complaint. The complaint was received on February 20. The plan was submitted on March 25. It must start by October 15.

6. **Agricultural Technician** You submitted the cleanup plan. When does the plan need to start?

F. by April 15

G. by February 20

H. by October 15

J. by March 25

K. by October 20

7. **Soil and Water Conservationist** You review this memo from the commissioner. Which event took place first?

A. the pollution complaint

B. the commissioners' meeting

C. the plan's implementation

D. the plan's submission

E. the plan's approval

E-mail Message

From: Mental Health Bill Advocates   Sent: July 1

To: Mental Health Professionals

Subject: We Need Your Support

We need your support for the mental health bill. The vote on the bill is on August 10. Please make phone calls to voters on July 21. The final hearing will be on August 6. We would like you to write letters of support. Please send the letters by July 15. Thank you for your support.

8. **Counseling Psychologist** You want to write a letter to support this bill. By which date should you send your letter?

   F. July 1

   G. July 15

   H. July 21

   J. August 6

   K. August 10

9. **Mental Health Counselor** You want to go to the final hearing. When is the hearing?

   A. July 1

   B. July 15

   C. July 21

   D. August 6

   E. August 10

10. **Community Service Director** You are sending this letter to your colleagues. On which date should people make phone calls?

    F. July 1

    G. July 15

    H. July 21

    J. August 6

    K. August 10

Level 1 Performance Assessment ▪ ▪ ▪

These problems are at a Level 1 rating of difficulty. They are similar to problems on a career readiness certificate test. For each question, you can check your answer. To do this, use the answer key. It is located on pp. 260–262 of this book. It explains each answer option. It also shows the lesson that covers that skill. You may refer to that lesson to review the skill.

E-mail Message

From: Accounting Department

To: Resort Workers

Subject: New Computer Time Clock for Workers

We have a new computer time clock for workers. Please remember to clock in and out during your work shift.

Follow these steps to clock in. First put your finger on the computer touch pad. Hold it there for 15 seconds. The computer will scan your fingerprint. Clock in at the beginning of your shift. Also remember to clock in after breaks. If you forget to clock in, tell a supervisor.

Clock out before breaks and at the end of your shift. If you forget to clock out, tell a supervisor.

---

1. You work at the front desk of a hotel. You receive this e-mail message from your boss. What is the main idea of the message?

   A. The accounting department tracks time worked.

   B. There is a new computer time clock for workers.

   C. The computer will scan your fingerprint.

   D. Hold it there for 15 seconds.

   E. Follow these steps to clock in.

2. You read the message. What is the main idea of the second paragraph?

   F. Follow these steps to clock in.

   G. First put your finger on the computer touch pad.

   H. Hold it there for 15 seconds.

   J. The computer will scan your fingerprint.

   K. If you forget to clock in, tell a supervisor.

3. You forget when you need to clock out. You read this e-mail again to figure out what to do. What is the main idea of the third paragraph?

   A. Clock out before breaks and at the end of a shift.

   B. Remember to clock in after breaks.

   C. Clock in at the beginning of your shift.

   D. If you forget to clock in, tell a supervisor.

   E. If you forget to clock out, tell a supervisor.

University Employee Safety

These guidelines cover rules for safety.

In Case of Injury

1. Immediately report the injury to a supervisor. Your supervisor will fill out the proper form.

2. Review and sign the form. Make sure it is correct. Initial any changes.

3. Document the injury. Go to the University Medical Center right away. If it occurs after hours, visit a hospital.

Workers' Compensation

Any worker injured on the job must report it immediately. The Workers' Disability Compensation Act provides medical payment for injuries. If you do not report your injury immediately, it may be hard to get compensation. All injuries must be reported. Report accidents too.

Workers' Compensation will <u>not</u> cover the first three days off. You will need to use sick days or vacation time for these days.

For questions, contact Human Resources. Call extension 345. Or e-mail hr@universitycenter.edu.

4. As a university groundskeeper, you receive these guidelines. The main idea of the guidelines is employee safety. What detail says what to do first after an injury happens?

   F. Review and sign the form.

   G. Go to the University Medical Center right away.

   H. Immediately report the injury to a supervisor.

   J. You will need to use sick days or vacation time for these days.

   K. For questions, contact Human Resources.

5. You worry about being paid if you are injured. You reread the guidelines. What detail provides facts about payment?

   A. Immediately report the injury to a supervisor.

   B. The Workers' Disability Compensation Act provides medical payment for injuries.

   C. Report accidents too.

   D. You will need to use sick days or vacation time for these days.

   E. Any worker injured on the job must report it immediately.

6. You want to know why it is important to report your injury right away. You reread the guidelines. What detail shows a reason for this?

   F. Any worker injured on the job must report it immediately.

   G. The Workers' Disability Compensation Act provides medical payment for injuries.

   H. If you do not report your injury immediately, it may be hard to get compensation.

   J. Workers' Compensation will <u>not</u> cover the first three days off.

   K. You will need to use sick days or vacation time for these days.

Fresh Tomato Salsa Recipe

Ingredients:

112 tomatoes

18 cups onions

20 cups cilantro

28 hot peppers

$\frac{3}{4}$ cup and 1 tsp. salt

$\frac{1}{2}$ cup olive oil

$1\frac{1}{2}$ cups and 1 tbsp. lime juice

Directions:

• Dice the tomatoes. Dice the onions. Finely chop the cilantro. Mix together in a large pot. Set aside.

• Separate the seeds from the peppers. Dice the peppers.

• Add the peppers to pot. Mix in salt. Mix in lime juice. Mix in oil.

• Pour into tubs. Seal tubs. Label with today's date. Refrigerate. Serve as needed.

7. As a cook at a Mexican restaurant, you make salsa. You follow this recipe. What word means the same as **chop**?

   A. mix

   B. dice

   C. add

   D. pour

   E. serve

8. You are adding the salt to the recipe. You check to make sure you have the right amount. What does the abbreviation **tsp.** stand for?

   F. tablespoon

   G. cup

   H. ounce

   J. teaspoon

   K. dash

9. You go over the directions again. You do not want to combine things incorrectly. What word in the recipe means the opposite of **combine**?

   A. mix

   B. add

   C. pour

   D. chop

   E. separate

E-mail Message

From: Foreman

To: Inspector

Subject: Inspector Guidelines

It is the inspector's job to verify the construction site is safe. She will inspect the site. This will show if it is safe. She will test the strength of the concrete. This will prove its safety.

Prior to beginning construction, the inspector should become familiar with the construction plan. She should attend preconstruction meetings. She should ask questions about the plan. She should review the materials list. She should check the contractor's schedule.

The inspector should be familiar with all local and national building codes. She should be prepared to make sure that the site complies with ordinances, regulations, and contract specifications.

10. In your work as a construction inspector, you inspect pavement construction. You read these guidelines for your job. You do not understand the word *verify*. Use context clues from the paragraph. What does **verify** mean?

   F. confirm

   G. review

   H. test

   J. disprove

   K. decide

11. You have trouble with the word *prior*. You do not know what it means. You read the surrounding sentence for context clues. Based on the sentence, what does the word **prior** mean?

   A. after

   B. before

   C. during

   D. beginning

   E. ending

MEMO

From: Principal

To: Teachers

In-Service Schedule

Tomorrow is our teacher in-service day. Students will have no classes. Teachers will follow the schedule below. Please review the schedule. For questions, contact the principal's office. I appreciate your cooperation in helping our in-service day to run as smoothly as possible. I hope you all learn a lot tomorrow and that you return to your classes ready to bring your new knowledge to your students.

Thank you.

8:15 a.m.–9:15 a.m.	Improving Communication with Parents
9:20 a.m.–10:15 a.m.	Nonverbal Communication
10:20 a.m.–11:15 a.m.	First Aid
11:20 a.m.–12:15 p.m.	Lunch
12:20 p.m.–1:25 p.m.	Materials Overview
1:30 p.m.–2:35 p.m.	New Standards Training
2:40 p.m.–3:15 p.m.	Staff Meeting

12. As a kindergarten teacher, you attend teacher trainings. You get this memo. Based on the memo, what happens on an **in-service day**?

    F. Students come to school for training.

    G. Teachers and students come to school for training.

    H. Teachers come to school for training, but students stay home.

    J. Teachers will teach classes as usual.

    K. Teachers and students come to school as usual.

13. You check the schedule. What activity happens right after lunch?

    A. First Aid

    B. Staff Meeting

    C. Improving Communication with Parents

    D. Materials Overview

    E. New Standards Training

MEMO

From: Management

To: Auditors

How to Check Payroll

An auditor should understand all payroll records. Here are steps to check a computerized payroll system.

First have a preaudit interview. Ask for computer documents. Study the general accounts.

Then get an explanation of the payroll format. Get printouts of data. Read them. Check for mistakes.

Finally study the printouts. Compare them with other data. Use canceled checks or time cards. Test a small sample of employees. Check for mistakes. Look harder if you find any mistakes. Ask about any red flags. Make sure any questions you have about any mistakes are fully answered.

14. You just got a job as a tax auditor. You will be auditing businesses. You get this instructional sheet about checking payroll. What is the second step on the list?

  F. Have a preaudit interview.

  G. Get an explanation of the payroll format.

  H. Study the printouts.

  J. Test a small sample of employees.

  K. Understand all payroll records.

15. You go over the instructions. Which word tells you the step that comes last in the instructions?

  A. finally

  B. then

  C. first

  D. steps

  E. next

Skill Support

Some words have more
than one meaning.
These are called
**multiple-meaning
words**. For example,
the word *light* may
mean what comes from
the sun. It may mean
a bright color. It may
refer to something that
has little weight, such
as a feather.

Remember!

Sometimes the
dictionary lists more
than one meaning
for a word. How do
you choose the right
meaning? Context
clues can help.

Lesson 6 ...
Recognize Multiple-Meaning Words

Skill: Recognize and define multiple-meaning words

Multiple-meaning words have more than one meaning. You use some of
these words at work. You can often tell the meanings by how the words
are used. The context clues help you find the meanings. Understanding
how to find the meanings of these words will help you read workplace
documents.

In order to understand multiple-meaning words, you must be able to do
the following:

- Identify main idea and details.
- Determine meaning from context.
- Recognize synonyms and antonyms.

Skill Examples ■ ■ ■

EXAMPLE 1 Identify multiple-meaning words.

This is a memo from a company's technology division. The memo
describes workers' new computer equipment. It uses the multiple-meaning
words *screen* and *mouse*. What do these words mean in this context?

From:	Technology Division
To:	All Office Workers

All employees should get their new computers today. Someone will bring your
new computer. This person will set it up for you. The new computers are laptops.
A laptop has a smaller screen than you are used to. You should get used to the
new screen quickly. Also, we are giving you a new wireless mouse to use with your
new laptop. You use this mouse the same way you used your old mouse. The
only difference is that this mouse is not connected to the computer with wires.

We hope you enjoy using your new computer. If you have any questions or
problems, please call tech support. Technical support can be reached at
extension 217.

- The fifth sentence contains the word *screen*. You may know that a
  screen is something you put in a window to keep the bugs out. In
  this memo, *screen* has a different meaning. It is part of a computer.
  A computer *screen* shows what you are working on.
- The word *mouse* is in the seventh sentence. You can tell that the
  memo writer does not mean a small animal. Look at the surrounding
  sentences. They talk about computers and wires. You know that this
  sentence refers to a computer mouse. A computer *mouse* controls
  what you do on a computer.

Screen and *mouse* both refer to computer hardware.

EXAMPLE 2 Use context clues to define multiple-meaning words.

Read the memo. What does the word **board** mean in this memo?

From:	Manager
To:	Employees

Board Meeting Report

There was a company board meeting last week. All the members of the board were there. They were delighted to hear that our firm is doing well. The head accountant gave his report. He said that the real estate we own appreciated more than 20 percent this year. Likewise, the company has grown in value.

This represents a record profit over previous years. For this reason, the board approved a larger end-of-year bonus for every employee.

Thank you all for your hard work.

- The word *board* is in the title. It is in the first and second sentences in the first paragraph. It is also in the last sentence of the second paragraph. Look at the words surrounding *board*. This is the context.
- From the context, you can tell that *board* does not mean "a plank of wood." In business, a company's board is "a group that helps direct and control the business."

Board is a business term meaning "group in control."

EXAMPLE 3 Use comparison clues to define multiple-meaning words.

Read the memo. What does the word **profile** mean?

From:	Human Resources
To:	Recruiters

We are looking to hire a new sales manager. This person will supervise all ongoing sales projects. He or she will create project overviews for each project. He or she will present these overviews to clients and management in business meetings.

The job also involves creating proposals for new projects.

If you have any candidates who fit this profile, please send their contact information to Human Resources. Likewise, if they fit the description, send us their job history.

- The word *profile* is in the third paragraph. Look at the context around *profile* to understand its meaning. In this memo, *profile* does not mean "side view of a person or object."
- Look for comparison clues. The next sentence begins with *likewise.* It says to send their job history if they fit the description. It compares *description* to *profile.*

Profile is a business term that means "description."

Skill Support

There are several kinds of context clues. One of them is a **comparison clue**. In a comparison clue, the new word is compared to another word or phrase you might know.

Certain words or phrases tell you that a comparison clue is being used. They include *in addition, also, too, like, another, other, likewise,* and *the same.* Consider an example: *Running a marathon is hard. Running a biathlon is difficult, too.* The word *too* is a comparison clue. It compares two types of races using the words *difficult* and *hard.* This tells you the meaning of *hard.*

Skill Practice ▪ ▪ ▪

Read the workplace documents. Then answer the questions.

From:	Alice Withers, Chief of Sales
To:	Sales Force
Subject:	Sales Steady

Everyone is aware of the weak state of the economy. While the general economy is depressed, sales at XYZ Company have been steady. Sales have declined somewhat. Yet net profits have increased by 2 percent. This increase is due to a decline in costs. I want to thank you all for keeping costs down. Without these cost savings, we would not have achieved this net profit.

1. You are a salesperson for this company. What does your boss mean when she uses the word **depressed** in this e-mail?

   A. XYZ Company is small.

   B. The salespeople are lazy.

   C. The general economy is weak.

   D. The workers at XYZ Company are unhappy.

   E. The general economy is sad.

   HINT: Find the word depressed *in the second sentence. Think about what this word means in this context. Look at the sentence before it.*

From:	Ricardo Suarez, Vice President of Production
To:	Lawrence Daniels
Subject:	Conference

This note is to remind you to double check my plans for next week's conference. Please make a reservation for me at the conference hotel. Remember to book a room that has a refrigerator and a microwave. Also double check that the airline has my first-class reservation. The reservation should be for a window seat. I don't want any problems when I get to the airport.

2. What does the word **book** mean in this e-mail?

   F. to arrange for something in advance

   G. to read a publication

   H. to write a manual showing the hotel offerings

   J. to request cooking facilities

   K. to produce a printed volume one can read

   HINT: The word book *is being used as a verb.*

Try It Out! ▪ ▪ ▪

Accounts Payable Assistant You are responsible for paying your company's bills. What does the word **liquid** mean in this e-mail?

From:	Management
To:	Accounting Department
Subject:	Bill Paying

You are all aware of the financial problems our firm has had. When the banks stopped lending, we found that our accounts were not liquid. We had little available cash. We therefore had to delay paying some bills for a few months.

Business has since picked up. Our balance sheet looks more positive these days. We are able to keep a greater amount of our profits liquid. Having more cash will make it easier to pay the money we owe. Please begin paying our overdue bills immediately.

A. fluid   **D.** ready to be used

B. slippery   **E.** tied up

C. abundant

 ## Understand the Question ▪ ▪ ▪

Complete the *Plan for Successful Solving.*

Plan for Successful Solving

What am I asked to do?	What are the facts?	How do I find the answer?
Find the meaning of the word *liquid*.	*Having more cash will make it easier to pay the money we owe.*	Look for clues in other words and sentences around the word *liquid*.

 ## Find Your Answer ▪ ▪ ▪

- First of all, remember that you are trying to find the meaning of a word.

- Notice the sentence with the phrase *having more cash*. Notice that *liquid* relates to being able to pay your bills. This is the context.

- *Liquid* means "ready to be used."

- **Select the correct answer: D.** ready to be used
  This e-mail explains one meaning of the word *liquid*. The cash is ready to be used. You looked at the context around the word *liquid* to determine its meaning.

Remember!
This note uses a word you are likely familiar with, *liquid*, in a new context. Use what you know about the familiar meaning of the word to help figure out the unfamiliar meaning.

Skill Support
Use related words to help you find the meaning of unknown words. Related words can share the same base word but are used in different ways. You don't need to know all the different uses—just one. For example, you know the word *refer* means "to submit for information." This will help you determine the meaning of related words. These may be *referral* or *reference*.

On Your Own ▪ ▪ ▪

Read the workplace documents and answer the questions.

News Script

The air force is cutting its budget. It is reducing the number of planes it uses. This means fewer planes stationed in West Virginia.

A local report tells us more.

The Martinsburg Air Base will lose 11 aircraft. But it will also get 8 new planes. The planes will be switched in 2015. This is according to the Pentagon's post.

We will continue to provide you with updates on this story.

---

1. **Broadcast News Reporter** You will deliver the news on the radio this evening. You read this script before you go on the air. What does **post** mean here?

   A. a delivery of mail
   B. a strong pillar
   C. part of an earring
   D. a job
   E. a published message

2. **News Editor** You are editing this news story. You want to be sure the story is accurate before it goes on air. What does **report** mean in this script?

   F. a rumor
   G. a complaint
   H. a news story
   J. a loud, sharp noise
   K. an academic paper

MEMO

From: Tech Support

To: All Staff

How to Use the Photocopier

First turn on the power switch. Allow the photocopier to warm up. It can take up to three minutes. Lift the cover and place your document on the glass. Close the photocopier cover.

Next choose the number of copies you want to make. Select black-and-white or color. Select the paper size on the control panel. You can also manually insert a single sheet of special-sized paper.

If you would like, you can press a button to reduce or enlarge the image. Other settings allow for two-sided copies or copying two documents on one page. Finally press the "Copy" button.

3. **Office Manager** You receive this memo about using the photocopier. What does **staff** mean in the memo?

   A. a process of hiring

   B. a group of employees

   C. a rod or baton

   D. a walking stick

   E. a line on which music is written

4. **Payroll Assistant** You need to use these instructions to print the company's payroll. What does **page** mean here?

   F. a piece of paper

   G. a way to contact someone

   H. a period in history

   J. a person who delivers messages

   K. a written record

5. **Administrative Assistant** You need to use special paper to copy something. What does **sheet** mean in this context?

   A. a sail

   B. a newspaper

   C. a piece of fabric used for bedding

   D. a piece of paper

   E. a large area of ice

E-mail Message

From: Bank Manager

To: Bank Tellers

Subject: Check Fraud

A bad check was cashed at the bank recently. We need to crack down on check fraud. There are several clues to fraudulent checks. Use these signs to screen for fakes:

- The check number is missing.
- The check number is low—between 101 and 400 for personal checks, between 1001 and 1500 for business checks.
- There are stains or marks on the check. This might mean somebody changed information on it.
- The numbers at the bottom of the check are shiny. This magnetic ink should be dull, not shiny.

6. **Teller** You read the e-mail closely. You want to make sure you understand what to do when you get a check. What does **screen** mean in the e-mail?

   F. to sort

   G. to block

   H. to hide

   J. to shield

   K. to examine

7. **Teller Coordinator** You read the e-mail. You want to be sure you completely understand the content. Use other words in the memo to help define *check*. What does **check** mean here?

   A. a written order for money from a bank

   B. a ticket or token identifying an item

   C. a bill showing the amount owed

   D. a measure against error

   E. a search or examination

MEMO

From: Kennel Manager

To: Kennel Staff

Keep Our Kennel Clean

People pay good money to board their cats here. Let's make sure their cats stay healthy. Using proper cleaning tools and methods helps keep cats healthy. Even healthy-looking cats can spread fleas and disease to other cats. Disinfect the kennel at the end of every shift. Check the written log of the areas needing extra cleaning. See the list of cleaning supplies. See the list of procedures for the proper steps to follow when cleaning the kennel.

8. **Animal Caretaker** The manager at the kennel where you work sends out this memo. What does he mean by **board**?

   F. to go aboard a ship

   G. to cover or seal with planks

   H. to keep

   J. to rent

   K. to sell

9. **Kennel Attendant** You read this memo from the kennel manager. You want to know where to find information about areas needing extra cleaning. What does **log** mean in this memo?

   A. a written record of information

   B. a part of a tree

   C. an account of screenshots for movies

   D. a shipping device

   E. a recording of distance or speed traveled

10. **Kennel Technician** Your boss holds a meeting about the information in this memo. She wants to make sure everyone understands what needs to be done each day. Use the surrounding text to define the word *shift*. What does **shift** mean here?

    F. a transfer or removal

    G. a change in direction

    H. a change from one group of people to another

    J. a change in position or place

    K. a scheduled period of work

Skill Support

A **cause** is an action or event that brings about another action or event. An **effect** is what happens as a result of the cause. It is important to recognize words and phrases that describe causes and effects. This will help you in the workplace.

Signal words can help you recognize the connection between cause and effect.

- Signal words may include *because, so, therefore,* and *when*.
- Signal phrases may include *as a result, for that reason,* and *so that*.
- Another signal is when *if* and *then* are used together in the same sentence.

Remember!

Cause and effect is in your daily life. Your alarm clock buzzed, so you woke up. It was cold outside, so you wore a jacket. Each pair of actions is connected.

Lesson 7
Identify Cause and Effect

Skill: Identify cause-and-effect relationships in workplace documents

In the workplace, employees are constantly making decisions to do or not do certain things. Each decision has a consequence, or an effect. For example, a worker offers to help another worker complete a task on time. The task gets done on time. As a result, the company runs smoothly and makes money. Deciding to help is a cause. A completed task and a well-run company are effects. Deciding not to help your coworker may be the cause of the company not filling an order. This effect may lose the company money.

In order to understand cause and effect, you must be able to do the following:

- Find relationships in text.
- Understand sequence.

Skill Examples

EXAMPLE 1 Identify cause-and-effect signal words.
What cause-and-effect signal words are used in this e-mail message?

From:	Hospital Administration
To:	All Personnel
Subject:	New billing system

Because our hospital has a new computer system, we have a new system for billing. Please follow these instructions in filling out the new forms.

The billing forms have a new format. Billing codes are now entered on the line to the RIGHT of the billing amount. Do not enter the codes on the left as we used to do. The system will reject forms with the old format. If the system rejects the form, then the hospital will not get paid.

Contact us if you have any questions. Thank you for your cooperation.

- *Because* is a cause-and-effect signal word. It lets you know there is a cause-and-effect relationship in the sentence. In the first sentence of the message, the cause is the hospital's new computer system. The effect is the new billing system.
- *If* and *then* together are also cause-and-effect signal words. *If* lets you know the cause, and *then* signals the effect. In the last sentence of the second paragraph, the cause is the system rejecting the form. The effect is the hospital not getting paid.

Because, if, and *then* are cause-and-effect signal words.

EXAMPLE 2 Identify the cause-and-effect relationships in a workplace document.

What is the effect of the new procedure for overtime work?

MEMO

From: Personnel

To: All Workers

Overtime Procedure

We have a new procedure for overtime work, so any worker who works overtime must follow these new rules.

Get permission from your boss. Your boss will fill out the correct form. He or she will time stamp it. You must sign the form before your overtime begins.

You may work up to six hours of overtime per day. No one may work more than six hours of overtime per day because company policy does not allow shifts longer than 14 hours.

When you finish your overtime work, see your boss. Your boss will time stamp your form. Sign the form before you leave.

Thank you all for following the new procedure.

- First look for cause-and-effect signal words. In the first sentence, *so* is a cause-and-effect signal word. It shows that there is a cause-and-effect relationship.
- The cause is the new procedure for overtime work. The signal word *so* connects this cause to an effect. Read the text after the word *so*.

The effect is that workers who work overtime must follow the new rules.

EXAMPLE 3 Identify the cause-and-effect relationships in a workplace document.

Read the memo again. What is the cause of limiting workers to six hours of overtime?

- The cause happens before the effect. However, sometimes the effect may be written before the cause.
- Look at the third paragraph. Find the sentence with the cause-and-effect signal word *because*. In this sentence, the effect is written first. The effect is that no one may work more than six hours of overtime per day.
- The signal word *because* connects the effect to a cause. Read the text after the word *because*.

The cause is that company policy does not allow shifts longer than 14 hours.

Skill Support

Many work documents have cause-and-effect scenarios. These scenarios help to clarify instructions. They will tell you what will happen (the effect) if you do a task correctly. They may also tell you what will happen if you do not do a task correctly.

Be sure you understand the cause-and-effect connections in work tasks. Ask yourself two questions:
- What will happen if I do this task the right way?
- What will happen if I do not do this task the right way?

Doing the task correctly or incorrectly is the cause. What happens is the effect.

Use prior knowledge
to help you determine
cause and effect. You
may already know
what will happen to
a cake if it is baked
too long. It will burn.
Use this knowledge to
identify other effects.
What might happen if
other time restrictions
are not followed?

Skill Support

Determining cause
and effect requires
two simple questions.
What action or event is
the cause? What effect
happens as a result of
the cause? For example,
the dog saw a car, *so* it
barked. "The dog saw
a car" is the cause. "It
barked" is the effect.
Fill in the blanks to
the following sentence
to make that decision.
_____ [cause] *so*
_____ [effect].

Skill Practice ▪ ▪ ▪

Read the workplace documents. Then answer the questions.

From: Lisa
To: All Staff
Subject: Lunchroom

Our lunchroom is a mess. Please keep our lunchroom clean. Eat at a table.
Clean up your table with a damp cloth after you have finished eating. Put your
trash in the bin. Clean up any food that you drop on the floor. There are many
crumbs in the lunchroom because people have not cleaned up after eating.

We are going to clean out the fridge on Friday. If you leave any food in the
fridge, then it will be thrown out. Old food rots and stinks. It is also a health
hazard. The janitor has complained about old, smelly food left in the lunchroom.

---

1. What is the effect of people not cleaning up after eating?

   A. Old food rots and stinks.

   B. You should put your trash in a bin.

   C. People have begun eating at tables.

   D. Any food left in the fridge on Friday will be thrown out.

   E. There are many crumbs in the lunchroom.

   HINT: *Look for a cause-and-effect signal word, such as* because.
   Remember that the effect might be written before the cause.

From: Dana Franks
To: Sherry
Subject: Conference Schedule

The attached file contains the conference schedule. Read the schedule and
edit it for typos and other mistakes. Make sure you send one hard copy of the
schedule to each department head. Finally e-mail each assistant a copy of the
file. If you have any questions, then you should call me on my cell phone.

---

2. Which sentence from the e-mail shows a cause and effect?

   F. Read the schedule and edit it for typos and other mistakes.

   G. Make sure you send one hard copy of the schedule to each
   department head.

   H. If you have any questions, then you should call me on my
   cell phone.

   J. The attached file contains the conference schedule.

   K. Finally e-mail each assistant a copy of the file.

   HINT: *The sentence needs to show a cause-and-effect relationship
   between two ideas.*

Try It Out! ▪ ▪ ▪

Shipping and Receiving Worker You help take inventory. What is the effect of the company knowing how much of each product is in stock?

To: Staff

From: Shipping and Receiving Manager

Inventory Process

You will be assigned one type of product to inventory. Inventory is stored in numerical order by product number. Write down the number of cartons. It is vital that you do a thorough job. If we know how much of each product we have in stock, then we will know how much of each product to order.

A. You will be assigned one type of product to inventory.

B. Inventory will be stored in numerical order by product number.

C. The company will know how much of each product to order.

D. You will write down the number of cartons.

E. You will do a thorough job.

 Step 1

Understand the Question ▪ ▪ ▪

Complete the *Plan for Successful Solving.*

Plan for Successful Solving

What am I asked to do?	What are the facts?	How do I find the answer?
Identify the effect of the company knowing how much of each product is in stock.	The message uses the cause-and-effect signal words *if* and *then.*	Find the effect identified by the cause-and-effect signal words.

 Step 2

Find Your Answer ▪ ▪ ▪

- First remember what you are looking for. What will happen if the company knows how much of each product is in stock?

- The memo contains the cause-and-effect signal words *if* and *then.* The cause is the company knowing how much of each product is in stock.

- **Select the correct answer: C.** The company will know how much of each product to order.
  You identified the effect. The company will know how much of each product to order.

Remember!

The cause is always something that happens before the effect. The cause is what makes the effect happen. What effect happens when the company knows how much of each product is in stock?

Skill Support

The words *if* and *then* are commonly used to show cause and effect. The action or event after *if* will show the cause. The action or event after *then* will show the effect. Use the following sentence as an example. *If it rains, then the crew will work inside.* "It rains" is the cause. "The crew will work inside" is the effect.

On Your Own ■ ■ ■

Read the workplace documents and answer the questions.

MEMO

From: Management

To: All Employees

Dress Code Violations

The reason for this memo is the increasing number of dress-code violations. You can only wear jeans on Fridays or on other special occasions when announced. Clothes may not be ripped or frayed. Clothes should not be wrinkled. If you need clarification, then please see the employee handbook.

---

1. **Data Entry Clerk** This memo was sent out to the employees where you work. What should you do if you need clarification on the dress code?

   A. Ask your supervisor.

   B. Ask a coworker.

   C. Ask the person who wrote the memo.

   D. There is no further clarification.

   E. See the employee handbook.

2. **Human Resources Manager** You have been asked to look over this memo before it is sent out. Which pair of words from the memo signals a cause-and-effect relationship?

   F. if; then

   G. reason; is

   H. may; not

   J. can; only

   K. or; other

Instructions for Internet Connection

The name of the library network is "1516 Main." We have made the network private because of security concerns. You can only access it if you have the password. The password is "Heron21." Enter the password when you are prompted. If you cannot connect, then contact the front desk for help. The front desk's hours are posted on the front door.

3. **Librarian** A library patron wants to access the Internet with her computer. What does she need to have in order to access the Internet?

   A. help from the front desk

   B. the name of the network

   C. the front desk's hours

   D. the password

   E. security clearance

4. **Children's Librarian** You work in the children's books department. You are helping a child access the Internet. Which of these words from the instructions signals a cause-and-effect relationship?

   F. have made

   G. can only

   H. because

   J. when prompted

   K. enter the password

5. **Reference Librarian** You are explaining the new Internet connection policy to a patron. What caused the library to make the network private?

   A. the network's name

   B. security concerns

   C. the front desk

   D. the password

   E. the front desk's hours

Instructions for Using a Smoker to Calm Bees

Light the smoker. When it is producing smoke, you may use it on the hive.

Blow smoke into the hive entrance and into any cracks. Wait a few moments.

Now blow smoke under the cover of the hive so you can remove it safely. If bees move to the top of the frames, then blow them down with smoke.

Use more smoke as you reassemble the hive.

6. **Beekeeper** You are preparing to harvest honey. Which of the following words from the instructions indicates a cause-and-effect relationship?

    F. blow

    G. may

    H. wait

    J. then

    K. use

7. **Beekeeper's Assistant** You are using a smoker to calm bees. Why would you blow smoke under the cover?

    A. because the smoker is lit

    B. so you can remove the cover safely

    C. because it will seal up the cracks

    D. to make the bees come up

    E. because you need to reassemble the hive

E-mail Message

From: Jane Moy Campaign

To: Friends of Jane Moy

Subject: The Fall Campaign

Dear Supporter,

I am running for Congress in our district. I need your support in the upcoming election. Because of the size of our district, media advertising is important. We are raising funds for television ads to be aired the week before the election. If we don't have ads, then I will be at a disadvantage. Please support the campaign with a donation.

Thank you,
Jane Moy

8. **Political Aide** You are helping the candidate write this e-mail. What is the effect of the size of the district?

   F. The candidate needs support.

   G. Media advertising is important.

   H. The candidate is raising funds for television ads.

   J. The ads will be aired a week before the election.

   K. Media advertising is expensive.

9. **Public Relations Specialist** You are reviewing this e-mail before it is sent out. Which words from the e-mail signal a cause-and-effect relationship?

   A. I; our   **D.** to; be

   B. we; are   **E.** if; then

   C. support; election

10. **Politician** You are writing this e-mail to send to supporters. What will happen if the campaign doesn't have ads?

    F. You will be at a disadvantage.

    G. The campaign will lose donations.

    H. The campaign will lose advertising.

    J. You will lose the primary.

    K. The campaign will not recover.

Skill Support

You **compare** things by identifying how they are the same.

- Certain words signal that things are being compared. These words include *same, alike, similar,* and *both.*
- Signal words let you know when things have something in common. For example, oranges are *similar* to tangerines. They are both citrus fruits.

You **contrast** things by looking for how they are different.

- Certain words signal that things are being contrasted. These words include *different, unlike,* and *dissimilar.*
- Signal words let you know when things are not alike. For example, oranges are *unlike* apples. They have different colors, tastes, and textures.

Remember!

You often compare and contrast. You may eat a dinner that is different from your lunch. You may wear an outfit that is similar to your coworkers' clothes.

Lesson 8 ...
Compare and Contrast

Skill: Compare and contrast details in workplace documents

Work documents often ask you to compare or contrast things. You may have to identify how two products are alike. You may have to identify how they are different. You may need to compare or contrast something you read. You can look for signal words. They can help you determine which things are similar and which ones are different.

In order to compare and contrast, you must be able to do the following:

- Understand context meaning.
- Identify details.
- Identify phrase and sentence meaning.
- Recognize synonyms and antonyms.

Skill Examples ■ ■ ■

EXAMPLE 1 Identify compare-and-contrast signal words.
In this e-mail, the head designer asks her design team to do something. What does she compare? What does she contrast?

> **E-mail Message**
>
> From: Missie Lang, Head Designer
> To: Design Team
> Subject: Window Themes
>
> I hope everyone has some ideas for next month's window display. Our spring theme is "Fun in the Sun." Please sketch out ideas for what we can include in our display. The designs should look similar to fun outdoor events. Make sure that your designs are different from those in our current display. We want a fresh look for our windows. Please submit your ideas to me by the end of the week.

- She uses the signal word *similar* in the fourth sentence. She wants a display that compares to fun outdoor events. These two things should look alike.
- She uses the signal word *different* in the fifth sentence. The designer wants a new display that contrasts with the current window. She asks her designers to think of something completely new and different.

In this passage, the writer compares designs with outdoor events. She says the designs should contrast with the current display.

EXAMPLE 2 **Understand comparative and superlative adjectives.**
Comparative adjectives show how one thing is different from another in a specific way. Superlative adjectives show how one thing stands out from a group of things. This flyer gives rules for meetings. Which superlative adjective is used? Which comparative adjective is used?

- The fourth sentence includes the word *biggest*. This is a superlative adjective. It contrasts Room A with Rooms B and C. Room A is the biggest of all the meeting rooms.

- Read the last sentence. This sentence uses the word *smaller*. This is a comparative adjective. It contrasts Rooms C and B. Room C is smaller than Room B.

> **Attention**
>
> There are new rules for meetings. Please be aware of the size of the group. Large groups may use Meeting Room A. This is the biggest room. Small groups do not need this room. They may use Meeting Room B or C. Meeting Room C is smaller than B.

The flyer uses the superlative adjective *biggest*. It uses the comparative adjective *smaller*.

EXAMPLE 3 **Compare and contrast information in a workplace document.**
The signal word *different* tells us that Sylvia's and José's numbers are not the same. However, Sylvia does not ask what José's numbers are. Instead, she asks him to stop by her office and show her how he got his numbers. What is to be contrasted?

From:	Sylvia Merron
To:	José Ramirez
Subject:	Monthly Report Numbers

Hi José,

When you have a minute, could you stop by my office? I want to talk about your monthly report. I keep getting different numbers each time I run the calculations. Some numbers are lower and some are higher. Can you show me how you got your totals? Thanks.

- José's numbers contrast with Sylvia's numbers. She wants to know how he got his numbers. To do this, she will contrast her working method with José's.

- The e-mail also uses the words *lower* and *higher*. These are comparative adjectives that contrast two things. What is being contrasted? Reread the sentence with these words. Sylvia is talking about the numbers she gets. The e-mail says she is looking at calculations in the monthly report. The comparative adjectives *lower* and *higher* contrast the numbers.

Sylvia contrasts her numbers with José's numbers. First she says that her numbers are *different* from his. She wants to contrast her method with his. This is why she asks him to show her how he got his totals. This is a general contrast. Then she uses the comparative adjectives *lower* and *higher* to explain how her numbers are different. This is a specific contrast.

Skill Support
Comparative adjectives contrast two nouns or pronouns. For example, Tichina is smaller than you. Dede is bigger than Harold. They show how one thing is different from another in a specific way. Adjectives may also combine with the words *more* or *less* to show contrast. For example, this test is *more difficult* than the last one. The dog was *less able* to walk than before.
Superlative adjectives contrast three or more nouns or pronouns. *Biggest, smallest, best,* and *worst* are examples. They show how one thing stands out from the others. Superlative adjectives may combine with the words *the most* or *the least*. This is *the most difficult* test I have ever taken. Jeremy is *the least happy* student in the class today.

Skill Practice

Read the workplace documents. Then answer the questions.

From:	Head Chef
To:	Line Cooks
Subject:	Choosing Which Dishes to Use

Please use the correct dishes when serving meals. We use different plates for hot and cold foods. Use the red plates for hot dishes. We have red bowls for soups, too. Use the blue plates for salads and cold meats. Use the same blue plates for sandwiches.

1. You are a line cook. What does the e-mail ask you to compare?

   A. the plates used for salads and the plates used for sandwiches

   B. the hot foods and the soups

   C. the red plates and the blue plates

   D. the hot foods and the cold foods

   E. the plates used for the sandwiches and the bowls used for the soups

   HINT: Look for things you might compare. Look for adjectives that indicate comparison.

From:	Clear Care Health Insurance
To:	All Employees

New Health Insurance

Thank you for choosing Clear Care Health Insurance. As part of your insurance package, you will receive membership cards. We offer the lowest rates on doctor visits. Like your previous insurance policy, you are still entitled to a free 24-hour health-care hotline. Call any time to ask health-related or insurance questions. Again, thank you for choosing Clear Care Health Insurance. We make things clear for you.

2. Your company offers new health insurance. You receive this memo. Which sentence contrasts this policy with others?

   F. As part of your insurance package, you will receive membership cards in the mail.

   G. We offer the lowest rates on doctor visits.

   H. Like your previous insurance policy, you are still entitled to a free 24-hour health-care hotline.

   J. Call at any time to ask any health-related or insurance questions.

   K. We make things clear for you.

   HINT: Look for the word that ends in -est.

Try It Out! ▪ ▪ ▪

Restock Clerk You work at Great Foods Market. Your manager sent you this memo. Which line tells you to contrast items?

| From: | Store Manager |
| To: | Restock Clerks |

Restocking

You are in charge of keeping the shelves tidy and up-to-date. When you restock an item, check the expiration date. If the dates are the same, make sure the items are put in neat rows. If the expiration dates are different, move the older items to the front of the shelf. If you run out of an item, check the storage area.

A. You are in charge of keeping the shelves tidy and up-to-date.

B. When you restock an item, check the expiration date.

C. If dates are the same, make sure the items are put in neat rows.

D. If expiration dates are different, move the older items to the front.

E. If you run out of an item, check the storage area.

Understand the Question ▪ ▪ ▪

Complete the *Plan for Successful Solving.*

Plan for Successful Solving		
What am I asked to do?	**What are the facts?**	**How do I find the answer?**
Find the sentence that asks you to contrast.	The topic is expiration dates.	Read the memo. Find the signal word.

Find and Check Your Answer ▪ ▪ ▪

- Review the facts. You need to find the contrast signal word. Use the topic to help figure out what to contrast.

- The signal word is *different* in the sentence, "If the expiration dates are different, move the older items to the front of the shelf."

- **Select the correct answer: D.** If the expiration dates are different, move the older items to the front of the shelf.
  You read the memo carefully. You needed to find the line that told you to contrast. You identified the topic. Then you identified the signal word that told you to contrast.

Skill Support

The adjectives *good* and *bad* have irregular forms. The comparative and superlative forms of *good* are *better* and *the best.* The comparative and superlative forms of *bad* are *worse* and *the worst.*

good	better	the best
bad	worse	the worst

On Your Own ■ ■ ■

Read the workplace documents and answer the questions.

MEMO

From: Show Manager

To: Performers

Rehearsal

Note the rehearsal changes. Please mark your calendars.

Modern Dance has moved from Sunday to Monday. Jazz Choir is still on Tuesday evenings. The time has changed. The old time was 3:00 to 5:00. The new time is 6:00 to 8:00.

Dress rehearsal is on Thursday night from 9:00 to 10:00. Unlike the earlier rehearsals, both dancers and singers will be needed for this rehearsal.

Remember, this is the last week before the show. Get plenty of rest. Take good care of yourself. Some of you have not been feeling healthy. We want performers feeling their best for the show.

Our show opens Friday night and will start at 7:30. All performers need to be here by 6:30. We are expecting the biggest crowd ever for opening night.

---

1. **Dancer** You get this e-mail about rehearsal changes for a show. What is the word **best** comparing in the fourth paragraph?

   A. performers' body types

   B. performers' appearances

   C. performers' roles

   D. performers' health

   E. performers' attitudes

2. **Singer** You mark your calendar with the rehearsal changes. What word signals a contrast in the third paragraph?

   F. changes

   G. earlier

   H. unlike

   J. needed

   K. this

Chemical Safety Guidelines

Use only the chemicals required for a specific process. Never substitute different chemicals. If a chemical is out of stock, place an order with the lab stocker.

Always properly identify a chemical before using it. Some chemicals may look similar to each other. They may even smell alike.

Wear proper eye protection. Use gloves. Accidents can happen. These safety measures help protect you from the worst injuries.

---

3. **Chemist** You receive these safety guidelines at your new job. In the first paragraph, which word signals a contrast?

   A. chemicals
   B. different
   C. substitute
   D. only
   E. if

4. **Chemical Technician** You need to use an unfamiliar chemical. In the second paragraph, what does the word **alike** compare?

   F. looks
   G. chemicals
   H. smells
   J. uses
   K. identifications

5. **Laboratory Technician** You check for eye protection in your lab. In the last paragraph, what does the word **worst** compare?

   A. injuries
   B. accidents
   C. gloves
   D. safety measures
   E. eye protection

E-mail Message

From: Lisa

To: Donna

Subject: Dad's 50th birthday party

Dear Donna,

Thank you for your help so far with planning my dad's 50th birthday party. I just talked to my sister last night. I need to make some changes to our plans.

My sister reminded me that my dad likes simple things to eat. We need to change the choice of appetizer. Shrimp cocktail is too fancy. My sister wants mini hot dogs. I think crackers and cheese taste better. What do you think?

Also, we need to discuss the seating chart. You have put Aunt Cheryl at the same table as Aunt Rose. They had a big fight a long time ago. They still do not get along. Seating them together is the worst thing that could happen. We should get together this week. Get back to me as soon as possible.

Thanks!
Lisa

6. **Event Planner** Why does Lisa's e-mail ask you to think about changing the choice of appetizer?

   F. Mini hot dogs taste better than crackers and cheese.

   G. Shrimp cocktail is too fancy.

   H. Crackers and cheese taste better than shrimp cocktail.

   J. Mini hot dogs are fancier than crackers and cheese.

   K. Mini hot dogs are not fancy enough.

7. **Events Manager** What do you need to do to make the seating chart better for the party?

   A. Let people sit wherever they want.

   B. Have more tables.

   C. Have fewer tables.

   D. Put Aunt Cheryl and Aunt Rose at different tables.

   E. Keep Aunt Cheryl and Aunt Rose at the same table.

Female Flight Attendant Dress Code

No more than two pairs of earrings are allowed. Earrings may only be gold or silver. Your rings must be similarly colored. Long hair must be in a ponytail. Instead of a rubber band, you can use a bow or scrunchie. You must wear navy pants or a navy skirt. You must wear a white shirt. You must wear black shoes.

---

8. **Flight Attendant** In your employee handbook, you read this dress code. In the fifth sentence, what does **instead of** mean?

   F. along with

   G. in addition to

   H. as a replacement for

   J. together with

   K. the same as

9. **In-Flight Crew Member** In the third sentence, what does **similarly** mean?

   A. different

   B. gold

   C. light

   D. silver

   E. alike

10. **Purser** The passage compares earrings and rings. Which sentence is correct?

    F. The earrings and rings must be the same colors.

    G. The earrings and rings all must be silver.

    H. The earrings must be bigger than the rings.

    J. The earrings must be shinier than the rings.

    K. The earrings and rings all must be small.

Skill Support

Workplace language
can be different than
everyday language.
It can have its own
words. For example,
employee is a word that
is only relevant to the
workplace. Workplace
language can also give
special meanings to
ordinary words. For
example, the term *firm*
can have two different
meanings. In business
it refers to a company.
It can also mean
"secure." Knowing
**common workplace
words** is important
in work settings. It
will improve the way
you communicate
with coworkers
and customers.

Remember!

Employers often
assume you know the
meaning of common
workplace terms.
They are not usually
defined in a document.
You must find the
meaning yourself,
usually from context.

Lesson 9
Define Common Workplace Words

Skill: Identify and define common workplace words

Some words are most commonly used in the workplace. For example, *employment* means "a job one does for money." *Employment* is a word used mainly at work. Other common workplace words include *policy* and *staff.* Acronyms are also common in the workplace. For example, *TBD* stands for "to be determined." Knowing how to figure out the meanings of these words and acronyms will help you understand workplace documents. This will help you succeed at work.

In order to understand common workplace words, you must be able to do the following:

- Define words using context.
- Identify main idea and details.

Skill Examples

EXAMPLE 1 Identify common workplace words.
This is an e-mail from a company's president. It contains two common workplace words. What are they?

From:	Company President R. Lawson
To:	All Workers
Subject:	Salary Increase

I have good news. Everyone will be getting a salary increase. Everyone's salary will increase 5 percent on January 1. We are very happy about this. However, we are not able to contribute more to benefits packages (health insurance and paid vacation). Benefits will stay the same. We hope that next year we can improve benefits.

Wishing you all a happy New Year.
Sincerely,
R. Lawson

- The second sentence uses the word *salary.* A *salary* is a "fixed payment." A salary is usually a yearly amount that is paid in installments every two weeks. Salaries are usually given in exchange for work.
- Several sentences use the word *benefits. Benefits* are another type of payment. Benefits can include services and time off. Health insurance is a service. Paid vacation and sick time are types of time off.
- Some workplace words are different than their everyday meanings. For example, *benefit* in everyday language refers to an advantage.

The e-mail contains the common workplace words *salary* and *benefits.*

EXAMPLE 2 Use context clues to define common workplace words.

This is a letter offering Mr. Johnson a job. It uses the common workplace words *hourly* and *full-time.* What do these words mean?

> Dear Mr. Johnson,
>
> Your application for employment with our company has been approved.
>
> We cannot offer you a full-time job now. We are offering you hourly work. We can pay you $20 an hour. You will work about 30 hours per week.
>
> Sincerely,
> Lamar Crawford

- The word *hourly* is in the second sentence of the second paragraph. Context helps you define the word. Context refers to the words and sentences surrounding the word. Mr. Johnson will be paid $20 an hour. He will work 30 hours each week. These details show that *hourly* means "by the hour."

- *Hourly* is used in contrast to another term, *full-time.* The document shows that hourly and full-time workers are treated differently. *Full-time* workers are paid a set salary for a full work week. Hourly workers are paid by the hour. In other words, if you work 10 hours, you get paid for 10 hours at a set fee.

Hourly means "by the hour." *Full-time* means "paid a set salary for a full work week."

EXAMPLE 3 Identify common workplace acronyms.

This memo contains two common workplace acronyms. What are they? What do they stand for?

> From: HR
> To: All Employees
> Subject: Employee Records
>
> FYI, we are updating our employee records. If you have moved or changed your home phone number in the last year, please send your new information to HR.
>
> Thank you.

- The memo says it is from *HR*. This acronym is also used in the second sentence of the memo. The memo asks employees to send their new information to *HR*. This stands for "Human Resources."

- The first sentence of the memo begins with the acronym *FYI*. This means "for your information." *HR* is letting the employees know that they are updating their records.

The memo uses the acronyms *HR* and *FYI.* They stand for *Human Resources* and *for your information.*

Skill Support

Some basic workplace words include:

- *agenda* – a list of items to be discussed in a meeting
- *contract* – a written or spoken agreement
- *compensation* – something given, typically money, in exchange for work
- *task* – a piece of work to be done

Remember!

Acronyms are common in the workplace. Here are some examples of common workplace acronyms:

- *AKA* – also known as
- *CEO* – Chief Executive Officer
- *EOM* – end of message
- *TBA* – to be announced
- *TBD* – to be determined

Read the workplace documents. Then answer the questions.

From: Marty Khoury, Foreman
To: All Employees
Subject: New Assignments

You know we are reorganizing our workforce. Some of you will be taught to perform new tasks. Do not worry about learning your new jobs. Your training will prepare you to do your new tasks well.

The training schedule is not yet final. Your supervisor will tell you when your training begins. Your supervisor will give you two days' notice. You should hear from your supervisor within the next two weeks. If not, ask him or her to check with me. Everyone will begin training within two weeks.

1. You work for this company. What does Marty mean by **training**?
   A. a promotion
   B. a raise in pay
   C. instruction to perform new tasks
   D. going back to school
   E. work hours

   HINT: Find the word training *in the first paragraph. How is it described? What does this tell you about the meaning of the word?*

From: Ricardo Suarez, Chief Financial Officer
To: All Employees
Subject: Good News

Hello Everyone,

I'm pleased to report last year's troubles are over. Our company is once again in good fiscal condition. The improvement in our financial situation is the result of increased profits.

Our company was able to adapt to changing market conditions. This is the key reason we have been so successful this year.

Our success will remain steady in the future.

2. What does the word **fiscal** refer to?
   F. improvement
   G. increased profits
   H. the financial situation
   J. changing market conditions
   K. profits that remain steady

   HINT: Find the word fiscal *in the message. Then read the sentence that follows it.*

Try It Out! ■ ■ ■

Production Line Worker Your company needs you to work extra hours. What does the word **compensation** mean in this memo?

From:	Bill Willis
To:	Production Line Workers

Overtime

We ask that you work overtime for the next month. Your compensation will increase based on the number of extra hours you work. You will be paid time and a half for all hours worked over 40 hours per week.

A. appreciation   D. payment for work

B. vacation time   E. time off later on

C. overtime hours

 Step 1 Understand the Question ■ ■ ■

Complete the *Plan for Successful Solving.*

Plan for Successful Solving

What am I asked to do?	What are the facts?	How do I find the answer?
Identify the meaning of *compensation* in this memo.	This memo is about working overtime and getting paid extra.	Look at the context to explain how *compensation* relates to the extra hours worked.

 Find Your Answer ■ ■ ■

- First remember what you are trying to find. You are trying to find the meaning of the word *compensation*.

- Review the facts. The memo is about working overtime. It explains that *compensation* will increase based on the amount of time worked. The sentences around *compensation* explain how much a worker is paid for extra work.

- Look for details to help explain the meaning of *compensation*.

- **Select the correct answer: D.** payment for work
  You read the memo carefully. You needed to find the meaning of *compensation*. You used context clues to define *compensation* as "payment for work."

Remember!

A workplace document may have a word you do not know. Look for clues in words and sentences near this word. What clues do other words and sentences give you? What information can help you figure out the meaning of the new word?

Skill Support

Some words may have multiple meanings in the workplace. For example, the word *desktop* may refer to the top of a desk. However, it may also refer to a computer that sits on the desk. It may even refer to the display on the computer. Use the context to determine the meaning.

On Your Own ■ ■ ■

Read the workplace documents and answer the questions.

E-mail Message

From: Angie Lee, Facilities Manager

To: New Custodian

Subject: Job Tasks

Welcome to the Rainy Town Elementary School custodial team.

As a reminder, remember to clean all areas of our facility each day. In our building, you will empty all the trash cans and sweep the floors. Clean the windows and sanitize all the desks and chairs. Finally, vacuum the carpets. You will also need to respond to calls about accidental spills and messes. In addition, you must keep an inventory of all your supplies. Send a list of needed supplies to the school administrator. The administrator is Mr. Perry.

After working with us for one month, if you do well, you will be eligible for a pay raise. We always reward our well-qualified employees.

Let me know if you have any questions.

Sincerely,
Angie Lee, Facilities Manager

---

1. **Custodian** You receive this memo from your new boss. In the second sentence, what does **facility** mean?

   A. area

   B. supplies

   C. building

   D. inventory

   E. assignments

2. **Facilities Manager** You write the new custodian that he will be eligible for a pay raise after one month. What does **eligible** mean?

   F. busy

   G. qualified

   H. paid

   J. spent

   K. rich

How to Send a Fax

First put the document face down into the document feeder. The feeder is on top of the fax machine. Second, dial the number as follows. Dial 5, then 9, and then the 10-digit fax number. Finally press the start button to begin the transmission. The fax communication should begin feeding through. If the line is busy, the machine will redial the number. It will do this automatically. You will not have to redial the number. A confirmation report will print if the fax transmission went through.

3. **Public Policy Analyst** These instructions are posted above the fax machine in our office. What does a **fax machine** do?

   A. sends a copy of your document to someone else

   B. makes a copy of your document for you

   C. prints documents in color

   D. saves a copy of your document to use later

   E. allows you to type documents

4. **Proofreader** Press the start button to begin the transmission. What is a **transmission**?

   F. an engine

   G. a communication

   H. a program

   J. a confirmation

   K. a machine

5. **Purchaser** If the line is busy, the fax machine will redial the number automatically. What does **automatically** mean?

   A. slowly

   B. lastly

   C. magically

   D. sweetly

   E. mechanically

E-mail Message

From: Bob Lindy

To: Tania Evangelista

Subject: Welcome

Dear Tania,

Welcome to the FutureTech team. As our name implies, we are a modern organization. Our company is always looking toward the future. We know that with you at the helm of our Robstown Branch, we will see great progress there.

One of our biggest projects this year is revamping our website. We want it to be more user friendly. We would like the Robstown Branch to spearhead this project.

We would not be in business today without dedicated employees. We look forward to your contribution to the success of FutureTech.

Sincerely,
Bob Lindy, President

6. **Office Manager** You receive this e-mail from your new supervisor. It says FutureTech is a modern organization. What is an **organization**?

   F. a building

   G. a class

   H. a company

   J. technology

   K. a project

7. **Office Clerk** FutureTech greatly values its employees. What are **employees**?

   A. computers

   B. workers

   C. offices

   D. websites

   E. branches

Dear Customer,

We hope you will take the time to explore Green Thumb's website. We sell many items that may interest you.

First, we sell supplies to help you build your own greenhouse. We also sell many accessories to make your greenhouse special. Ornaments create a fun space that represents you. Second, we sell many kinds of bulbs and seeds. If you want to grow it, I bet we sell it. Third, we sell herbicides and pest controls. You need to protect your plants from weeds and unwanted pests.

Finally, we are firm believers in education. We love helping people learn about horticulture.

Happy growing.
—Green Thumb Sales Team

8. **Nursery Grower** You receive this letter from a supplier. The Green Thumb company believes in education. What does **education** mean?

   F. garden

   G. growth

   H. digging

   J. teaching

   K. sales

9. **Nursery Worker** The Green Thumb sells supplies for greenhouses. What are **supplies**?

   A. materials

   B. plants

   C. windows

   D. shovels

   E. seeds

10. **Sales Person** You sell many accessories to customers for their greenhouses. What are **accessories**?

    F. essential items

    G. bulbs

    H. window decorations

    J. basic supplies

    K. nonessential items

Skill Support

Sometimes information
is not directly stated.
It is implied, or
suggested, in the text.
An **inference** is a
guess based on what
you read and what you
already know.

To make an inference,
you must first identify
stated information.
Then you must figure
out the relevant
unstated information.

Making inferences
requires **prior
knowledge**. This is
the information you
already know.

Remember!

A writer may not state
some information. It
is assumed that you
will infer certain
information. Be sure
to consider both
stated and unstated
information when
reading a document.

Lesson 10 ...
Make Inferences

Skill: Make inferences to draw conclusions from workplace documents

You often make inferences when you read workplace documents. You
must combine your own experience with information from the text. You
then draw a conclusion that is not stated in the text. This is called making
an *inference*.

For example, you might get an e-mail informing you that you have
been hired as a temporary worker. You can infer that you will not get
any benefits.

In order to make inferences, you must be able to do the following:

- Understand stated concepts.
- Use prior knowledge.
- Identify cause and effect.
- Draw conclusions.

Skill Examples ...

**EXAMPLE 1 Identify information that is stated, identify information
that is not stated, and make inferences.**
What information is stated in the e-mail? What information is not stated?
What inference can you draw?

From:	Management
To:	All Staff
Subject:	Parking Lot

The employee parking lot will be closed this week. Workers are repainting the
lines. There is limited street parking available outside the building.

- First identify information that is stated. The e-mail states that the
  employee parking lot will be closed this week.
- Next you must "read between the lines," or look for unstated
  information. The e-mail states that the employee parking lot will be
  closed this week. It does not state that employees cannot park in the
  lot if it is closed. This is unstated information.
- You can combine the stated and unstated information to make the
  inference that you will have to park somewhere else this week.

The e-mail states that the employee parking lot will be closed this week.
The unstated information is that you cannot park in the lot. You can infer
that you will have to park somewhere else this week.

EXAMPLE 2 Identify information that is stated.

This is a message from Human Resources to a job applicant. What information is stated?

E-mail Message

From: Human Resources

To: Applicant

Subject: Job Offer

Thank you for meeting with us last week about our editor position. We were impressed with your interview. We are writing to offer you a job at our company. Your first three months of work will be a trial period. After that time, we will decide if you will become a full-time employee.

Please let us know if you wish to accept the job. We request that you respond within three days. Feel free to call us if you have any questions. Our number is 555-0121. Thank you.

- Look for information that is stated directly in the e-mail.
- You must read the whole e-mail to find information. The subject line can contain valuable information. The subject line tells you that you are receiving a job offer.
- The first paragraph has further information about the job offer.

The e-mail states that your first three months will be a trial period. It states that you could become a full-time employee after three months.

EXAMPLE 3 Identify information that is not stated.

Read the message again. What information is not stated?

- Figure out what information is not directly stated in the e-mail.
- The e-mail states that you are being offered a job. It does not directly state that you will be a temporary worker for the first three months. This is unstated information.

The unstated information is that you are being hired as a temporary worker.

EXAMPLE 4 Make inferences.

What inference can you draw from this message?

- The e-mail states that you could become a full-time employee after three months. This is the stated information. You will be a temporary worker until then. This is the unstated information.
- Combine these two pieces of information with your prior knowledge. You might know that full-time employees receive benefits. They also receive a salary. Temporary workers usually do not receive benefits.

You can infer that you will not receive benefits for the first three months.

Skill Support

After you make inferences, you can draw a conclusion. A **conclusion** is based on more than one observation or fact combined with prior knowledge. A conclusion is a form of educated guess. A conclusion is slightly different from an inference. A conclusion is based on more than one clue. You can make an inference using only one clue.

If you see a man at a bus stop, you can infer that he needs to go somewhere. You used one clue to make an inference. What if you see a man at a bus stop wearing business attire and holding a briefcase? You have several clues. You can draw a conclusion that he is going to work.

Skill Practice ▪ ▪ ▪

Read the workplace documents. Then answer the questions.

From:	Project manager
To:	Employee
Subject:	Benson Project Status Report

The Benson project is almost finished. There are three phases. We have completed Phase 1 and Phase 2. Once you complete your part, the project will be finished. Thank you for all your work on this project.

1. You are working on the Benson project. What is the stated information about your role?

  A. The project is almost finished.

  B. There are three phases.

  C. We have completed Phase 1 and Phase 2.

  D. Once you complete your part, the project will be finished.

  E. Thank you for your work on the project.

  HINT: Identify the stated information that refers to you.

2. What can you infer from this document?

  F. Your part is Phase 1.   **J.** You completed your part.

  G. Your part is Phase 2.   **K.** You do not need to complete your part.

  H. Your part is Phase 3.

  HINT: How many phases are there? How many phases are already completed? Use this information to make an inference.

From:	Management
To:	Groundskeeper
Subject:	Watering Schedule

The watering schedule is changing. Currently, the lawn is watered every weekday. From now on, it will be watered only on Tuesdays and Thursdays.

3. You are a groundskeeper. What important information is not stated?

  A. the days that the lawn does not need to be watered

  B. the changing watering schedule

  C. the previous watering schedule

  D. the days the lawn needs to be watered

  E. why the watering schedule changed

  HINT: You need to know which days you don't have to water the lawn.

Try It Out! ▪ ▪ ▪

Dry Cleaner You need to clean a suit. You find the following memo from your manager attached to the suit. What can you infer from this memo?

From:	Management
To:	All Workers

Guidelines for Cleaning Suits

We have a new policy for cleaning suits. We will no longer clean the jacket and pants separately. Please follow this guideline when cleaning all suits.

A. You should first clean the pants and then clean the jacket.

B. You should first clean the jacket and then clean the pants.

C. You should clean the jacket but not the pants.

D. You should not clean the jacket or the pants.

E. You should clean the jacket and pants together.

 Step 1 **Understand the Question** ▪ ▪ ▪

Complete the *Plan for Successful Solving.*

Plan for Successful Solving

What am I asked to do?	What are the facts?	How do I find the answer?
Make an inference based on the information in the memo.	The memo states, "We will no longer clean the jacket and pants separately."	Identify stated information. Identify relevant unstated information. Then make an inference.

 Step 2 **Find Your Answer** ▪ ▪ ▪

- You need to make an inference. Use the stated information to help.

- The stated information is, "We will no longer clean the jacket and pants separately." The unstated information is that you should still clean the jacket and pants. You can infer that you should clean them together.

- **Select the correct answer: E.** You should clean the jacket and pants together.
  You read the memo carefully. You identified the stated and unstated information. Then you made an inference.

Remember!

You likely make inferences and draw conclusions every day. You see that the weather is bad. You may infer that traffic will also be bad. Use that experience to make inferences and draw conclusions in the workplace.

Skill Support

When making an inference, clearly identify stated information. The *Try It Out!* memo states that pants and jackets will no longer be cleaned separately. It also states that there will be a new policy.

Clearly identifying the stated information will help you make the correct inference.

On Your Own ▪ ▪ ▪

Read the workplace documents and answer the questions.

Attendance Policy

Excellent work attendance is expected at Scent It. We take our work seriously. On-time flower delivery depends on you.

All employees get 2.15 hours of emergency personal time per pay period. This is 56 hours a year. To use it, call when you miss a shift. This call must happen no later than one hour after your shift starts. When a new year begins, you get a bonus for unused emergency personal time. The bonus depends on the amount of time left at the end of the year.

Let me know if you have any questions.
Jerome Lesle, owner

---

1. **Cashier** You just got a job at Scent It Flower Shop. You are reading over the work attendance policy. What inference can you make based on the information in the policy?

   A. Emergency personal time is not meant to be used at the end of the year.

   B. Emergency personal time is not meant to be used at the beginning of the year.

   C. Emergency personal time is not meant to be used for vacations.

   D. Emergency personal time is not meant to be used for two shifts in a row.

   E. Emergency personal time is not meant to be used for medical reasons.

2. **Florist** You work at Scent It. The attendance policy has recently changed. You read this copy of the new policy. What information is stated in the policy?

   F. You get a smaller bonus for less unused emergency personal time.

   G. You get a bigger bonus for more unused emergency personal time.

   H. You get 2.15 hours of emergency personal time a year.

   J. You get 56 hours of emergency personal time per pay period.

   K. You get a bonus for unused emergency personal time.

Reading for Information   Basic Skills for the Workplace

> **MEMO**
>
> From: Management
> To: All Staff
>
> ### Flu Prevention Tips
>
> A yearly flu vaccine is recommended. The vaccine protects against the three most common flu viruses. People at high risk for flu complications include pregnant women and older adults.
>
> If you get sick, stay home for at least 24 hours after your fever is gone. Only leave your house to get medical care or for other necessities.

3. **Middle School Teacher** Many teachers have been out sick lately. You receive this memo in your mailbox. What information is stated in the memo?

   A. Pregnant women are at high risk for flu complications.

   B. Pregnant women should not get a flu vaccine.

   C. Pregnant women should get a flu vaccine.

   D. Pregnant women are more likely to get the flu.

   E. Pregnant women are less likely to get the flu.

4. **Computer Network Specialist** You work in the information technology department at a large office. This memo about the flu was just sent to all the office departments. You read the memo. What unstated information can you infer from the memo?

   F. The flu vaccine protects against the three most common flu viruses.

   G. The flu vaccine does not protect against all types of flu.

   H. Older people are at high risk for flu complications.

   J. There are only three types of flu viruses.

   K. A yearly flu vaccine is recommended.

5. **Receptionist** The office manager of the firm shares this memo with you. It is about how to prevent the flu. What inference can you make based on the memo?

   A. Do not get a vaccine if you already have the flu.

   B. Do not get out of bed if you have the flu.

   C. Do not get a vaccine if you are an older adult.

   D. Do not leave the house to go to work if you have the flu.

   E. Do not leave the house to go to the doctor if you have the flu.

E-mail Message

From: Building and Grounds Supervisor

To: All Window Cleaners

Subject: Equipment Safety

Equipment safety is very important on the job. We will provide all cleaning equipment. Use only equipment labeled "for commercial use." Equipment labeled "recreational or rescue use only" is not allowed. Equipment alterations are only safe if the changes are based on instructions from the manufacturer. Before beginning a shift, check your equipment. If you have questions, refer to the manufacturer manuals. Alert your supervisor to any problems.

---

6. **Building and Grounds Supervisor** You sent this e-mail. What information did you state in the message?

   F. The company will check all cleaning equipment.

   G. The company will provide all cleaning equipment.

   H. The company will make specific changes to cleaning equipment.

   J. The company will write manuals for equipment safety.

   K. The company will label all equipment.

7. **Window Washer** You want to make sure you follow the equipment safety instructions. You read this e-mail. Which of the following is unstated information that is supported by the message?

   A. Equipment alterations are always safe.

   B. Always use equipment labeled "rescue use only."

   C. Do not bring in your own equipment.

   D. Alter equipment as you prefer.

   E. Only use equipment labeled "recreation use only."

8. **Heavy Duty Custodian** After reading this e-mail, you check the equipment you will be using. Which of the following is an inference you can make from the message?

   F. Always question equipment labeled "for commercial use."

   G. Use equipment labeled "for recreational or rescue use only."

   H. Do not check any equipment provided by the company.

   J. Alert a supervisor about equipment labeled "for recreational or rescue use only."

   K. Do not refer to the manufacturer manuals.

E-mail Message

From: State Animal Health Commission

To: State Licensed Veterinarians

Subject: Pet Identification

Thousands of pets go missing each year. The law requires pet identification tags. Collars with tags are good, but they can fall off. Microchips are an excellent way to identify lost pets. All state animal shelters now scan animals for microchips. Encourage clients to microchip their pets. This will help shelters return them to their owners faster.

9. **Veterinarian** A client is concerned about his new cat. He wants to protect his pet from getting lost. What unstated information about pet identification is supported in this notice?

    A. Collars with tags are the best way to identify a pet.

    B. Microchips can only be read at some state animal shelters.

    C. Microchips cannot be read at state animal shelters.

    D. Collars with tags are not the best way to identify pets.

    E. Microchips are not the best way to identify a pet.

10. **Veterinary Technician** You share information from this notice with your client. You talk about what to do if a pet is lost. What is one inference you can make from the notice about finding lost pets?

    F. Many lost pets are identified through collars with tags.

    G. Microchips are not as effective as collars with tags for identifying pets.

    H. Many lost pets with microchips are never identified.

    J. Many lost pets with collars and tags are never identified.

    K. Microchips help shelters identify lost pets.

Level 2 Performance Assessment ■ ■ ■

These problems are at a Level 2 rating of difficulty. They are similar to problems on a career readiness certificate test. For each question, you can check your answer. To do this, use the answer key. It is located on pp. 262–264 of this book. It explains each answer option. It also shows the lesson that covers that skill. You may refer to that lesson to review the skill.

E-mail Message

From: System Administrator

To: Computer Technicians

Subject: System Diagnostic Testing

We will be running a system diagnostic test on the computer server at 12:30 p.m. Please make sure all workers log off their computers before lunch. If not, log them off. The test will not run correctly if any computers are logged on.

This test will help us monitor any bugs or other problems with the network. It should last about 15 minutes. For questions on what to do, contact the administrator.

---

1. You are a computer support technician in an office. You receive this e-mail from the computer system administrator. What does the word **server** mean in the e-mail? Use surrounding words to help define it.

    A. a person who brings food or drink

    B. a tennis player

    C. the main computer in a network

    D. a person who serves legal papers

    E. a wide fork or spoon

2. You read the e-mail again. You want to make sure you know what will be happening with the diagnostic test. What does the word **running** mean in the e-mail?

    F. moving quickly by foot   J. flowing

    G. performing   K. occurring over and over

    H. escaping

3. A coworker asks you what the diagnostic test is for. You refer to this e-mail. What does the word **bugs** mean here? Use clues from the surrounding text for the meaning.

    A. small insects   D. hidden listening devices

    B. nonspecific sicknesses   E. germs

    C. defects or flaws

> **MEMO**
>
> From: State Court System
>
> To: Goody & Burns, Attorneys at Law
>
> ### EZ Filing Closure Notice
>
> The state is having financial trouble. The court system has cut its budget, so it cannot fund the EZ Filing system. That means you may not file court forms online. This change takes effect July 1. Complete all online filings by the end of June.
>
> As of July 1, all forms must be filed in person or by mail. If you try to file online, then the forms will not be accepted. Incorrectly filed forms can lead to problems. Your clients may be fined. They may face legal action.
>
> Please inform all staff at your law firm of these changes. It has been a pleasure serving you. We look forward to seeing you in person. For questions, contact the nearest state court. A clerk will be happy to help you.

4. As a lawyer, you file documents in court. You receive this notice from the state court system. You read it to find out why EZ Filing is closing. Which sentence in the notice uses a cause-and-effect signal word?

F. The court system has cut its budget, so it cannot fund EZ Filing.

G. Complete all online filings by the end of June.

H. Your clients may be fined.

J. It has been a pleasure serving you.

K. We look forward to seeing you in person.

5. You explain to your assistant how to file court papers now that the EZ Filing is closing. You tell him why this is so important. Which is a cause-and-effect relationship explained in the notice?

A. Your clients may face legal action.

B. For questions, contact the nearest state court.

C. Inform all staff at your law firm of these changes.

D. If you file the forms online, then they will not be accepted.

E. As of July 1, all forms must be filed in person.

Choose the Right Brush

Different dogs have different kinds of coats. Therefore, we use specific brushes for each kind. Look at the fur before choosing a brush. Please choose the right brush for the dog you are working on.

Use rake brushes for dogs with a soft undercoat. These dogs have long, sturdy outer hair. Rakes are good for both golden retrievers and Siberian huskies.

Use pin brushes for dogs with curly hair. These are wire brushes with round heads. Unlike rakes, pin brushes are used for sensitive skin. They are also gentle.

You can use a bristle brush on any type of dog. Different bristle brushes have different lengths of bristles and different spacing between the bristles. Use bristle brushes with widely spaced, long bristles on dogs with longer coats. For dogs with coarse fur, make sure the bristles are stiff enough to brush the coat.

Consider using a slicker brush for dogs with long, thick coats. These brushes are good for removing tangles.

6. You just got a job as a dog groomer. You get these descriptions on grooming brushes at work. Which sentence uses a cause–and–effect signal word?

   F. Use pin brushes for dogs with curly hair.

   G. These are wire brushes with round heads.

   H. Therefore, we use specific brushes for each kind.

   J. Use rake brushes for dogs with a soft undercoat.

   K. Please choose the right brush for the dog you are working on.

7. You use a pin brush on some dogs. Other dogs need a rake. What signal word is used to signal a difference between rakes and pin brushes?

   A. different

   B. good

   C. both

   D. used

   E. unlike

Clinical Trial Guidelines

All medical clinical trials are similar in that they follow standard rules. These rules state the best way to perform the trials.

There must be a safety plan for clinical trials. This plan keeps participants safe. It also protects the outcome of the study.

There is a control group for all trials. Different from the rest of the participants, this group does not get the experimental treatment.

The participants are placed into groups randomly to decide who is in the control group and who gets the experimental treatment.

The participants do not know whether they are in the control group or in the group that receives the experimental treatment.

Researchers or doctors closely monitor participants. A participant can leave the trial at any time.

8. You are a scientist. You are setting up a clinical trial for a new medicine. You read these guidelines to help you. Which sentence explains whether your trial should be set up in the same way or differently from other trials?

   F. All medical clinical trials are similar in that they follow standard rules.

   G. Researchers or doctors closely monitor participants.

   H. There must be a safety plan for clinical trials.

   J. A participant can leave the trial at any time.

   K. Different from the rest of the participants, this group does not get the experimental treatment.

9. You want to know how these guidelines were developed. You would like to know if other rules were ever compared. Which of the following is a comparison signal word in the guidelines?

   A. any

   B. must

   C. best

   D. all

   E. also

> **MEMO**
>
> From: Human Resources
>
> To: All Employees
>
> ### Insurance Benefits Overview
>
> Here are the insurance plans for employees. These plans, along with your salary, are part of your total compensation package. They are your reward. Thank you for working for our company. You have earned these benefits.
>
> If you are hired to work full time, you get basic insurance. The basic policy offers:
>
> • a medical plan with prescription medication coverage
>
> • $20,000 basic life insurance
>
> • $20,000 accidental death or injury insurance
>
> Remember, these plans are only the basic package. You can also sign up for the select package. With the select package, you get more coverage. Children and spouses may be covered. Schedule an appointment with Human Resources to learn more.

10. You are a graphic designer. You were hired to work at an advertising company. You receive this information about insurance benefits. What does the word **benefits** mean?

    F. help

    G. aid

    H. payments

    J. kind deeds

    K. events to raise money

11. You read the overview. What does the word **compensation** refer to? Look for context clues in the text.

    A. salary and other benefits

    B. reimbursement for injuries

    C. medical coverage

    D. basic life insurance

    E. family coverage

12. You want to know more about your possible insurance coverage. What does the word **schedule** mean in the overview?

    F. to register

    G. to list

    H. to plan for a certain time

    J. to enroll

    K. to create a timetable

E-mail Message

From: School Construction Project Manager

To: McKinley School Principal

Subject: Construction Status

Construction on the McKinley School site is almost done. The bathrooms are 98 percent finished. Construction will be complete August 15. Your staff can begin entering the building at that time. There will be a generator available for daytime electricity use. Permanent power will be turned on the week of August 30. At that point, we will sign off on the project.

13. You are the secretary at McKinley School. The school has been closed for construction repairs during the summer. You receive this e-mail from the construction manager. What information is stated in the e-mail?

   A. The bathrooms are not yet usable.

   B. Construction will be complete August 15.

   C. Staff should not enter the building at this time.

   D. There is no power in the building yet.

   E. The toilets are not in the bathrooms yet.

14. You are concerned about the reopening of the school site. You need to give the staff instructions on building use. What information is not directly stated in the e-mail?

   F. The staff can enter the building on August 15.

   G. Permanent power will be turned on the week of August 30.

   H. There will be no permanent power before August 30.

   J. Construction on the bathrooms is 98 percent finished.

   K. The construction crew will sign off on the project the week of August 30.

15. You read the e-mail again. What can you infer from this document?

   A. Construction is almost done.

   B. Staff should not enter the building before August 15.

   C. The project will be finished on August 15.

   D. The bathrooms are the most difficult part of construction.

   E. Staff can enter the building on August 15.

Applied Mathematics ...

Applying mathematics in the workplace is an essential skill. The level of mathematics you need is often basic. For example, you might need to give change to a customer. You might have to add up the cost of an order. At other times you may need to perform more difficult tasks. You might need to identify the correct operation for solving a problem.

Workplace Skills: Basic Skills for the Workplace contains lessons that will help you improve your mathematical skills. It will also help you to apply them in the workplace. The questions in the lessons are pulled from real workplace situations. Each lesson includes step-by-step examples of how to perform a skill. You then have the opportunity to try the skill on your own. You will also learn to use the two-step approach to problem solving. This is shown on the next page.

Level 1

Lesson 1: Understand Number Basics

Lesson 2: Add Whole Numbers

Lesson 3: Subtract Whole Numbers

Lesson 4: Understand Decimals

Lesson 5: Read Time

Level 2

Lesson 6: Multiply Whole Numbers

Lesson 7: Divide Whole Numbers

Lesson 8: Use Measurements

Lesson 9: Understand Fractions

Lesson 10: Choose the Correct Operation

Photo: Jamie Grill/Getty Images

Two–Step Approach ▪ ▪ ▪

It is important to learn how to approach mathematical problems. Different problems require the use of different skills. However, you can solve all problems using two necessary steps. First you must be sure you understand the problem. You must identify important information and key words. Then you need to find and check your answer.

The two-step approach to problem solving is an easy-to-follow model. You can use it to solve workplace problems. It can also be used on a career readiness certificate test.

Here is an example. You work at a repair shop. A customer requested an oil change and a tire rotation. The oil change costs $29. The tire rotation costs $17. What is the total amount the customer will be charged before tax?

 ## Understand the Problem ▪ ▪ ▪

Complete the *Plan for Successful Solving.*

Plan for Successful Solving

What am I asked to do?	What are the facts?	How do I find the answer?
Determine the solution you are being asked to find.	Identify information in the problem that leads you to a solution.	Identify how to solve the problem.
You need to find the total amount to charge the customer.	oil change $29 tire rotation $17	You need to add the two numbers to find the total.

 ## Find and Check Your Answer ▪ ▪ ▪

- Write the numbers in columns. Align by place value.

- Draw a line under the numbers. You will write the sum (total) under this line.

$$\begin{array}{r} \overset{1}{} \$29 \\ +\ \ 17 \\ \hline \$46 \end{array}$$

- Add the digits in the far right column. This is the ones column. You need to regroup 1 to the column to the left.

- Now move one column to the left. This is the tens column. Add these digits and the 1 you regrouped.

The sum is 46. The customer owes $46 altogether.

Key Words:
*whole number, digit,
place value, round*

Skill Support

Whole numbers are the numbers 0, 1, 2, 3, 4, 5, etc. Ten **digits** are used to write all numbers: 0, 1, 2, 3, 4, 5, 6, 7, 8, and 9.

Numbers follow a **place value** system. The value of a digit depends on its place in the number. The diagram below shows the place value of each digit in the number 2,594.

$$\begin{array}{cccc} \text{thousands} & \text{hundreds} & \text{tens} & \text{ones} \\ 2, & 5 & 9 & 4 \end{array}$$

The 4 is in the ones place. It means 4 ones. The 9 is in the tens place. It means 9 tens, or 90. The 5 is in the hundreds place. It means 5 hundreds, or 500. The 2 is in the thousands place. It means 2 thousands, or 2,000. In large numbers, commas separate digits into groups of three: 2,594.

Remember!

> means "greater than."
< means "less than."
= means "equal to."

Lesson 1 ...
Understand Number Basics

Skill: Understand number basics such as counting, comparing, ordering, and rounding

You use numbers in most jobs.

- You must *count* items. Store clerks count the items on a shelf.
- You must *compare* numbers. Salespeople compare prices of products.
- You must *order*, or arrange, items. You can arrange items from least to greatest or from greatest to least.
- Sometimes you must estimate numbers. *Rounding* is a way to estimate. Hotel cooks estimate amounts when they order food.

In order to use number basics to solve problems, you must be able to do the following:

- Read and understand whole numbers.
- Understand place values in whole numbers to thousands.
- Round whole numbers to the nearest place value.

Skill Examples ▪ ▪ ▪

EXAMPLE 1 Count numbers.
Counting numbers means finding how many. Count the number of nails.

There are 17 nails.

EXAMPLE 2 Compare numbers.
Compare 1,296 and 1,269. Numbers are greater than, less than, or equal to other numbers. Which is greater: 1,296 or 1,269?

- Identify the place value by writing the numbers in columns. Place ones under ones, tens under tens, and so on.

$$\begin{array}{cccc} \text{thousands} & \text{hundreds} & \text{tens} & \text{ones} \\ 1, & 2 & 9 & 6 \\ 1, & 2 & 6 & 9 \end{array}$$

- Compare each column. Begin with the column on the far left. This is the thousands column. Compare the numbers in the thousands column. 1 = 1.
- Compare the numbers in the hundreds column. 2 = 2.
- Compare the numbers in the tens column. 9 > 6. We do not even need to look at the ones column. 1,296 > 1,269.

EXAMPLE 3 Order numbers.

Compare 97, 538, 912, 535, and 583. Place them in order from least to greatest.

- Align the numbers. Place ones under ones, tens under tens, and so on.

- Compare the number of digits. Begin with the digits in the column on the far left. This is the hundreds column. 97 has no digit in this column. That means 97 is less than 100. It is the least number. Place 97 at the beginning of the list.

    97, ____, ____, ____, ____

- Compare the other digits in the hundreds column. 9 is the greatest digit. Place 912 at the end of the list.

    97, ____, ____, ____, 912

- Look at the three remaining digits in the hundreds column. They are all 5. This does not help you compare the numbers. You must move to the tens column. 3 < 8. Place 583 to the left of 912.

    97, ____, ____, 583, 912

- Two numbers remain. Compare the digits in the ones column. 5 < 8. Place 535 to the right of 97.

hundreds	tens	ones
	9	7
5	3	8
9	1	2
5	3	5
5	8	3

hundreds	tens	ones
	9	7
5	3	5
5	3	8
5	8	3
9	1	2

The numbers from least to greatest are 97, 535, 538, 583, 912.

EXAMPLE 4 Round numbers.

Rounding is a way to estimate. This means you give a number that is about equal to an actual number. Round 1,537 to the nearest ten. Round 1,745 to the nearest hundred.

- Round 1,537 to the nearest ten. The digit in the tens column is 3. Look at the digit to its right. 7 > 5.

- Add 1 to the digit in the tens column. 3 + 1 = 4. Then change the digit to the right to a zero.

thousands	hundreds	tens	ones
1,	5	3	7

Round up: 1,540

- Round 1,745 to the nearest hundred. The digit in the hundreds column is 7. Look at the digit to its right. 4 < 5.

- Keep the digit in the hundreds column the same. Change the digits to the right to zeros.

thousands	hundreds	tens	ones
1,	7	4	5

Round down: 1,700

Remember!

To compare two whole numbers, look at the digits. Count the number of digits. The number with more digits is always greater: 250 > 95.

The whole number with fewer digits is always less: 999 < 1,000.

Skill Support

To **round** a whole number, follow these steps:

- Find the place you are rounding to. Underline this digit.
- Look at the digit to its right. If it is 5 or greater, round up. If it is less than 5, round down.

Remember!

If you are rounding to the nearest ten, the number will have at least 1 zero. Examples:

- 40
- 120
- 500

If you are rounding to the nearest hundred, the number will have at least 2 zeros. Examples:

- 200
- 700
- 1,000

Skill Support

This is a number line. It can help you decide whether to round up or down.

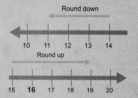

15 is halfway to 20. 16 is more than halfway. So it is closer to 20 than to 10. To round 16 to the nearest ten, you should round up to 20.

Skill Practice ▪ ▪ ▪

1. Put the numbers in order from least to greatest.
913   1,113   1,311   931   999

	thousands	hundreds	tens	ones
		9	1	3
	1,	1	1	3
	1,	3	1	1
		9	3	1
		9	9	9

A. 913   931   999   1,113   1,311
B. 931   913   999   1,113   1,311
C. 913   931   999   1,311   1,113
D. 1,311   1,113   913   931   999
E. 1,311   1,113   999   931   913

HINT: *913, 931, and 999 have no digit in the thousands column. They are less than 1,113 and 1,311.*

2. Round 16, 85, and 134 to the nearest ten.

	hundreds	tens	ones
		1	6
		8	5
	1	3	4

F. 10   80   130
G. 10   90   130
H. 20   80   130
J. 20   90   130
K. 20   90   140

HINT: *Look at the digits in the ones column. If the digit is less than 5, round down. If the digit is 5 or greater, round up.*

3. Compare the following numbers. Which is the greatest?   649   3,340   3,965   852   4,213

	thousands	hundreds	tens	ones
		6	4	9
	3,	3	4	0
	3,	9	6	5
		8	5	2
	4,	2	1	3

A. 4,213   **D.** 3,965
B. 649   **E.** 3,340
C. 852

HINT: *Start with the digits in the column with the greatest value. This is the thousands column.*

4. Look at the pencils. Some of them are shaded gray. Count the number of gray pencils.

F. 1
G. 5
H. 7
J. 8
K. 15

HINT: *Count only the pencils that are shaded gray.*

Try It Out! ▪ ▪ ▪

Construction Worker You work at Sturdy Construction. You are building a fence. You need about 55 posts. The lumber yard sells posts in bundles. The posts come in bundles of 50, 60, 70, 80, and 90 posts. How many posts should you buy?

A. 50   **B.** 60   **C.** 70   **D.** 80   **E.** 90

 Step 1 Understand the Problem ▪ ▪ ▪

Complete the *Plan for Successful Solving.*

Plan for Successful Solving

What am I asked to do?	What are the facts?	How do I find the answer?
You need to determine how many posts to buy.	You need about 55 posts. They are sold in bundles of 50, 60, 70, 80, and 90.	The key word is *about.* It tells you that you are going to estimate. You must use rounding to solve this problem. Round to the nearest ten. This will tell you how many posts you should buy.

 Step 2 Find and Check Your Answer ▪ ▪ ▪

- Confirm your understanding of the problem. Revise your plan as needed.

- Decide how to solve the problem. *I need to estimate how many posts to buy. I must round to the nearest ten. To round to the nearest ten, I look at the ones column. The digit is 5. I should round up.*

- Before selecting an answer, read the question again. Be sure your answer makes sense.

- **Select the correct answer: B.** 60
  The digit in the ones column is 5, so you round up. To round 55, you add 1 to the digit in the tens column. The digit in the ones column becomes 0.

Remember!
This problem deals with workplace quantities. Think carefully about when to round up or down. In this case, the ones column digit is 5. So you round up.

Suppose you rounded down. You would not have bought enough posts.

Level 1
Applied Mathematics

Skill Support
This is a multiple-choice question. Eliminate any unlikely choices. The choice, 90, is much greater than 55. Suppose you bought a bundle of 90 posts. You would have too many unused posts. So, eliminate 90 as an answer choice.

On Your Own ▪ ■ ■

Read and solve the following problems.

1. **Restaurant Manager** You are scheduling your waitstaff for this week. You look at how much they worked last week. You want to balance the hours. People who worked more last week will work less this week. Ben worked 22 hours last week. Cole worked 34 hours. Juanita worked 40 hours. Mei worked 28 hours. Vladimir worked 26 hours. Who worked the most hours?

   A. Ben   D. Mei

   B. Cole   E. Vladimir

   C. Juanita

2. **Sociologist** You are studying population groups. You read statistics on US households. There are 4,687 Asian and Pacific Islander households in your area. You predict the number of households will rise to the nearest hundred in 2 years. What do you predict the number of households will be?

   F. 4,600   J. 4,900

   G. 4,700   K. 5,000

   H. 4,800

3. **Software Developer** You are developing software for a new company. You need to buy a database package to complete your work. The packages you find cost $38, $53, and $51. You want to know which one is the least expensive and which one is the most expensive. Put the prices in order from least to greatest.

   A. $38, $51, $53

   B. $51, $38, $53

   C. $38, $53, $51

   D. $51, $53, $38

   E. $53, $51, $38

4. **Political Aide** You are raising money for a campaign. You have received donations of $50, $80, and $65. You are making a list of donations. You list the highest amount first. Put the donations in order from highest to lowest.

   F. $80, $65, $50

   G. $80, $50, $65

   H. $50, $65, $80

   J. $50, $80, $65

   K. $65, $80, $50

5. **Painter** You paint houses. You give customers estimates before you start the jobs. Your estimates are to the nearest hundred dollars. You find that one house will cost $4,560. What was your estimate?

   A. $4,000   D. $5,000

   B. $4,500   E. $5,560

   C. $4,600

6. **Automotive Specialty Technician** You fix radiators at an auto repair shop. A customer needs a new radiator cap for her car. Your estimate of the cost was to the nearest ten dollars. The cap costs $28. What amount did you estimate?

   F. $10

   G. $20

   H. $30

   J. $40

   K. $50

7. **Farm Manager** You order grain once a week. Your cows eat 57 pounds of grain each week. You order grain in 10-pound bags. You order the grain by weight. How many pounds must you order each week?

A. 10 pounds

B. 50 pounds

C. 55 pounds

D. 60 pounds

E. 100 pounds

8. **Photographer** You have a modeling shoot. You print photos from the job. Your client wants 365 pictures. Photos are available in bundles of hundreds. How many photos should she order?

F. 100

G. 200

H. 300

J. 400

K. 500

9. **Account Manager** You are checking the deposits from a local company. Last week the company deposited $1,500 on Monday. On Wednesday the deposit was $1,000. On Friday the deposit was $1,250. Order the deposits from least to greatest.

A. $1,000, $1,500, $1,250

B. $1,500, $1,000, $1,250

C. $1,250, $1,000, $1,500

D. $1,250, $1,500, $1,000

E. $1,000, $1,250, $1,500

10. **Legal Secretary** You are taking notes for a lawyer. You need to buy 35 legal pads. The legal pads are sold in sets of 10. Which set should you buy?

F. a set of 10

G. a set of 20

H. a set of 30

J. a set of 40

K. a set of 50

WORKSPACE

Key Words:

addition, addends, sum, regrouping

Remember!

Addition is combining, or adding, numbers. The plus sign (+) tells you what to add. The numbers that are added are called **addends.** The answer is called the **sum** or total.

There are different ways to write an addition problem.

$$6 + 4 = 10$$

$$\begin{array}{r} 6 \\ + 4 \\ \hline 10 \end{array}$$

Skill Support

When you add numbers on paper, you add from right to left, starting with the ones column. However, when you add using a calculator, you must type the numbers into the calculator from left to right.

Lesson 2 ⬛⬛⬛
Add Whole Numbers

Skill: Use addition of whole numbers to solve problems

You add to combine numbers. You probably do it every day. For example, you may add the number of hours you work each day. You may add the number of hours you work in a week. You know how many men and how many women work in your office. You may add to find the total number of workers.

In order to use addition to solve problems, you must be able to do the following:

- Understand place value.

- Understand basic addition facts.

- Add numbers with regrouping.

Skill Examples ⬛⬛⬛

EXAMPLE 1 Add two numbers.
Add: 645 + 153

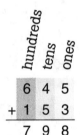

- Write the numbers in columns. Write the ones under ones. Write the tens under tens. Write the hundreds under hundreds.

- Draw a line under the numbers. You will write the sum (total) under this line.

- Begin by adding the digits in the far right column. This is the ones column. 5 + 3 = 8. Write 8 under the line in the ones column.

- Now move one column to the left. This is the tens column. Add these digits. 4 + 5 = 9. Write 9 under the line in the tens column.

- Finally add the digits in the far left column. This is the hundreds column. 6 + 1 = 7. Write 7 under the line in the hundreds column.

The sum is 798.

EXAMPLE 2 Use regrouping to add two numbers.
Add: 2,356 + 917

Sometimes the sum of the numbers in a column is 10 or more. If so, you must **regroup**, or carry. To regroup numbers, follow these steps:

	thousands	hundreds	tens	ones
	1		1	
	2,	3	5	6
+		9	1	7
	3,	2	7	3

- Write the numbers in columns based on place value. Begin by adding the digits in the ones column. 6 + 7 = 13. The sum is greater than 10. You must regroup. Write 3 under the line in the ones column. Regroup 1 ten to the tens column.

- Now add the digits in the tens column. Be sure to add the 1 you regrouped. 1 + 5 + 1 = 7. Write 7 below the line in the tens column.

- Next add the digits in the hundreds column. 3 + 9 = 12. The sum is 10 or more. You must regroup. Write 2 under the line in the hundreds column. Regroup 1 thousand to the thousands column.

- Finally add the digits in the thousands column. There is no digit in the thousands column for 917. Be sure to add the 1 you regrouped. 1 + 2 = 3. Write 3 under the line in the thousands column.

The sum is 3,273.

EXAMPLE 3 Add more than two numbers.
Add: 59 + 37 + 481 + 153

	hundreds	tens	ones
	2	2	
		5	9
		3	7
	4	8	1
+	1	5	3
	7	3	0

- Align the numbers in columns. Begin by adding the digits in the ones column. Group pairs that add up to 10.

- Add the digits in the ones column. Write 0 under the line in the ones column. Regroup 2 tens to the tens column.

- Look at the digits in the tens column. Group pairs that add up to 10.

- Add the digits in the tens column. Write 3 under the line in the tens column. Then regroup 2 to the hundreds column.

- Add the digits in the hundreds column. 2 + 4 + 1 = 7.

The sum is 730.

Remember!

You can add numbers in any order. Changing the order does not change the sum.

4 + 3 = 7

3 + 4 = 7

Skill Support

Look for pairs of numbers that add up to 10. Change the order of the numbers if you find them. This method does not work with every problem, but it makes adding much easier when it does work.

10
↓   ↓
9 + 7 + 1 + 3 = 20
↑   ↑
10

10
↓   ↓
2 + 5 + 3 + 8 + 5 = 23
↑   ↑
10

Skill Practice ...

1. Add two numbers.
31 + 65 =

A. 86

B. 96

C. 97

D. 99

E. 105

HINT: Align the numbers in columns by place value.

	tens	ones
	3	1
+	6	5

2. Use regrouping when adding.
475 + 332 =

F. 707

G. 797

H. 807

J. 817

K. 907

HINT: Regroup if the numbers in a column add up to 10 or more.

	hundreds	tens	ones
	4	7	5
+	3	3	2

3. Add more than two numbers.
1,000 + 429 + 351 =

A. 1,770

B. 1,780

C. 1,870

D. 1,880

E. 8,880

HINT: Align numbers in columns. Then add each column. Begin with the ones column on the right. Then move to the columns on the left.

	thousands	hundreds	tens	ones
	1,	0	0	0
		4	2	9
+		3	5	1

4. Add more than two numbers.
62 + 243 + 7 + 81 =

F. 293

G. 383

H. 393

J. 403

K. 456

HINT: Look for pairs of numbers that add up to 10.

	hundreds	tens	ones
		6	2
	2	4	3
			7
+		8	1

Try It Out! ▪ ■ ■

Baker You work at the First Street Bakery. It is the end of the day. You must count all the goods that have not sold. You look in the case to see what items are left. There are 6 pies. There are 11 cakes. There are 9 loaves of rye bread. There are 2 loaves of white bread. How many items in all are left at the end of the day?

A. 17   **B.** 18   **C.** 19   **D.** 26   **E.** 28

 Step 1 ## Understand the Problem ▪ ■ ■

Complete the *Plan for Successful Solving.*

Plan for Successful Solving

What am I asked to do?	What are the facts?		How do I find the answer?
Find the total number of items that are left.	pies cakes rye bread white bread	6 11 9 2	The key words *in all* tell you that you are looking for the total. You must add to solve this problem.

 Step 2 ## Find and Check Your Answer ▪ ■ ■

- First remember what you are looking for. You need to find the total number of items left.

- Review the facts. You need to know how many items are left at the end of the day. You must add to find the total.

- Be sure you aligned the digits by place value.

```
     tens ones
      1
        6  ←— pies
      1 1  ←— cakes
        9  ←— rye bread
    +   2  ←— white bread
    ─────
    2 8
```

- Check that you included all regrouped numbers in the sum of each column.

- Before selecting an answer, read the question again. Be sure your answer makes sense.

- **Select the correct answer: E. 28**
  You added the number of items left. You have found the total number of unsold items.

Level 1
Applied Mathematics

On Your Own ▪ ■ ■

Read and solve the following problems.

1. **Video Editor** You are adding a sound track to a video. The sound track must be the same length as the video. You use three songs. The first song is 272 seconds long. The second song is 351 seconds. The third song is 128 seconds. How long is the sound track?

   A. 681 seconds
   B. 721 seconds
   C. 751 seconds
   D. 781 seconds
   E. 821 seconds

2. **Auditor** You work for the IRS. You are auditing a freelance writer. You read her tax records. Last year she paid $2,754 in taxes. This year she paid $1,523 in taxes. How much money did she pay in taxes for both years?

   F. $3,277
   G. $4,277
   H. $5,277
   J. $6,277
   K. $7,277

3. **Coach** You are training runners for a cross-country race. You have them run on a schedule. On Monday they ran 2 miles. On Tuesday they ran 10 miles. On Wednesday they ran 4 miles. On Thursday they ran 12 miles. On Friday they ran 3 miles. How many total miles did they run this week?

   A. 28
   B. 29
   C. 30
   D. 31
   E. 32

4. **Fence Installer** You installed two fences this week. One fence used 164 feet of material. The other used 25 feet of material. You need to restock the supplies you used for the jobs. How many feet of fencing material did you use altogether?

   F. 185
   G. 186
   H. 187
   J. 188
   K. 189

5. **Grain Buyer** You are calculating how much money you spent this month. You bought wheat for $251. You bought corn for $247. You bought barley for $149. What were your total expenses?

   A. $547
   B. $647
   C. $674
   D. $746
   E. $799

6. **Recycling Worker** You are sorting bottles and cans into different bins. You need to keep a count of how many containers you fill. You fill 43 containers with bottles and 32 containers with cans. How many total containers do you fill?

   F. 75
   G. 76
   H. 85
   J. 86
   K. 87

7. **Photographer** You work as a wedding photographer. Last weekend you photographed two weddings. The first couple bought 340 photos. The second couple bought 425 photos. How many total wedding photos did you sell last weekend?

   A. 765
   B. 770
   C. 775
   D. 865
   E. 870

8. **Postal Service Mail Carrier** Your postal route is downtown. You deliver mail to three city blocks. There are 26 buildings on the first block. There are 22 buildings on the second block. There are 24 buildings on the third block. To how many total buildings do you deliver mail?

   F. 46
   G. 48
   H. 50
   J. 62
   K. 72

9. **Jeweler** You work at Glittery Gems. You set gemstones in jewelry. You just received a shipment of stones. You got 12 diamonds. You got 26 rubies. You got 18 emeralds. How many gems did you get altogether?

   A. 56
   B. 58
   C. 60
   D. 66
   E. 69

10. **Teller** A bank customer deposits three checks. The first check is for $152. The second check is for $43. The third check is for $248. You give him a receipt. How much money did the customer deposit?

    F. $343
    G. $434
    H. $443
    J. $453
    K. $543

WORKSPACE

Skill Support

The answer to a subtraction problem is called the **difference**. This is the amount left after a part is removed.

With subtraction, the order of numbers is important. Write the number you are subtracting <u>under</u> the number you are subtracting from. Or write it after.

This is a vertical subtraction problem. Always write the starting amount on the top.

$$\begin{array}{r} 8 \\ -\ 6 \\ \hline 2 \end{array}$$

This is a horizontal subtraction problem. Always write the starting amount first.

$$8 - 6 = 2$$

Remember!

The symbol (–) means to subtract. It is called the minus sign.

Sometimes you will subtract zero from a number. The difference will be the number you started with.

$$7 - 0 = 7$$

Lesson 3 ...
Subtract Whole Numbers

Skill: Use subtraction of whole numbers to solve problems

When you **subtract,** you take something away. You find out what is left. Sometimes the bottom digit is too large to subtract from the digit above it. Then you have to borrow from the next column to the left. **Borrowing** is called regrouping.

Many jobs require you to use subtraction. For example, a truck driver may drive from New York to Boston for a delivery. His total trip will be 225 miles. He has driven 58 miles. He subtracts 58 miles from 225 miles. This will tell him how many miles he has left to drive.

In order to use subtraction to solve problems, you must be able to do the following:

- Understand place value.
- Know basic subtraction facts.
- Subtract with regrouping.

Skill Examples ■ ■ ■

EXAMPLE 1 Subtract one number from another.
You have loaded your truck with 29 bags of fertilizer. You unload 18 bags of fertilizer. How much fertilizer is left? You need to subtract 18 from 29.

You could remove 18 bags from the total and count. Count all the bags that are not whited out. There are 11 bags left.

You can also use subtraction to find how much is left.

- Align the numbers by place value. Place ones under ones. Place tens under tens.

- First subtract the digits in the right column. This is the ones column. $9 - 8 = 1$. Write 1 under the line in the ones column.

- Now move to the left column. This is the tens column. Subtract these digits. $2 - 1 = 1$. Write 1 under the line in the tens column.

$$\begin{array}{r} \overset{\text{tens ones}}{} \\ 2\ \ 9 \\ -\ 1\ \ 8 \\ \hline 1\ \ 1 \end{array}$$

The difference is 11. You have 11 bags of fertilizer left.

EXAMPLE 2 Subtract one number from another with regrouping.
Subtract: 479 − 296

Sometimes the digit in the bottom number is too large to be subtracted from the digit above it. In this case, you need to *regroup* from the next column to the left. Regrouping is also called borrowing.

```
        hundreds  tens  ones
           3      17
           4̶      7̶     9
        −  2      9     6
        ─────────────────
           1      8     3
```

- Align the numbers by place value.

- Subtract the digits in the ones column. 9 − 6 = 3. Write 3 in the ones column.

- Look at the tens column. The bottom digit is larger than the top digit. You need to regroup.

- Borrow 1 hundred from the hundreds column. This leaves 3 hundreds.

- Now add 1 hundred to the 7 tens in the tens column. Remember, 1 hundred = 10 tens. 10 tens + 7 tens = 17 tens. Now the top number in the tens column is 17.

- Subtract the tens column. 17 − 9 = 8. Write 8 in the tens column.

- Finally look at the digits in the hundreds column. Remember you regrouped 1 hundred from the tens column. The top digit is now 3. Subtract the hundreds column. 3 − 2 = 1. Write 1 in the hundreds column.

The difference is 183.

EXAMPLE 3 Subtract a two-digit number from a three-digit number.
Subtract: 391 − 97

```
        hundreds  tens  ones
                  18
           2      8̶     11
           3̶      9̶     1̶
        −         9     7
        ─────────────────
           2      9     4
```

- Look at the digits in the ones column. The top digit is less than the bottom digit. You need to regroup. Borrow 1 from the tens column. Add it to the ones column. 10 + 1 = 11. There are now 11 ones.

- Subtract the ones column. 11 − 7 = 4. Write 4 in the ones column.

- Next subtract the digits in the tens column. Remember you borrowed 1 for the ones column. The top digit is now 8. The top digit is less than the bottom digit. You need to regroup again.

- Borrow 1 from the hundreds column. Add it to the tens column. 10 + 8 = 18.

- There are now 18 tens. Subtract the digits in the tens column. 18 − 9 = 9. Write 9 in the tens column.

- Finally subtract the digits in the hundreds column. Remember you borrowed 1 for the tens column. The top digit is now 2. Subtract. 2 − 0 = 2. Write 2 in the hundreds column.

The difference is 294.

Use subtraction when you take things away. It can tell you how many are left. You also use subtraction to compare two amounts (how many more, how many less).

Level 1
Applied Mathematics

Skill Support
You can check the answer to a subtraction problem. Add the difference to the bottom number. The sum should be the top number.

Example:
```
    46
  − 25
  ────
    21
```

To check, add:
```
    25
  + 21
  ────
    46
```

Skill Practice ▪ ▪ ▪

1. Subtract two numbers.
$82 - 61 =$

A. 20

B. 21

C. 23

D. 31

E. 143

tens	ones
8	2
− 6	1

HINT: First subtract the digits in the ones columns. Then subtract the digits in the tens column.

2. Use regrouping when subtracting.
$58 - 19 =$

F. 31

G. 38

H. 39

J. 41

K. 49

tens	ones
5	8
− 1	9

HINT: Is the bottom digit greater than the top digit? If so, you will need to regroup.

3. Subtract three-digit numbers using regrouping.
$472 - 153 =$

A. 319   **D.** 329

B. 321   **E.** 419

C. 323

hundreds	tens	ones
4	7	2
− 1	5	3

HINT: In the ones column, the bottom digit is greater than the top digit. You need to regroup. Regroup 1 from the tens column.

4. Subtract three-digit numbers using regrouping.
$321 - 286 =$

F. 34

G. 35

H. 45

J. 55

K. 135

hundreds	tens	ones
3	2	1
− 2	8	6

HINT: The top digit is less than the bottom digit in the ones and tens columns. You must regroup twice.

Try It Out! ■ ■ ■

Sales Associate You work at Pages Bookstore. You took inventory on Monday night. You counted 523 mystery books. On Tuesday you sold 86 mystery books. How many mystery books are left?

A. 436   **B.** 437   **C.** 447   **D.** 537   **E.** 547

Understand the Problem ■ ■ ■

Complete the *Plan for Successful Solving.*

Plan for Successful Solving

What am I asked to do?	What are the facts?	How do I find the answer?
Find the total number of mystery books that are left.	starting count 523 books sold 86	The key word *left* tells you that you are looking for the difference. You must subtract to solve this problem.

Find and Check Your Answer ■ ■ ■

- Review the facts. You need to know how many mystery books are left. You must subtract to find the difference.

- Write a subtraction problem. Be sure to line up the digits by place value.

- Subtract the digits in the ones column. The bottom digit is greater than the top digit. You must regroup.

- Subtract and regroup numbers in the ones, tens, and hundreds columns.

$$
\begin{array}{c}
\overset{\text{hundreds}}{} \ \overset{\text{tens}}{} \ \overset{\text{ones}}{} \\
\overset{4}{\cancel{5}} \ \overset{11}{\cancel{2}} \ \overset{13}{\cancel{3}} \quad \leftarrow \text{Starting count} \\
- \quad 8 \ \ 6 \quad \leftarrow \text{Books sold} \\
\hline
4 \ \ 3 \ \ 7
\end{array}
$$

- Before selecting an answer, read the question again. Be sure your answer makes sense.

- **Select the correct answer: B.** 437
  You sold 86 mystery books on Tuesday. You started the day with 523. You subtracted to find the number of mystery books left.

On Your Own ▪ ▪ ▪

Read and solve the following problems.

1. **Accountant** You are preparing a two-month report for a small business. The business earned $8,532 in February. It had sales of $4,910 in March. How much greater were sales in February than in March?

   A. $3,412
   B. $3,442
   C. $3,622
   D. $4,422
   E. $4,622

2. **Warehouse Manager** You are checking the inventory for your warehouse. In August, 826 printers were in stock. In September, 515 were in stock. How many printers were shipped?

   F. 301
   G. 311
   H. 401
   J. 411
   K. 421

3. **Animal Caretaker** You are feeding the dogs at your kennel. You keep track of how much food is available. You open a 30-pound bag of food. You pour 12 pounds of food for the dogs. How many pounds of food are left in the bag?

   A. 8
   B. 12
   C. 18
   D. 22
   E. 28

4. **Teacher Assistant** You have 26 students in your algebra class. You are taking attendance. Only 18 students are in class today. How many are missing?

   F. 8
   G. 10
   H. 12
   J. 14
   K. 18

5. **Baker** You baked 48 pies this morning. You sold 7 pies. You are taking inventory. How many pies do you still have?

   A. 21
   B. 29
   C. 31
   D. 39
   E. 41

6. **Logistician** You are planning a shipping route with 24 stops. You have planned 17 stops already. How many more stops do you still have to plan?

   F. 7
   G. 11
   H. 13
   J. 17
   K. 23

7. **Forest Technician** You need to report information about a fire. The fire burned 562 acres of the forest. The size of the forest is 900 acres. How many acres were not burned?

   A. 338
   B. 348
   C. 362
   D. 448
   E. 462

8. **Tile Setter** You are installing a bathroom floor. You had 150 tiles. You used 86 tiles. How many tiles do you have left?

   F. 64
   G. 66
   H. 74
   J. 76
   K. 164

9. **Planner** You are planning to expand a public parking lot. There are 120 spaces in the parking lot now. It will be expanded to 196 spaces. How many spaces do you need to add?

   A. 24
   B. 34
   C. 66
   D. 76
   E. 86

10. **Research Associate** You are conducting a survey of 830 people for a company. You have questioned 620 people. How many people do you still have to question?

    F. 110
    G. 210
    H. 220
    J. 310
    K. 1,450

WORKSPACE

Skill Support

A **decimal** is a number with a decimal point. This is a small dot like a period. A **decimal point** separates the whole number from an amount less than 1.

Whole number part

12.86

decimal part

decimal point

The whole number is on the left. The decimal part shows a value less than a whole. This is on the right.

Place value is important. It sets the value of a digit. This depends on the position of the decimal point.

For 14.893, 8 represents 8 tenths. For 148.93, 8 represents 8 ones.

Remember!

The symbol $ is used for the **dollar sign**.

Lesson 4 ...
Understand Decimals

Skill: Add and subtract decimals to solve problems

Decimals are common when working with money. Using decimals is a way to be accurate. Costs are shown in dollars and cents. Decimals help cashiers find the amounts owed. Cashiers add the cost of each item in dollars and cents. Decimals also help them find correct change. Cashiers subtract the amount owed from the amount paid.

Decimals show parts of a whole. Decimal place names mirror whole number places. The decimal names have *-ths* at the end. Look at the decimal point below. The first column to its right is the tenths column. The next column to the right is the hundredths column. The far right column is the thousandths column.

hundreds	tens	ones	.	tenths	hundredths	thousandths
6	2	3	.	4	8	5

In order to use decimals to solve problems, you must be able to do the following:

- Understand place value.

- Understand addition facts.

- Understand subtraction facts.

Skill Examples ...

EXAMPLE 1 Add money amounts with decimals.
You work at a store. You need to find the total cost of two items.
Add: $12.76 + $6.27

- Align the numbers at the decimal points. Hundredths are under hundredths. Tenths are under tenths. Ones are under ones. Tens are under tens. Look at the decimal point. The first column to the right is the tenths column. The next column to the right is the hundredths column.

	tens	ones		tenths	hundredths
				1	
$	1	2	.	7	6
+		6	.	2	7
$	1	9	.	0	3

- First add the digits in the hundredths column. 6 + 7 = 13. Regroup 1 to the tenths column.

- Now move one column left to the tenths column. Be sure to add the 1 that you regrouped. 1 + 7 + 2 = 10. Regroup 1 to the ones column. Bring down the decimal point.

- Next add the digits in the ones column. Be sure to add the 1 that you regrouped. 1 + 2 + 6 = 9.

- Finally add the digits in the tens column. The bottom number has no digit in the tens column. 1 + 0 = 1. Bring down the dollar sign ($).

The sum is $19.03.

EXAMPLE 2 Subtract two numbers with decimals.
Subtract: 8.65 − 2.522

- Align the numbers at the decimal points. Tenths are under tenths. Hundredths are under hundredths. And so on.

- Subtract the digits in the thousandths column. The top number has 0 thousandths. The top digit is less than the bottom digit. You need to regroup. Now the top digit is greater than the bottom digit. Subtract the digits in the thousandths column. 10 − 2 = 8.

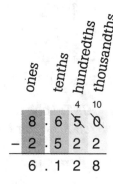

- Move one column left to the hundredths column. You regrouped, or borrowed, 1 to the thousandths column. The top digit is now 4. Subtract. 4 − 2 = 2.

- Move one column left to the tenths column. Subtract the digits in this column. 6 − 5 = 1. Bring down the decimal point.

- Finally move one more column left to the ones column. Subtract the digits in this column. 8 − 2 = 6.

The difference is 6.128.

EXAMPLE 3 Subtract money amounts with decimals.
Subtract: $5.04 − $2.29

- Align the numbers at the decimal points.

- Look at the digits in the hundredths column. The top digit is less than the bottom digit. You need to regroup 1 from the tenths column. The digit in the tenths column is 0. So you need to borrow 1 from the ones column.

- Regroup 1 from the tenths column. Now the top digit is greater than the bottom digit. You can subtract the hundredths. 14 − 9 = 5.

- Move one column left to the tenths column. Remember you regrouped. The top digit is now 9. 9 − 2 = 7. Bring down the decimal.

- Look at the ones column. Remember you regrouped. The top digit is now 4. Subtract. 4 − 2 = 2. Bring down the dollar sign.

The difference is $2.75.

Remember!
Sometimes numbers have a different number of decimal places. The decimals need the same number of digits. Add zeros after the last digit. The value of the decimal is the same. 8.65 = 8.650

Level 1
Applied Mathematics

Skill Support
Each number to the right of the decimal point has a different value.
- 1 one = 10 tenths
- 1 tenth = 10 hundredths
- 1 hundredth = 10 thousandths

Skill Practice ■ ■ ■

1. Add money amounts with decimals.
   $9.08 + $1.47 =

   A. $7.61

   B. $9.45

   C. $9.55

   D. $10.45

   E. $10.55

	ones	tenths	hundredths
$	9 .	0	8
+	1 .	4	7

   HINT: Look at the hundredths column. The sum is more than 10. You need to regroup. Remember that 1 is carried to the tenths column.

2. Subtract money amounts with decimals.
   $5.15 – $1.65 =

   F. $3.40

   G. $3.50

   H. $4.40

   J. $4.50

   K. $6.80

	ones	tenths	hundredths
$	5 .	1	5
–	1 .	6	5

   HINT: Look at the tenths column. Regroup when the digit on the top is less than the bottom digit. Borrow from the column to the left.

3. Add two decimal numbers.
   8.97 + 0.636 =

   A. 1.533

   B. 9.506

   C. 9.60

   D. 9.606

   E. 15.33

ones	tenths	hundredths	thousandths
8 .	9	7	0
+ 0 .	6	3	6

   HINT: Align at the decimal points. 8.97 has no digit in the thousandths place. Put 0 there.

4. Subtract two decimal numbers.
   8.213 – 3.659 =

   F. 4.553   J. 4.654

   G. 4.554   K. 5.554

   H. 4.564

ones	tenths	hundredths	thousandths
8 .	2	1	3
– 3 .	6	5	9

   HINT: Regroup when the top digit in a column is less than the bottom digit. Sometimes you have to regroup more than once.

Try It Out! ■ ■ ■

Cashier You work at a home improvement store. Your customer's purchases total $13.45. He gives you a $20 bill. How much change do you need to give him?

    A. $6.54   **B.** $6.55   **C.** $6.65   **D.** $16.55   **E.** $16.65

 Understand the Problem ■ ■ ■

Complete the *Plan for Successful Solving.*

Plan for Successful Solving

What am I asked to do?	What are the facts?	How do I find the answer?
Find the difference.	paid $20.00 owed $13.45	The key word is *change.* It tells you that you are looking for the difference. Subtract the amount owed from the amount paid.

 Find and Check Your Answer ■ ■ ■

- Review the facts. The customer paid $20. He owed $13.45. You need to subtract to find the change.

- Look at the digits in the hundredths column. The top digit is less than the bottom digit. You need to regroup.

- Borrow 1 from the tenths column. There are no tenths to regroup. Borrow 1 from the ones column. There are no ones to regroup. Borrow 1 from the tens column. Regroup 1 to the ones. Regroup 1 to the tenths. Regroup 1 tenth to the hundredths.

$$\begin{array}{r} \overset{\text{tens}}{} \overset{\text{ones}}{} \overset{\text{tenths}}{} \overset{\text{hundredths}}{} \\ \$\ \ 2\ 0\ .\ 0\ 0 \leftarrow \text{Paid} \\ -\ \ \ 1\ 3\ .\ 4\ 5 \leftarrow \text{Owed} \\ \hline \$\ \ \ \ \ 6\ .\ 5\ 5 \end{array}$$

- You can now subtract the digits in the columns. Remember the numbers you regrouped.

- Bring down the decimal and the dollar sign.

- **Select the correct answer: B.** $6.55
  You found the amount of change due. You took the amount paid. Then you subtracted the amount owed from it.

Skill Support

You are looking for the change owed. Find the amount the customer owed. Then subtract that amount from the amount the customer gave to the cashier. The amount given is a whole number. Add a decimal point after the whole number. Add two zeros. $20 = $20.00

Level 1
Applied Mathematics

Remember!

To solve the problem, first identify what you are asked to do. Look for the sentence with a question mark. Then identify the facts. Look for the sentences with numbers. Finally determine how to find the answer. Look for key words, such as *total* and *change.*

On Your Own ▪ ■ ▪

Read and solve the following problems.

1. **Producer** You are producing a TV show. You hire a production assistant. You pay the production assistant $14.75 an hour. You also hire a video engineer. You pay the video engineer $18.50 an hour. What will it cost per hour to pay both people?

   A. $32.25
   B. $33.25
   C. $33.75
   D. $34.25
   E. $34.75

2. **Executive Secretary** You work for a university president. She recently took a business trip. You are preparing her expense report. She spent $147.99 on a rental car. She spent $87.65 on a business dinner. What were her total expenses?

   F. $235.54
   G. $235.64
   H. $236.54
   J. $236.64
   K. $245.64

3. **Elementary School Teacher** You teach first grade. You reward your students with stickers for good behavior. You buy a new sheet of stickers for the class. It costs $12.80. You pay with a $20 bill. How much change do you get?

   A. $6.10
   B. $6.20
   C. $7.00
   D. $7.10
   E. $7.20

4. **Veterinary Assistant** A client brought her dog in for an appointment. You write a bill for the appointment. The basic exam cost $58.50. The lab waste fee is another $4.99. How much does the client owe altogether?

   F. $53.49
   G. $62.49
   H. $63.49
   J. $63.59
   K. $64.49

5. **Physician Assistant** A patient is in for a checkup. You look at his medical records. Last year he weighed 176.8 pounds. This visit he weighs 187.4 pounds. How much weight has he gained?

   A. 9.4 pounds
   B. 9.6 pounds
   C. 9.8 pounds
   D. 10.4 pounds
   E. 10.6 pounds

6. **Fishing Vessel Operator** You are buying new fishing nets. The nets cost $210.90. Lead weights for the nets cost $156.25. You must record the total cost. How much do the nets and weights cost together?

   F. $366.75
   G. $366.85
   H. $366.95
   J. $367.05
   K. $367.15

7. **Speech Language Pathologist** You visit a client who has a stuttering problem. You charge $65.25 for the visit. The client gives you a $100 bill. How much change do you give back?

A. $34.25

B. $34.50

C. $34.75

D. $35.25

E. $35.75

8. **Loan Officer** A married couple wants a home loan. You need to know if they qualify for the loan. The husband makes $3,045.50 a month. The wife earns $3,345.75 a month. How much money do they make together each month?

F. $6,390.25

G. $6,391.25

H. $6,481.25

J. $6,490.25

K. $6,491.25

9. **Asbestos Abatement Worker** You are removing asbestos from a building. The building originally contained 386.7 pounds of asbestos. You have removed 73.3 pounds. How many pounds of asbestos remain?

A. 213.4

B. 313.4

C. 313.7

D. 373.4

E. 373.7

10. **Bicycle Repairer** You are working on a customer's bicycle. The bike needs a brake repair. New brake shoes cost $18.88. A new brake lever costs $20.98. What is the cost for both parts?

F. $37.86

G. $38.68

H. $38.86

J. $39.68

K. $39.86

WORKSPACE

Skill Support

To tell time on a clock, remember these facts:

An **analog clock** shows time using hands. The longer hand is the **minute hand**. It takes this hand 5 minutes to move from one number to the next. Each number equals 5 minutes.

1 = 5 minutes
2 = 10 minutes
3 = 15 minutes
4 = 20 minutes
5 = 25 minutes
6 = 30 minutes
7 = 35 minutes
8 = 40 minutes
9 = 45 minutes
10 = 50 minutes
11 = 55 minutes
12 = 60 minutes

The shorter hand is the **hour hand**. It takes this hand 1 hour to move from one number to the next. Each number equals 1 hour. One hour is 60 minutes.

A **digital clock** shows time using digits. A colon (:) divides two sets of digits.

Lesson 5
Read Time

Skill: Read time using a clock and a calendar

Clocks and calendars are useful in the workplace. They can help you keep track of activities. For example, you can use a clock to see if you are on time for a company meeting. You can use a calendar to show your daily schedule.

Clocks show hours, minutes, and sometimes seconds. Analog clocks usually have circular faces with the numbers 1–12. The numbers are arranged around the inside edge of the circle. Digital clocks show time using digits. Calendars show days, weeks, months, and sometimes hours.

In order to read time, you must be able to do the following:

- Understand time facts.
- Understand calendar facts.
- Count by fives and tens.

Skill Examples

EXAMPLE 1 Use a digital clock to tell time.
You deliver packages. You need to make deliveries on time. What time is it?

- Digital clocks show time using digits. A colon (:) divides two sets of digits.

- The digits to the left of the colon show the hour.

- The digits to the right of the colon show the minutes.

The time is 7:15 or 7 hours and 15 minutes.

EXAMPLE 2 Use an analog clock to tell time.
What time is it?

- Analog clocks use hands to tell hours and minutes.

- Look at the number the hour hand is pointing at. It is pointing between 2 and 3. When this happens, pick the number before the hour hand. The number of hours is 2.

- Next find the number of minutes. Each number means 5 minutes.
- Look at the number the minute hand is pointing at. It is pointing at 6. You could count each tick until you reach the minute hand. There is a quicker method. Count by fives. Start at 1 on the clock. Stop at 6. The number of minutes is 30.

The time is 2:30.

- One hour is 60 minutes. A quarter hour is 15 minutes. A half hour is 30 minutes.
- You can use phrases with *quarter* and *half* to describe time. *Quarter to* means "15 minutes before the hour." *Quarter past* means "15 minutes after the hour." *Half past* means "30 minutes after the hour."

The time is half past 2.

EXAMPLE 3 Use a monthly calendar.
Your office has a meeting on the third Thursday in June. What day of the month is that?

- Use a monthly calendar showing the days of the week. This calendar is for the month of June. It has 30 days.
- Look for the column marked Thursday. The dates in this column are 2, 9, 16, 23, and 30. They fall on a Thursday during this month.
- Count down the rows. Find the third date in the Thursday column. The third date in the column is 16.

June						
Sunday	Monday	Tuesday	Wednesday	Thursday	Friday	Saturday
			1	2	3	4
5	6	7	8	9	10	11
12	13	14	15	16	17	18
19	20	21	22	23	24	25
26	27	28	29	30		

The third Thursday in June is the 16th.

EXAMPLE 4 Use a weekly calendar.
You have a meeting during the fourth time slot on Wednesday. What time is that?

- Use a weekly calendar showing the hours. This calendar is for the week of the 20th. Each day has 9 time slots. Each slot is for 1 hour.

	20 Monday	21 Tuesday	22 Wednesday	23 Thursday	24 Friday
8 a.m.					
9:00					
10:00					
11:00					
12 p.m.					
1:00					
2:00					
3:00					
4:00					

- Look for the column marked Wednesday. The time slots in this column are 8:00 a.m., 9:00 a.m., 10:00 a.m., and so on.
- Count down the rows to the fourth time slot in the Wednesday column. The fourth time slot in the column is 11:00 a.m.

The meeting is at 11:00 a.m. on Wednesday.

Remember!
There are different types of calendars. You can use them to organize your time.

- A daily calendar shows one day per page. It is divided into hours.
- A weekly calendar shows one week per page. It is divided into days and hours.
- A monthly calendar shows one month per page. It is divided into days.

Remember!
Use these facts to read a calendar:

- Monthly calendars have seven columns. Each column is a day of the week: Sunday, Monday, Tuesday, Wednesday, Thursday, Friday, and Saturday.
- The dates change with each month.
- Each month has 28 to 31 days.

Remember!

Look at an analog clock. Look at the number the hour hand points at. This is the hour. Look at the number the minute hand points at. Count by fives to that number. Always start at the number 1 on the clock. These are the minutes.

You use a.m. after the hour for morning. You use p.m. after the hour for afternoon and evening. Noon is 12 p.m.

Skill Support

The minute hand may not always point at a number. To read time to the nearest minute:

- Read the time to the nearest 5 minutes. Do not count past the minute hand.
- Then add 1 minute for each tick mark.

The minute hand is just past the 2. The 2 represents 10 minutes. The minute hand is two tick marks past the 2. Add 2 minutes to 10 minutes. The clock shows 12 minutes after the hour.

Skill Practice ▪ ▪ ▪

1. What time is it?

   A. 10:15   D. 3:00
   B. 11:03   E. 3:55
   C. 11:15

   HINT: *This is a digital clock. The digits on the right of the colon show minutes. The digits on the left of the colon show hours.*

2. Today is Monday, March 19. What date is next Monday?

   F. March 11
   G. March 18
   H. March 24
   J. March 25
   K. March 26

   HINT: *You are looking for a Monday. Look at the second column. Then look at the row directly below 19.*

March						
Sunday	Monday	Tuesday	Wednesday	Thursday	Friday	Saturday
				1	2	3
4	5	6	7	8	9	10
11	12	13	14	15	16	17
18	19	20	21	22	23	24
25	26	27	28	29	30	31

3. What is another way to state the time shown on the clock?

   A. 3 o'clock
   B. a quarter past 3
   C. a quarter to 4
   D. 4 o'clock
   E. a quarter past 4

   HINT: *Remember the alternative way to say the number of minutes.*

4. What is the sixth time slot on Tuesday the 21st?

   F. 8:00 a.m.
   G. 11:00 a.m.
   H. 12:00 p.m.
   J. 1:00 p.m.
   K. 4:00 p.m.

	20 Monday	21 Tuesday	22 Wednesday	23 Thursday	24 Friday
8 a.m.					
9:00					
10:00					
11:00					
12 p.m.					
1:00					
2:00					
3:00					
4:00					

   HINT: *Locate the column marked Tuesday. Next look at the sixth row to find the sixth time slot on Tuesday.*

Try It Out! ▪ ▪ ▪

Production Clerk You work at the Miller Bag Factory. Each month there is an employee meeting. It is on every third Tuesday. You must attend the employee meetings. In October, when is the employee meeting?

A. October 18

B. October 19

C. October 25

D. October 26

E. October 27

October						
Sunday	Monday	Tuesday	Wednesday	Thursday	Friday	Saturday
						1
2	3	4	5	6	7	8
9	10	11	12	13	14	15
16	17	18	19	20	21	22
23	24	25	26	27	28	29
30	31					

Remember!
You are looking for a date that falls on a Tuesday. The date must be in the Tuesday column. This is the third column from the left.

 Step 1 Understand the Problem ▪ ▪ ▪

Complete the *Plan for Successful Solving*.

Plan for Successful Solving

What am I asked to do?	What are the facts?	How do I find the answer?
Find the date of the employee meeting.	The day is Tuesday. The week is the third week of the month. The month is October.	The key word *when* tells that you are looking for the date. You must read the calendar to solve the problem.

 Step 2 Find and Check Your Answer ▪ ▪ ▪

- Review the facts. You need to know what date the meeting is in October. You must read the calendar to find the answer.

- Look at the calendar. Find the column labeled Tuesday.

- Locate the third date in the Tuesday column.

- Before selecting an answer to the problem, read the question again. Be sure your answer makes sense.

- **Select the correct answer: A.** October 18
  By reading the calendar, you discovered the date of the employee meeting in October.

Level 1 Applied Mathematics

Skill Support
This is a monthly calendar. The dates in each column fall on the same day of the week. As you read down a column, the number of each date is increased by 7.

The first Tuesday in October is the 4th. The second Tuesday will be the 11th. 4 + 7 = 11.

The third Tuesday will be the 18th. 11 + 7 = 18.

The fourth Tuesday will be the 25th. 18 + 7 = 25.

On Your Own ■ ■ ■

Read and solve the following problems.

March						
Sun	Mon	Tues	Wed	Thurs	Fri	Sat
1	2	3	4	5	6	7
8	9	10	11	12	13	14
15	16	17	18	19	20	21
22	23	24	25	26	27	28
29	30	31				

1. **Interior Designer** You are working on a kitchen redesign. You told the client the design would be done March 9. What day of the week is this?

   A. Monday

   B. Tuesday

   C. Wednesday

   D. Thursday

   E. Friday

2. **Astronomer** You monitor meteor showers. A meteor shower is predicted to be on the second Sunday in March. What date is this?

   F. March 7

   G. March 8

   H. March 9

   J. March 15

   K. March 22

1.

4.

2.

5.

3.

3. **Artist** You are painting a portrait. You need to quit working at 4:30. Which clock shows 4:30?

   A. Clock 1   D. Clock 4

   B. Clock 2   E. Clock 5

   C. Clock 3

4. **Spa Manager** A client is coming in for a massage. You booked the massage for 1:15. Which clock shows 1:15?

   F. Clock 1   J. Clock 4

   G. Clock 2   K. Clock 5

   H. Clock 3

5. **Librarian** You need to announce the library is closed. The clock shows the library closing time. What time does it show?

   A. 4:00   D. 5:30

   B. 4:30   E. 6:00

   C. 5:00

1.

2.

3.

4.

5.

September						
Sun	Mon	Tues	Wed	Thurs	Fri	Sat
				1	2	3
4	5	6	7	8	9	10
11	12	13	14	15	16	17
18	19	20	21	22	23	24
25	26	27	28	29	30	

6. **Carpet Installer** You are scheduled to install a carpet at 3:15. Which clock shows 3:15?

   F. Clock 1
   G. Clock 2
   H. Clock 3
   J. Clock 4
   K. Clock 5

7. **Certified Public Accountant** You are editing a quarterly earnings report. It is due by 5:30 today. Which clock shows 5:30?

   A. Clock 1
   B. Clock 2
   C. Clock 3
   D. Clock 4
   E. Clock 5

8. **Politician** You are holding a campaign fund-raiser. It is scheduled for September 27. What day of the week is that?

   F. Monday   J. Thursday
   G. Tuesday   K. Friday
   H. Wednesday

9. **Equal Opportunity Officer** You review contracts. You study complaints. You have a scheduled meeting with management on the third Thursday of each month. What date will this be in September?

   A. 8   B. 14   C. 15   D. 22   E. 29

	20 Monday	21 Tuesday	22 Wednesday	23 Thursday	24 Friday
8 a.m.					
9:00					
10:00					
11:00					
12 p.m.					
1:00					
2:00					
3:00					
4:00					

10. **Motorcycle Mechanic** You are repairing a motorcycle for a customer. You tell her it will be repaired by Thursday. What date is this?

   F. 20   J. 23
   G. 21   K. 24
   H. 22

Level 1 Performance Assessment ■ ■ ■

These problems are at a Level 1 rating of difficulty. They are similar to problems on a career readiness certificate test. For each question, you can check your answer. To do this, use the answer key. It is located on pp. 264–266 of this book. It explains each answer option. It also shows the lesson that covers that skill. You may refer to that lesson to review the skill.

1. You work as a carpet installer. The carpet comes in rolls that are 10 feet long. You must decide how many rolls you need. The floor you are covering is 27 feet long. What is this number rounded to the nearest ten?

   A. 10   **B.** 25   **C.** 30   **D.** 40   **E.** 100

2. You receive three large packages during your shift as a shipping agent. One weighs 146 pounds. Another is 165 pounds. The third is 78 pounds. You load them on a shipping cart. The packages must be loaded with the heaviest on bottom. Put the weights in order from least to greatest.

   F. 78, 165, 146

   G. 78, 146, 165

   H. 146, 165, 78

   J. 146, 78, 165

   K. 165, 146, 78

3. The electricity is not working in a home. As an electrician, you are called to repair it. You need 183 feet of cable for the repair. It comes in lengths of 100 feet. Determine how many lengths you should use. What is 183 rounded to the nearest hundred?

   A. 100   **B.** 150   **C.** 180   **D.** 190   **E.** 200

4. As a bookkeeper, you keep track of business expenses. You are writing a monthly report. You need to identify the largest expense for this report. The business you work for spends $450 on insurance each month. About $534 is spent on electricity. Another $99 is spent on office supplies. Trash pickup costs $245. Advertising is $550. What is the largest monthly expense?

   F. $99

   G. $245

   H. $450

   J. $534

   K. $550

5. You begin your shift as a busser. You work at a restaurant. You are assigned 12 inside tables. You are also assigned 7 tables outside. How many tables are you assigned altogether?

   A. 5   **B.** 7   **C.** 12   **D.** 18   **E.** 19

6. As a truck driver, you are paid for the miles you drive. You drove 65 miles last hour. This hour, you drive 53 miles. How many total miles is this?

F. 115

G. 117

H. 118

J. 128

K. 138

7. You are a sales associate. You work at a clothing store. You are restocking shirts. You stock 12 blue shirts, 14 red shirts, and 7 white shirts. How many shirts is this in total?

A. 23

B. 31

C. 32

D. 33

E. 43

8. You are a computer technician. You are upgrading programs in the office. You need to upgrade 11 computers in marketing. The front desk has 2 computers to upgrade. There are 5 computers in human resources needing updgrades. How many total computers need upgrades?

F. 17

G. 18

H. 19

J. 20

K. 28

9. You are a roofer. You have 100 roofing shingles. You use 65 on a section of roof. How many shingles are left over?

A. 30

B. 35

C. 40

D. 45

E. 165

10. You are a third-grade teacher. You have 20 students. Of the 20 students, 13 of them got As on the math test. The other students get a chance for extra credit. You calculate how many students this is. How many students did not get As?

F. 5

G. 6

H. 7

J. 17

K. 33

11. You check inventory in the warehouse that you manage. Last month there were 58 bags of gravel. This month there are 22. How many bags of gravel are gone?

   A. 26

   B. 35

   C. 36

   D. 38

   E. 80

12. You work at a doughnut shop. You sold 1,600 doughnuts today. You started out with 2,800. How many doughnuts do you have left to sell?

   F. 900

   G. 1,200

   H. 1,300

   J. 1,600

   K. 1,800

13. A chicken sandwich costs $4.19 in the restaurant where you work as a server. A customer gives you $10. How much change do you give him?

   A. $4.81

   B. $4.95

   C. $5.80

   D. $5.81

   E. $14.19

14. As a graphic designer, you need to know the total size of two digital images. The first one is 2.6 megabytes. The second one is 4.5 megabytes. You add the two sizes. How many megabytes are both images together?

   F. 6.1

   G. 7.0

   H. 7.1

   J. 7.2

   K. 8.1

15. In your job as an airport parking lot attendant, you take payments for parking. A driver parks her car for a week. She owes $32.50. She pays with a $50 bill. How much change do you give her?

   A. $7.50

   B. $17.45

   C. $17.50

   D. $18.50

   E. $27.50

16. You are mixing hair dye in your work as a hairdresser. The applicator bottle is 2.5 ounces. You put 1.25 ounces of dye in it. The rest you fill with water. How many ounces of water do you need?

   F. 1.05   **G.** 1.15   **H.** 1.20   **J.** 1.25   **K.** 2.25

17. You end your shift as an assembly worker at 5 p.m. You look at the clock at work. What time is it now?

   A. 2:10

   B. 2:20

   C. 2:40

   D. 4:10

   E. 4:40

18. You work as a receptionist. You need to lock the front office door at 5 p.m. What time is it now?

   F. 3:34

   G. 3:44

   H. 4:34

   J. 4:43

   K. 4:44

19. As a human resources specialist, you meet with new employees. Someone was just hired in marketing. You schedule a meeting with her. It is on February 3. What day of the week is this?

   A. Monday

   B. Tuesday

   C. Wednesday

   D. Thursday

   E. Friday

February						
Sunday	Monday	Tuesday	Wednesday	Thursday	Friday	Saturday
1	2	3	4	5	6	7
8	9	10	11	12	13	14
15	16	17	18	19	20	21
22	23	24	25	26	27	28

20. You schedule hour-long appointments as a massage therapist. A client wants the second time slot on Tuesday. What time is that?

   F. 8:00 a.m.

   G. 9:00 a.m.

   H. 10:00 a.m.

   J. 11:00 a.m.

   K. 12:00 p.m.

Calendar and Appointments						
File Edit View Calendar Appointments Find						
First Day of Week [Monday ▾] ☐ Day View ☐ Week View ☐ Month View						
Start Time [8:00 a.m. ▾]						
End Time [4:00 p.m. ▾]						
	21 Monday	22 Tuesday	23 Wednesday	24 Thursday	25 Friday	26 Saturday
8 a.m.						
9:00						
10:00						
11:00						
12 p.m.						
1:00						
2:00						
3:00						
4:00						

Level 1
Applied Mathematics

Skill Support

To **multiply** means to perform repeated addition. To set up a multiplication problem, follow these steps:

- Align the numbers in columns by place value. Place ones under ones and tens under tens.
- The symbol (×) is a multiplication sign. It reads as "times." For example, three *times* three equals nine.
- **Factors** are the numbers being multiplied.
- Draw a line under the numbers. You will write the **product** (the answer) under this line.

Remember!

Zero times a number is zero. One times a number is that number.

$5 \times 0 = 0$

$8 \times 1 = 8$

Lesson 6 ...
Multiply Whole Numbers

Skill: Use multiplication of whole numbers to solve problems

When you multiply, you add the same number over and over again. $3 + 3 + 3 + 3 = 12$. Likewise, $3 \times 4 = 12$. Use multiplication when each group is the same size. For example, in your building, you know there are 10 offices on each floor. You also know that there are 5 floors. You can find the total number of offices by using multiplication. $5 \times 10 = 50$. There are 50 offices in your building.

In order to use multiplication to solve problems, you must be able to do the following:

- Understand place value.
- Understand multiplication facts.
- Multiply with regrouping.

Skill Examples ■ ■ ■

EXAMPLE 1 Multiply numbers with no regrouping.

You are stocking apples in a grocery store. You have 4 cases of apples. There are 12 apples in each case. You need to know the total number of apples. You need to multiply.

Multiply: 12×4

- Align the numbers in columns by place value. Write 12 as the top factor and 4 as the bottom factor.

- Look at the ones column of the top factor. There is a 2 in the ones column. Multiply this by the 4 in the bottom factor. $2 \times 4 = 8$. Now write 8 in the ones column.

- Now look at the tens column of the top factor. There is a 1 in the tens column. Multiply this by the 4 in the bottom factor. $1 \times 4 = 4$. Write 4 in the tens column.

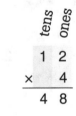

$$
\begin{array}{cc}
\text{tens} & \text{ones} \\
1 & 2 \\
\times & 4 \\
\hline
4 & 8
\end{array}
$$

The product is 48. You have 48 apples.

EXAMPLE 2 Multiply numbers with regrouping.
Multiply: 28×7

- Align the numbers in columns by place value. Place 28 as the top factor and 7 as the bottom factor.

- Multiply the ones column of both factors. $8 \times 7 = 56$. 56 is 6 ones and 5 tens. Write 6 in the ones column. Regroup the 5 to the tens column.

- Now multiply the tens column of the top factor by the bottom factor. $2 \times 7 = 14$.

- Add the 5 you regrouped to 14. $14 + 5 = 19$. Write 9 in the tens column and 1 in the hundreds column.

The product is 196.

	tens	ones
5		
	2	8
×		7
1	9	6

EXAMPLE 3 Multiply two 2-digit numbers with regrouping.
Multiply: 12×84

You are multiplying two 2-digit numbers. You should always follow a two-step process. First multiply the top factor's digits by the bottom factor's ones column. Then multiply the top factor's digits by the bottom factor's tens column.

- Align the numbers in columns by place value.

- Begin by multiplying the ones column of both factors. $2 \times 4 = 8$. Write 8 in the ones column.

- Look at the top factor in the tens column and the bottom factor in the ones column. Multiply these numbers. $1 \times 4 = 4$. Write 4 in the tens column. The partial product is 48.

- Now you will work with the tens column of the bottom factor. You need to write a placeholder zero in the ones column below the first product. Multiply the top factor in the ones column by the bottom factor in the tens column. $2 \times 8 = 16$. Write 6 in the tens column. Regroup 1 to the hundreds column.

- Next multiply the top factor in the tens column by the bottom factor in the tens column. $1 \times 8 = 8$. Add the 1 you regrouped. $8 + 1 = 9$. Write 9 in the hundreds column.

- The second partial product is 960. Draw a line under 960. Finally add the two products. $48 + 960 = 1,008$.

The product is 1,008.

		tens	ones
1			
		1	2
×		8	4
		4	8
+	9	6	0
1,	0	0	8

Level 2
Applied Mathematics

Skill Support
You are multiplying two 2-digit numbers. First find the product for each digit. You will multiply four times. There will be two partial products. The top factor is actually multiplied by 80, not 8. To see this, break the entire problem, 12×84, into two problems. You write zero in the ones column as a placeholder.

$$\begin{array}{r} 12 \\ \times\ 84 \end{array} = \begin{array}{r} 12 \\ \times\ 4 \end{array} + \begin{array}{r} 12 \\ \times\ 80 \end{array}$$

Skill Support

Regrouping in multiplication is a lot like regrouping in addition. Regroup when a product is 10 or more. Regroup to the next column to the left.

Remember!

Always multiply from right to left. Start with the ones column. Finish with the column farthest to the left. For example, for the problem, 23 × 4, multiply in this order:

3 × 4

2 × 4

Skill Practice ▪ ▪ ▪

1. Multiply two numbers.
   23 × 4 =

   A. 82

   B. 87

   C. 92

   D. 97

   E. 102

	tens	ones
	2	3
×		4

   HINT: Remember to regroup the 1 to the tens column.

2. Multiply two numbers using regrouping.
   16 × 24 =

   F. 98

   G. 320

   H. 374

   J. 378

   K. 384

	tens	ones
	1	6
×	2	4

   HINT: Be sure to write the zero as a placeholder when you multiply the tens column of the bottom factor.

3. Multiply two numbers.
   23 × 3 =

   A. 26

   B. 46

   C. 66

   D. 69

   E. 99

	tens	ones
	2	3
×		3

   HINT: First multiply the top factor's ones column by the bottom factor.

4. Multiply two numbers using regrouping.
   53 × 47 =

   F. 583   J. 2,493

   G. 2,481   K. 5,830

   H. 2,491

	tens	ones
	5	3
×	4	7

   HINT: Multiply the top factor by the bottom factor's ones column first. Then multiply the top factor by the bottom factor's tens column.

Try It Out! ▪ ▪ ▪

Counter Clerk You work at the Midtown Donut Shop. A customer orders 5 boxes of doughnuts. You place 12 doughnuts in each box. What is the total number of doughnuts the customer orders?

A. 12   **B.** 36   **C.** 48   **D.** 60   **E.** 65

 Step 1 Understand the Problem ▪ ▪ ▪

Complete the *Plan for Successful Solving.*

Plan for Successful Solving

What am I asked to do?	What are the facts?	How do I find the answer?
Find the total number of doughnuts.	boxes 5 doughnuts per box 12	The key word *total* tells you that you are looking for the product. You are combining multiple groups of the same size. You must multiply to solve this problem.

 Step 2 Find and Check Your Answer ▪ ▪ ▪

- First remember that you are looking for the total number of doughnuts.

- Write a multiplication problem. Be sure to line up the digits.

$$
\begin{array}{cc}
 & \overset{\scriptstyle\text{tens}}{}\overset{\scriptstyle\text{ones}}{} \\
 & \overset{1}{} \\
 & 1\ 2 \quad\leftarrow \text{Doughnuts per box}\\
\times & 5 \quad\leftarrow \text{Boxes}\\
\hline
 & 6\ 0
\end{array}
$$

- Multiply the top factor's ones column by the bottom factor. Because the product is 10 or more, you must regroup.

- Write zero in the ones column. Regroup 1 to the tens column.

- Multiply the top factor's tens column by the bottom factor. Be sure to add the 1 ten that you regrouped from the ones column.

- Write 6 in the tens column.

- **Select the correct answer: D.** 60
  By multiplying the number of doughnuts per box by the number of boxes, you have found the total number of doughnuts.

Skill Support
In this problem, you need to find the total number of doughnuts. You know how many boxes the customer ordered. You know how many doughnuts are placed in each box. Each box has the same number of doughnuts. Because of this, you can multiply to find the total number of doughnuts.

Level 2
Applied Mathematics

Remember!
When dealing with workplace problems, be sure you understand what you are being asked. Read the question carefully. Review all elements of the question. Be sure your answer fits the question.

On Your Own ▪ ■ ▪

Read and solve the following problems.

1. **Property Manager** You manage a business office. You need to purchase new air-conditioning units for each floor. The units cost $280 each. You buy a total of 3. What will be the total cost of the air-conditioners?

   A. $460

   B. $560

   C. $640

   D. $840

   E. $940

2. **Personal Chef** You are cooking for a large party. You are making a side dish with jasmine rice. You need 8 pounds of rice. The rice costs $2 a pound. What is the total cost of the rice?

   F. $10

   G. $12

   H. $16

   J. $18

   K. $20

3. **Order Filler, Retail Sales** You work for a mail-order toy company. You package orders placed online. You can package 4 orders an hour. There are 7 workers filling orders. If everyone can fill 4 orders an hour, how many total orders can be filled in an hour?

   A. 28

   B. 29

   C. 34

   D. 35

   E. 38

4. **Administrative Assistant** You are ordering pizzas for a staff lunch meeting. You order 4 large pizzas. Each pizza costs $19. What is the total cost for all the pizzas?

   F. $38

   G. $56

   H. $57

   J. $66

   K. $76

5. **Tutor** You work at Main School Tutoring Center. You tutor elementary students in reading and writing. You charge $25 for a one-hour session. You have 20 of these sessions each week. How much money do you earn each week?

   A. $450

   B. $500

   C. $550

   D. $600

   E. $650

6. **Greenhouse Grower** You work for Rattlesnake Gardens. The company has decided to use a new kind of fertilizer. The fertilizer costs $18 a bag. You buy 12 bags of it. What is your total cost?

   F. $18

   G. $36

   H. $144

   J. $216

   K. $324

7. **Bank Teller** A customer is making a deposit. He has 3 checks to deposit. Each is for $250. How much money does he deposit in total?

   A. $350
   B. $500
   C. $550
   D. $700
   E. $750

8. **Bell Captain** You work at the Midtowner Hotel. A family of 5 people has just checked in to the hotel. You carry all of their bags to their hotel rooms. Each person in the family has 2 bags. How many bags is this in total?

   F. 7
   G. 10
   H. 11
   J. 12
   K. 15

9. **Astronomer** You work at the National Telescope Lab. You have just discovered a new planet around a star 28 light years away. You then discover another planet around another star that is 4 times farther away. How many light years away is the second planet you discovered?

   A. 112
   B. 114
   C. 118
   D. 120
   E. 122

10. **Survey Researcher** You are conducting a research study in a downtown neighborhood. You have 16 people doing door-to-door survey interviews. They each interviewed 18 people. How many total interviews did they conduct?

    F. 274
    G. 288
    H. 318
    J. 344
    K. 398

WORKSPACE

Skill Support

To solve division problems, you will need to understand some key terms.

- The **dividend** is the number that you want to divide.
- The **divisor** is the number dividing the dividend.
- The **quotient** is the answer to the division problem. It is the number of times the divisor goes into the dividend.
- The **remainder** is any part left over. When the number you are dividing cannot be divided evenly, you have a remainder.

Remember!

Use division to find how many times one number will go into another. Suppose you have 9 tasks and 3 workers. Divide the tasks by the number of workers. This tells you how many tasks each worker can complete. There are two ways to write a division problem:

$9 \div 3 = 3 \qquad 3\overline{)9}^{\,3}$

Lesson 7 •••
Divide Whole Numbers

Skill: Use division of whole numbers to solve problems

When you divide, you separate an amount into equal parts or groups. Division can help you in the workplace. For example, you are paid $120 to work 8 hours at a store. To find your hourly pay, use division. Divide the dollar amount by the number of hours you worked. $120 \div 8 = 15$. You make $15 per hour. The division sign ($\div$) tells you that these two numbers will be divided. You can also set up your problem vertically: $8\overline{)120}^{\,15}$.

In order to divide whole numbers, you must be able to do the following:

- Understand basic multiplication facts.
- Understand basic division facts.
- Understand basic subtraction facts.

Skill Examples ■ ■ ■

EXAMPLE 1 Use basic division facts.
Divide: $10 \div 2$

How many times will 2 go into 10? To figure this out, look at the 10 boxes below. You need to put the boxes on shelves. You can fit 2 boxes on each shelf. How many shelves will you need?

- Set up the problem vertically.

  $2\overline{)10}^{\,5}$

- Use subtraction to help you answer the division problem. How many times can you subtract 2 from 10?

$$10 - 2 = 8$$
$$8 - 2 = 6$$
$$6 - 2 = 4$$
$$4 - 2 = 2$$
$$2 - 2 = 0$$

- 2 can be subtracted from 10 five times. The quotient is 5.

You will need 5 shelves for the boxes.

EXAMPLE 2 Divide whole numbers by a single digit.
Divide: $12 \div 3$

- Set up the problem vertically.

- You cannot divide 3 into 1. Write 0 in the quotient as a placeholder. Multiply: $0 \times 3 = 0$. Write 0 under 1 in the dividend.

- Draw a line under the product. Subtract: $1 - 0 = 1$. Write 1 under the line.

$$\begin{array}{r} 04 \\ 3\overline{)12} \\ -\ 0 \\ \hline 12 \\ -\ 12 \\ \hline 0 \end{array}$$

- Bring down the 2 from the dividend. The new number is 12. You can divide 3 into 12 four times. Write 4 in the quotient. Multiply: $4 \times 3 = 12$. Write 12 under 12.

- Draw a line under the product. Subtract: $12 - 12 = 0$. The difference is 0. That means there is no remainder.

The quotient is 4.

EXAMPLE 3 Divide whole numbers with no remainder.

Divide: $427 \div 7$

- Set up the problem vertically.

- You cannot divide 7 into 4. Write 0 in the quotient as a placeholder. Multiply: $0 \times 7 = 0$. Write 0 below 4.

$$\begin{array}{r} 061 \\ 7\overline{)427} \\ -\ 0 \\ \hline 42 \\ -\ 42 \\ \hline 07 \\ -\ 07 \\ \hline 0 \end{array}$$

- Subtract: $4 - 0 = 4$. Write 4 under the line.

- Bring down the 2 from the dividend. The new number is 42. Divide: $42 \div 7 = 6$. Write 6 in the quotient. Multiply: $6 \times 7 = 42$. Write 42 under 42.

- Subtract: $42 - 42 = 0$. Write 0 under the line.

- Bring down the 7 from the dividend. The new number is 7. Divide: $7 \div 7 = 1$. Write 1 in the quotient. Multiply: $1 \times 7 = 7$. Write 7 under 7.

- Subtract: $7 - 7 = 0$. Write 0 under the line. There is no remainder.

The quotient is 61.

EXAMPLE 4 Divide whole numbers with a remainder.

Divide: $87 \div 6$

- Set up the problem vertically.

- You can divide 6 into 8 once. Write 1 in the quotient. Multiply: $1 \times 6 = 6$. Write the product below the 8.

$$\begin{array}{r} 14\,R3 \\ 6\overline{)87} \\ -\ 6 \\ \hline 27 \\ -\ 24 \\ \hline 3 \end{array}$$

- Subtract: $8 - 6 = 2$. Write 2 under the line.

- Bring down the 7 from the dividend. The new number is 27. You can divide 6 into 27 four times. Write 4 in the quotient. Multiply: $4 \times 6 = 24$. Write 24 under 27.

- Subtract: $27 - 24 = 3$. Write 3 under the line.

- You cannot divide 6 into 3. You must add 3 as the remainder. Add the letter R to the quotient. Add the number 3 after the R.

The quotient is 14 R3. This can also be said as 14, remainder 3.

Remember!

The division sign (÷) tells you that two numbers will be divided.

When you divide any number by 1, the quotient will be the same as the number you are dividing.

$$6 \div 1 = 6$$

Zero divided by any non-zero number equals 0.

$$0 \div 12 = 0$$

When you divide any number by itself, the quotient will be 1.

$$8 \div 8 = 1$$

You cannot divide by zero.

Skill Support

You are dividing 6 into 27. How many 6s are in 27?

- $1 \times 6 = 6$
- $2 \times 6 = 12$
- $3 \times 6 = 18$
- $4 \times 6 = 24$
- $5 \times 6 = 30$

With 27 there is enough to make 4 groups of 6. There is not enough to make 5 groups of 6. There will be a remainder of 3.

Skill Support

Check your division work with multiplication. For quotients without a remainder, multiply the quotient by the divisor. If the product equals the dividend, then your answer is correct.

Problem:
$$4\overline{)156} \quad \frac{39}{}$$

Check:
$$\begin{array}{r} 39 \\ \times\ 4 \\ \hline 156 \end{array}$$

For problems with a remainder, multiply the quotient by the divisor. Then add the remainder to the product. If the sum equals the dividend, then your answer is correct.

Problem:
$$4\overline{)159} \quad \frac{39\,R3}{}$$

Check:
$$\begin{array}{r} 39 \\ \times\ 4 \\ \hline 156 \\ +\ 3 \\ \hline 159 \end{array}$$

Skill Practice ▪ ▪ ▪

1. Divide two numbers.
   $15 \div 3 =$ or $3\overline{)15}$

   A. 3

   B. 5

   C. 6

   D. 12

   E. 18

   HINT: When solving a division problem, set your problem up vertically.

2. Divide two numbers.
   $123 \div 6 =$ or $6\overline{)123}$

   F. 2

   G. 19 R3

   H. 20 R3

   J. 21

   K. 117

   HINT: Be sure to bring down each digit in the dividend.

3. Divide two numbers.
   $1,536 \div 3 =$ or $3\overline{)1536}$

   A. 510

   B. 511

   C. 512

   D. 522

   E. 523

   HINT: Look at the first digit in the dividend. It cannot be divided by the divisor. Place a 0 above it in the quotient.

4. Divide two numbers.
   $254 \div 5 =$ or $5\overline{)254}$

   F. 40 R4

   G. 45

   H. 45 R4

   J. 50

   K. 50 R4

   HINT: 5 does not divide into 254 evenly. There will be a remainder.

Try It Out! ▪ ▪ ▪

Stock Clerk You work at a department store. Your manager asks you to stock 4 empty shelves with a new delivery of glassware. Each shelf should contain the same number of glasses. The total shipment contains 152 pieces of glassware. How many glasses should you place on each shelf?

A. 23   **B.** 32   **C.** 35   **D.** 38   **E.** 43

 Step 1 ## Understand the Problem ▪ ▪ ▪

Complete the *Plan for Successful Solving.*

Plan for Successful Solving

What am I asked to do?	What are the facts?	How do I find the answer?
Find the number of glasses to be placed on each shelf.	There are 4 shelves. There are 152 glasses.	The key words *on each shelf* tell you that you are looking to divide the total number of glasses into groups. You must divide to solve this problem.

 Step 2 ## Find and Check Your Answer ▪ ▪ ▪

- Set up the division problem vertically.

- You cannot divide 4 into 1. Write 0 in the quotient. Multiply: 0 × 4 = 0. Write 0 under 1 in the dividend.

- Subtract: 1 − 0 = 1. Write 1 under the line.

- Bring down the 5. You can divide 4 into 15 three times. Write 3 in the quotient. Multiply: 3 × 4 = 12. Write 12 under 15.

- Subtract: 15 − 12 = 3. Write 3 under the line.

- Bring down the 2. The new number is 32. Divide: 32 ÷ 4 = 8. Write 8 in the quotient. Multiply: 8 × 4 = 32. Write 32 under 32.

- Subtract: 32 − 32 = 0. Write 0 under the line. There is no remainder.

Shelves

$$\begin{array}{r} 038 \\ 4\overline{)152} \\ -\underline{0} \\ 15 \\ -\underline{12} \\ 32 \\ -\underline{32} \\ 0 \end{array}$$ ← Glasses

- **Select the correct answer: D.** 38
  You divided the number of glasses by the number of shelves. The answer tells you the equal number of glasses to place on each shelf.

Remember!
Division can be helpful in workplace situations. For example, you have 100 packages to deliver and 4 workers. You can divide 100 by 4 to equal 25. Each worker can be responsible for delivering 25 packages.

100 ÷ 4 = 25

Level 2
Applied Mathematics

Skill Support
In addition and subtraction, you start with the digits in the least place value column. Then you work to the left. In division, however, you always start dividing the digit in the greatest place value column. Then you work to the right.

On Your Own ■ ■ ■

Read and solve the following problems.

1. **Parking Garage Attendant** The parking garage where you work costs $3 an hour. You just charged a customer $48 when she left the garage. How many hours was she parked?

   A. 15
   B. 16
   C. 18
   D. 19
   E. 29

2. **Truck Driver** You are delivering a shipment to a warehouse. The warehouse is 165 miles away. The trip takes you 3 hours. On average, how many miles an hour do you drive?

   F. 45
   G. 50
   H. 55
   J. 60
   K. 65

3. **Painter** You are working on a painting project that uses disposable foam brushes. You have 35 brushes. You have a crew of 9 people. Each person needs the same number of brushes. How many brushes can you give to each person in your crew? How many brushes will be left over?

   A. 2 brushes, 8 left over
   B. 3 brushes, 2 left over
   C. 3 brushes, 8 left over
   D. 4 brushes, 1 left over
   E. 4 brushes, 2 left over

4. **Caterer** You are making apple pies for an event. You have 75 apples to use, and each pie needs 6 apples. How many apple pies can you make? How many apples will be left over?

   F. 11 pies, 3 apples left over
   G. 12 pies, 0 apples left over
   H. 12 pies, 1 apple left over
   J. 12 pies, 3 apples left over
   K. 13 pies, 3 apples left over

5. **Registered Nurse** You are ordering new supplies for the month. You ordered 9 large boxes of cotton swabs. The total cost is $108. How much did each box cost?

   A. $12
   B. $13
   C. $15
   D. $16
   E. $17

6. **Brick Mason** You are laying bricks for a wall. One row of bricks must measure 297 inches. Each brick, with mortar, is 9 inches long. How many bricks can you place in each row?

   F. 12
   G. 29
   H. 31
   J. 33
   K. 37

7. **Florist** You are making flower arrangements for a wedding. Each arrangement will use 9 white roses. You have 46 white roses available. How many arrangements can you make? How many roses will be left over?

A. 4 arrangements, 1 rose left over

B. 4 arrangements, 3 roses left over

C. 4 arrangements, 9 roses left over

D. 5 arrangements, 1 rose left over

E. 5 arrangements, 2 roses left over

8. **Tax Preparation Specialist** You have 152 clients who use simple tax returns. You can complete 8 of these returns in a business day. How many business days will it take to complete the simple tax returns?

F. 14

G. 16

H. 17

J. 18

K. 19

9. **Security Guard** You are hired to work at a venue with 640 people. You recommend there be one guard per 80 people in the crowd. How many guards should work the venue?

A. 7

B. 8

C. 9

D. 12

E. 16

10. **Dock Worker** You and your crew are unloading a ship full of cargo containers. There are 224 containers that need to be unloaded. You have 8 hours to unload them. You want to keep a steady pace. How many containers do you need to unload every hour?

F. 24

G. 25

H. 26

J. 28

K. 33

WORKSPACE

Remember!

Temperature tells
you how hot or cold
something is. **Length**
tells you how long
something is. **Distance**
tells how far it is
between two things
or places.

Skill Support

Temperature is
measured in degrees.
In the United States,
temperature is
measured in degrees
Fahrenheit (°F). In
countries that use
the metric system,
temperature is
measured in degrees
Celsius (°C).

Length and distance
use the same units of
measurement. People
in the United States
measure length and
distance in inches, feet,
yards, and miles. Other
countries may use
centimeters, meters,
and kilometers.

Lesson 8 ...
Use Measurements

Skill: Identify and measure temperature, length, weight, and volume

You use measurements to say how heavy or hot something is. You also use
measurements to identify height, distance, and volume. Bakers measure
the volume of liquid ingredients. They also measure oven temperature to
bake cakes. Carpenters measure length to build cabinets. A nurse might
measure your height and weight.

In order to use measurements, you must be able to do the following:

- Understand basic temperature facts.

- Understand basic length and distance facts.

- Understand basic weight facts.

- Understand basic volume facts.

Skill Examples ■ ■ ■

EXAMPLE 1 Read temperature.
What is the temperature?

- The tool for measuring temperature is a thermometer.
  Temperature is measured in degrees. Each tick on the
  thermometer represents 2 degrees.

- Look at the thermometer and find where the filled-in
  line ends. The line ends at two ticks above 60. This
  represents 4 degrees above 60.

The temperature is 64 degrees Fahrenheit.

EXAMPLE 2 Measure length and distance.
How long is the pen?

- To measure short lengths or distances, use inches. To measure
  medium lengths or distances, use feet. To measure long lengths or
  distances, use miles.

- The tool for measuring short lengths is a ruler. Each large tick
  represents 1 inch.

- Look at the ruler and find where the pen ends. Compare this point to
  the numbers on the ruler. The pen ends at the tick marked 5.

The pen is 5 inches long.

EXAMPLE 3 Measure weight.

How much does the pumpkin weigh?

- A scale is used for measuring weight. Each tick on this scale represents one pound.

- This is a mechanical scale. Find the number that matches up with where the pointer falls on the scale. This represents the number of pounds the pumpkin weighs.

- The pointer is at the tick between 12 and 14 pounds.

The pumpkin weighs 13 pounds.

EXAMPLE 4 Measure volume.

How much water is this?

- A measuring cup is used to measure volume in fluid ounces (fl. oz.). Each line on the cup represents 4 fl. oz.

- Find the line that matches up with the highest point of the liquid. Now find the number that aligns with this point.

- The water reaches the line marked 20 oz.

The volume of the water is 20 fluid ounces.

Weight tells you how heavy something is. Grocers measure the weight of vegetables they sell.

Volume tells you how much space something takes up. When you buy a gallon of gas, you are using volume.

Skill Support

Weight is measured in pounds in the United States. In countries that use the metric system, weight is measured in kilograms. We use a scale to measure weight. A scale can be mechanical or digital.

Volume is measured in fluid ounces (oz.) in the United States. It can also be measured in cups, quarts, and gallons. In the metric system, volume is measured in liters or milliliters.

Skill Practice ▪ ▪ ▪

1. What is the temperature?

A. 30 degrees Fahrenheit

B. 33 degrees Fahrenheit

C. 34 degrees Fahrenheit

D. 35 degrees Fahrenheit

E. 36 degrees Fahrenheit

HINT: Remember that each tick equals 2 degrees.

2. How long is this hammer?

F. 4 inches

G. 6 inches

H. 8 inches

J. 10 inches

K. 12 inches

HINT: Count the large ticks on the ruler. Each large tick represents 1 inch.

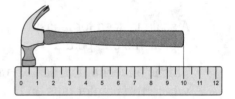

3. How much does the sugar weigh?

A. 5 pounds

B. 6 pounds

C. 10 pounds

D. 15 pounds

E. 50 pounds

HINT: Each tick on the scale represents one pound.

4. How much water is in the cup?

F. 24 fluid ounces

G. 26 fluid ounces

H. 28 fluid ounces

J. 30 fluid ounces

K. 30 fluid ounces

HINT: Each line on the cup represents 4 fluid ounces. If the water is halfway between 2 lines, that equals 2 oz.

Try It Out! ▪ ▪ ▪

Cook You work at the City Café and Restaurant. You are in charge of making muffins every morning. The recipe has many ingredients. Two ingredients are 16 pounds of flour and 30 fluid ounces of water. How will you measure the correct amounts of these ingredients?

A.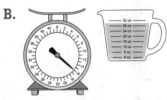

D.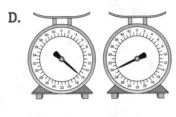

B.

E.

C.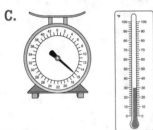

 Step 1 ## Understand the Problem ▪ ▪ ▪

Complete the *Plan for Successful Solving.*

Plan for Successful Solving

What am I asked to do?	What are the facts?	How do I find the answer?
Find the correct tools and measurements.	You need 16 pounds of flour. You need 30 fluid ounces of water.	The key word *measure* tells you that you will use measurements to solve this problem.

Step 2 ## Find and Check Your Answer ▪ ▪ ▪

- To measure the weight of the flour, use a scale. To measure the volume of water, use a measuring cup.

- **Select the correct answer: B**
  By using the right types of measurements, you were able to measure the correct amounts of both ingredients.

Remember!
Measurement tools often show both US and metric units. Thermometers show degrees Fahrenheit. They also show degrees Celsius. Rulers show inches and centimeters. Measuring cups show fluid ounces and milliliters.

Skill Support
Measuring correctly is important in many jobs. To measure correctly, follow these tips:

- Always measure at the closest point. Do not round to the highest or lowest number unless asked to do so.
- Sometimes it can be hard to line up the measurement with your eyes. Use a straightedge, like a piece of paper, to match up each point.

On Your Own ▪ ▪ ▪

Read and solve the following problems.

1. **Tow Truck Driver** You have just picked up a car that broke down. You need to keep a record of the distance you tow the car. Which unit of measurement should you write down?

   A. feet   D. inches

   B. pounds   E. miles

   C. degrees

2. **Animal Breeder** You breed chickens and sell them to farmers. New chicks have just hatched. You are checking on the temperature of the incubator. You want to make sure they are not too warm or too cold. How many degrees does the thermometer show?

   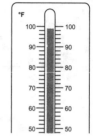

   F. 97   J. 100

   G. 98   K. 101

   H. 99

3. **Landscaper** You are picking up a load of cedar mulch for a customer. It is sold by the pound. You weigh the mulch before paying. How many pounds does the scale show?

   A. 35   D. 50

   B. 40   E. 55

   C. 45

4. **Carpenter** You need to buy lumber to build a deck for a client. You must measure the length of the space for the deck before you buy the lumber. What unit of measurement should you use?

   F. pounds   J. miles

   G. degrees   K. ounces

   H. feet

5. **Dietician** You are showing a client what a serving of dry cereal looks like. You pour the cereal into a measuring cup. How many ounces are in the serving?

   A. 4

   B. 6

   C. 8

   D. 10

   E. 12

6. Carpet Installer You are installing carpet in a bedroom. You calculate the amount of carpet you will need to cover the floor. You want to have a few extra inches of carpet just to be safe. The tick marks above the ruler shows the amount of extra inches you want. How many inches do the tick marks show?

F. 1   G. 5   H. 6   J. 8   K. 10

7. Seamstress You are making living room drapes for a client. You need to order fabric for the drapes. What unit of measurement do you use when ordering the fabric?

A. degrees   D. pounds

B. ounces   E. miles

C. yards

8. Insurance Sales Agent A construction company needs liability insurance for a project. You are checking the site before approving the policy. You need to check the height of the building. Which unit of measurement would you use for this?

F. gallons   J. degrees

G. ounces   K. feet

H. pounds

9. Ski Patrol You are making a report on the snowfall from last night. You need to measure the depth of the snow. Which unit of measurement should you use?

A. ounces   D. degrees

B. miles   E. inches

C. pounds

10. Shipping Clerk You are preparing a box for shipment. The shipper needs to know how much it weighs. How many pounds does the scale show?

F. 41   J. 44

G. 42   K. 45

H. 43

Lesson 9 ...
Understand Fractions

Skill: Understand fractions and fraction parts

A fraction is a part of a whole or a group that has been divided equally. Cooks use fractions to measure ingredients. A recipe calls for $\frac{1}{4}$ cup of water. Carpenters use fractions to measure length and height. A piece of wood needs to be $\frac{15}{16}$ inch thick. When you say, "I will be there in one half hour," you are using a fraction.

In order to understand fractions, you must be able to do the following:

- Understand basic multiplication facts.
- Understand basic division facts.

Skill Examples ...

EXAMPLE 1 Name the fraction.
What fraction of the circle is shaded?

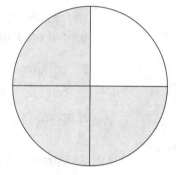

- The circle is divided into 4 equal parts, or fourths. Four fourths make one whole.

- Count the number of shaded parts. Three parts are shaded. This is the numerator. Write 3 above the line.

- Count the total number of parts. There are 4 parts of the circle. This is the denominator. Write 4 below the line.

The fraction of the circle that is shaded is $\frac{3}{4}$.

EXAMPLE 2 Name the fraction.
What fraction of the boxes is shaded?

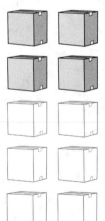

- Count the number of shaded boxes. Four boxes are shaded. This is the numerator. Write 4 above the line.

- Count the total number of boxes. This includes the shaded and nonshaded boxes. There are 10 boxes. This is the denominator. Write 10 below the line.

The fraction of the boxes that are shaded is $\frac{4}{10}$.

EXAMPLE 3 Find equivalent fractions by multiplying.
Rename the fraction $\frac{4}{5}$.

There is more than one way to write a fraction to show a given amount. Equivalent fractions are equal parts of one whole. Although they are written differently, they are the same amount.

You can find an equivalent fraction by multiplying. This is called raising a fraction to *higher terms*.

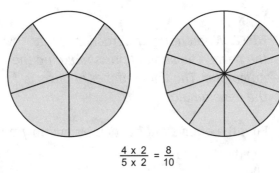

$$\frac{4 \times 2}{5 \times 2} = \frac{8}{10}$$

- Multiply both the numerator and the denominator by the same number.

- Rewrite the fraction as $\frac{4 \times 2}{5 \times 2}$. Next multiply the number in the numerator. $4 \times 2 = 8$. Write 8 in the numerator.

- Then multiply the number in the denominator. $5 \times 2 = 10$. Write 10 in the denominator.

You can rename $\frac{4}{5}$ as $\frac{8}{10}$. These are equivalent fractions.

EXAMPLE 4 Find equivalent fractions by dividing.
Rename the fraction $\frac{9}{12}$.

You can also find equivalent fractions by dividing. This is called reducing the fraction to *lower terms*.

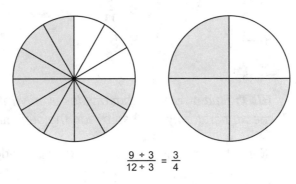

$$\frac{9 \div 3}{12 \div 3} = \frac{3}{4}$$

- Divide both the numerator and the denominator by the same number. You need to find a digit that divides evenly into 9 and 12. Both 9 and 12 can be divided by 3.

- Rewrite the fraction as $\frac{9 \div 3}{12 \div 3}$.

- Next divide the numbers in the numerator. $9 \div 3 = 3$. Write 3 in the numerator.

- Then divide the numbers in the denominator. $12 \div 3 = 4$. Write 4 in the denominator.

You can rename $\frac{9}{12}$ as $\frac{3}{4}$. These are equivalent fractions.

Remember!
The denominator of a fraction is how many parts there are. The numerator is how many parts you describe.

Level 2
Applied Mathematics

Skill Support
Equal fractions can have different numerators and denominators. Look at: $\frac{1}{2}$, $\frac{2}{4}$, and $\frac{4}{8}$.
$\frac{1}{2} = \frac{2}{4} = \frac{4}{8}$
These fractions all equal $\frac{1}{2}$.

Because these numbers are equal parts of one whole, they are called **equivalent fractions**.

Fractions can also be
written in words. Below
are some examples
of how fractions are
written as words.

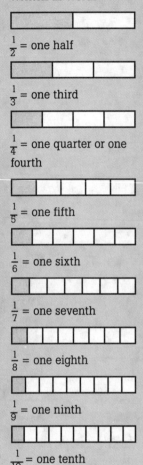

$\frac{1}{2}$ = one half

$\frac{1}{3}$ = one third

$\frac{1}{4}$ = one quarter or one
fourth

$\frac{1}{5}$ = one fifth

$\frac{1}{6}$ = one sixth

$\frac{1}{7}$ = one seventh

$\frac{1}{8}$ = one eighth

$\frac{1}{9}$ = one ninth

$\frac{1}{10}$ = one tenth

Remember!

When saying a fraction
out loud, read the
numerator first. Read
the denominator
second.

$\frac{1}{4}$ = one fourth

$\frac{2}{9}$ = two ninths

$\frac{12}{28}$ = twelve twenty-
eighths

Skill Practice ∎ ∎ ∎

1. Name the fraction of this circle that is shaded.

    A. $\frac{1}{10}$ **D.** $\frac{2}{10}$

    B. $\frac{1}{9}$ **E.** $\frac{9}{2}$

    C. $\frac{2}{9}$

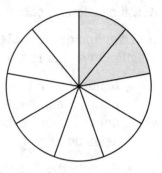

    *HINT: When naming a fraction, count
    the parts. The shaded parts make up the
    numerator. The total number of parts is
    the denominator.*

2. Find the equivalent fraction by multiplying.
    $\frac{4}{7}$ is the same as

    F. $\frac{8}{15}$ **J.** $\frac{12}{21}$

    G. $\frac{17}{17}$ **K.** $\frac{12}{28}$

    H. $\frac{8}{21}$

    *HINT: Multiply the numerator and denominator by the same number.
    Start with the number 2 to see if the fraction matches the choices. If it
    doesn't, increase the multiplier by 1.*

3. Find the equivalent fraction by dividing.
    $\frac{25}{60}$ is the same as

    A. $\frac{4}{12}$ **D.** $\frac{5}{13}$

    B. $\frac{5}{12}$ **E.** 5

    C. $\frac{6}{12}$

    *HINT: Find a number that divides evenly into both 25 and 60. Divide
    the numerator by 5. Then divide the denominator by 5 also.*

4. Name the fraction of this circle that is shaded.

    F. $\frac{1}{9}$ **J.** $\frac{7}{8}$

    G. $\frac{1}{8}$ **K.** $\frac{8}{7}$

    H. $\frac{1}{4}$

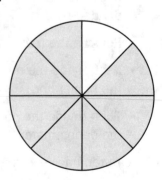

    *HINT: Count the number of shaded parts.
    This is the numerator. The total number of
    parts is the denominator. The numerator is
    placed above the denominator.*

Try It Out! ■ ■ ■

Business Manager You work for a cleaning company. You have 2 jobs to complete. You have 20 employees. You need 5 people for job A. You need 15 people for job B. What fraction of your employees will work on each job?

A. $\frac{1}{4}$ on job A, $\frac{3}{4}$ on job B   D. $\frac{1}{5}$ on job A, $\frac{1}{2}$ on job B

B. $\frac{1}{4}$ on job A, $\frac{1}{2}$ on job B   E. $\frac{1}{5}$ on job A, $\frac{3}{4}$ on job B

C. $\frac{1}{2}$ on job A, $\frac{3}{4}$ on job B

 ## Understand the Problem ■ ■ ■

Complete the *Plan for Successful Solving*.

Plan for Successful Solving

What am I asked to do?	What are the facts?	How do I find the answer?
Find the fraction of your employees who will work on each job.	There are 20 employees. You need 5 people for job A. You need 15 people for job B.	The key word *fraction* tells you that you will use fractions to solve this problem.

 ## Find and Check Your Answer ■ ■ ■

- You want to find out what fraction of your employees is assigned to each job. The total number of people in your group is 20. Five will work on job A. You can rewrite this as $\frac{5}{20}$

- Use division to rewrite $\frac{5}{20}$ in lowest terms. Divide the numerator by 5. Then divide the denominator by 5 also.

- $\frac{5 \div 5}{20 \div 5} = \frac{1}{4}$. One-fourth of the employees will work on job A.

- Fifteen people will work on job B. You can write this as $\frac{15}{20}$.

- Use division to rewrite $\frac{15}{20}$ in lowest terms. Divide the numerator by 5. Then divide the denominator by 5 also.

- $\frac{15 \div 5}{20 \div 5} = \frac{3}{4}$. Three-fourths of the employees will work on job B.

- **Select the correct answer: A.** $\frac{1}{4}$ on job A, $\frac{3}{4}$ on job B
  You found out what fraction of your employees will work on each job.

Remember!

Sometimes the numerator and denominator are the same number. When this happens, the fraction equals 1.
$$\frac{4}{4} = 1$$

Skill Support

When a fraction cannot be divided further, it is reduced to *lowest terms*. This is the most basic form of a fraction.

The fractions $\frac{3}{4}$ and $\frac{9}{12}$ are equal in value. $\frac{3}{4}$ is in lowest terms. It cannot be reduced any further.

On Your Own ▪ ■ ▪

Read and solve the following problems.

1. **Reservation Agent** You are booking rooms for a hotel. Sixteen rooms have a view of the ocean. A group reserved 14 of these rooms. What fraction of the rooms with ocean views did this group reserve?

   A. $\frac{1}{4}$

   B. $\frac{1}{3}$

   C. $\frac{1}{2}$

   D. $\frac{7}{8}$

   E. $\frac{8}{10}$

2. **Veterinarian** You are seeing several animals with skin allergies today. You want to see if you have enough medication on hand for them. You check your appointment book. You have 8 appointments today. You have enough skin allergy medication for 4 animals. What fraction of the animals can receive skin allergy medication today?

   F. $\frac{3}{8}$ J. $\frac{6}{8}$

   G. $\frac{4}{8}$ K. $\frac{7}{8}$

   H. $\frac{5}{8}$

3. **Butcher** You are looking at how much of each type of meat to stock. You go over recent sales. Today you had 12 sales. Of these, 7 were cuts of lamb. What fraction shows the number of lamb cuts sold out of the total?

   A. $\frac{3}{12}$ D. $\frac{6}{12}$

   B. $\frac{4}{12}$ E. $\frac{7}{12}$

   C. $\frac{5}{12}$

4. **Motorboat Operator** You are hired to take people waterskiing. You had 10 sessions scheduled today. You have completed 8 of them. You need to keep track of your progress. What fraction shows the number of sessions that you have completed?

   F. $\frac{6}{10}$

   G. $\frac{7}{10}$

   H. $\frac{8}{10}$

   J. $\frac{9}{10}$

   K. $\frac{10}{8}$

5. **Psychologist** A client owes you $1,000 for previous sessions. The client can afford to pay you $100 now and will pay you the rest when he is able. What fraction of the total owed can the client afford to pay you now?

   A. $\frac{1}{10}$

   B. $\frac{1}{7}$

   C. $\frac{1}{5}$

   D. $\frac{1}{3}$

   E. $\frac{1}{2}$

6. **Bicycle Mechanic** You work at a bicycle shop. You need to replace some gears on a broken bike. You need to know what fraction of the gears to replace. The bike has a total of 10 gears. You are replacing 4 gears. What fraction of the gears are you replacing?

   F. $\frac{2}{10}$ J. $\frac{8}{10}$

   G. $\frac{4}{10}$ K. $\frac{10}{4}$

   H. $\frac{6}{10}$

7. **Logger** You are cutting down trees in a forest. You need to keep track of the fraction of trees you are cutting. The trees you are to cut down have all been marked. There are markings on 2 out of 8 trees. What is an equivalent fraction to 2 out of 8?

A. $\frac{1}{4}$

B. $\frac{1}{3}$

C. $\frac{1}{2}$

D. $\frac{2}{4}$

E. $\frac{2}{3}$

8. **Actor** You are about to shoot a movie scene. You rehearse before shooting. You go over the dialogue in the scene. You have 9 lines. There are a total of 16 lines. What fraction represents your lines out of the total in the scene?

F. $\frac{5}{16}$

G. $\frac{6}{16}$

H. $\frac{7}{16}$

J. $\frac{8}{16}$

K. $\frac{9}{16}$

9. **Bill and Account Collector** You work for a debt collection agency. You earn money for bills you collect on. You get a bonus for having a high success rate. You have a success rate of 25 collected bills per 100 bills. What is an equivalent fraction for this rate?

A. $\frac{1}{25}$

B. $\frac{1}{5}$

C. $\frac{1}{4}$

D. $\frac{1}{3}$

E. $\frac{1}{2}$

10. **Lifeguard** You work at the city pool. Pool rules allow no more than 4 children for every 5 people at the pool. You count 9 children out of 15 people. What fraction is equivalent to 9 out of 15?

F. $\frac{1}{5}$

G. $\frac{1}{3}$

H. $\frac{1}{2}$

J. $\frac{3}{5}$

K. $\frac{4}{5}$

WORKSPACE

Key Words:

total, equation, calculator

Remember!

The entire amount of something is called a **total**. When asked to find a total, create an **equation**, or math problem. An equation is a number sentence that states equal amounts.

Skill Support

Look out for key words when choosing a mathematical operation.

Addition
- total or sum
- all together
- how many in all

Subtraction
- how many are left
- how many more than
- how many less than
- take away

Multiplication
- total or product
- multiplied by

Division
- quotient
- shared equally
- split

Lesson 10 ▪ ▪ ▪
Choose the Correct Operation

Skill: Choose the correct math operation to solve a workplace problem

When using math in the workplace, you must decide which operation to use. This may be adding, subtracting, multiplying, or dividing.

In order to choose the correct operation, you must be able to do the following:

- Understand number operations.

- Add and subtract whole numbers.

- Multiply and divide whole numbers.

Skill Examples ▪ ▪ ▪

EXAMPLE 1 Choose the correct operation to find the total.
A cashier at a dry cleaner must decide how much to charge a customer. The customer had a coat cleaned for $15 and a dress cleaned for $25. Which equation will show how to find the total to charge the customer?

- Write an equation that shows how to find the total. There are two amounts. To find the total to charge, you need to find the sum.

Coat Cleaning $15	+	Dress Cleaning $25

- The equation the cashier needs to use is 15 + 25 = 40.

Add:
$$\begin{array}{r} 15 \\ +25 \\ \hline 40 \end{array}$$

The customer owes a total of $40.

EXAMPLE 2 Choose the correct operation to find the total of multiple groups of the same size.
A human resources representative prepares orientation packets for new employees. Each new employee gets 3 packets. There are 12 new employees. Which equation should she use to find how many packets to prepare?

- You need to find the total number of packets she needs. She needs to give 3 packets to each of 12 employees. When counting multiple groups of the same size, use multiplication.

Number of Packets 3	×	Number of Employees 12

- Write an equation that shows how to find the total. To find the total amount of packets, you need to find the product.

Multiply: 12
          × 3
          36

- The equation she should use is 3 × 12 = 36.

She must prepare 36 packets.

EXAMPLE 3 Choose the correct operation to find the difference between two numbers.

A grocer must find out how many cases of melons sold last week. On Monday he had 39 cases of melons. On Sunday he has 6 cases left. Which equation should he use to find how many cases of melons were sold?

- The grocer wants to know how many cases of melons he sold. You know how many he had at the start of the week. You also know how many he has now.

| Beginning Cases 39 | – | Ending Cases 6 |

- Write an equation that shows how to find the difference. To find the difference, you need to subtract.

Subtract: 39
        – 6
        33

- The equation the grocer should use is 39 – 6 = 33.

The grocer sold 33 cases of melons.

EXAMPLE 4 Choose the correct operation to split a number into equal groups.

A baker in a cupcake shop baked 60 cupcakes. All of them will be used to fill 4 orders. Each order is for the same number of cupcakes. Which equation will show how many cupcakes to place in each order?

- Each order should receive the same number of cupcakes. The baker needs to split 60 cupcakes among 4 orders.

| Number of Cupcakes 60 | ÷ | Number of Orders 4 |

- Write an equation that shows how to find the number in each order. To separate into equal-size groups, you need to divide.

Divide: 15
        4)60
        – 4
         20
       – 20
          0

- The equation he should use is 60 ÷ 4 = 15.

Each order should receive 15 cupcakes.

Remember!

Operation	Symbol
addition	plus sign +
subtraction	minus sign –
multiplication	multiplication or times sign ×
division	division sign ÷

When asked to find the total, you need to find the sum or the product. This means you need to add or multiply.

When asked to find the amount remaining, you need to find the difference. This means you need to subtract.

When asked to split numbers into multiple groups of the same size, you need to find the quotient. This means you need to divide.

**Level 2
Applied Mathematics**

Skill Support

A **calculator** is often helpful for solving problems. When you add or multiply, the order *does not* matter. You can enter numbers in any order. When subtracting or dividing, the order *does* matter. Enter the larger number first when subtracting or dividing with a calculator.

Remember!

Find the sum or total with addition. Find the difference with subtraction. Find the product with multiplication. Find the quotient with division.

Skill Support

Use a pen or pencil to keep track of key information in a word problem. Underline information and key words in the problem. Useful information for math problems contains numbers.

- $9 an hour
- worked 36 hours

Key words tell something about the operation. In the first problem, the key word is *total*.

Before answering the question, be sure you used all of the information and key words.

36 hours × $9 = product (total)

Skill Practice ■ ■ ■

Choose the correct operation.

1. An office assistant earns $9 an hour. This week he worked 36 hours. You need to find his total earnings for the week. Which equation do you use to find the total earnings?

   A. $36 \div 9 = 4$

   B. $36 - 9 = 27$

   C. $9 + 36 = 45$

   D. $9 \times 9 = 81$

   E. $9 \times 36 = 324$

   HINT: You need to find the total. Use the operation for finding the total of multiple groups of the same size.

2. He worked 36 hours this week. He worked on 4 projects during the week. He spent an equal amount of time on each project. Which equation do you use to find how many hours he spent on each project?

   F. $36 \div 4 = 9$

   G. $36 - 4 = 32$

   H. $36 + 4 = 40$

   J. $36 - 36 = 0$

   K. $36 \times 4 = 144$

   HINT: You need to find 4 equal amounts of hours. You will want to use the operation that splits a number into equal amounts.

3. You are a DJ planning to work at a weekend event. Saturday will be longer than Sunday, so the fees are different. For Saturday, you are charging $250. For Sunday, you are charging $200. Which equation tells you the total amount you should charge? Use a calculator to find your answer.

   A. $250 - 200 = 50$

   B. $200 \times 2 = 400$

   C. $250 + 200 = 450$

   D. $250 + 250 = 500$

   E. $250 \times 2 = 500$

   HINT: Each day's rate is different, and you must find the total.

4. You are a wind turbine technician. Last week you worked on 48 turbines. This week you worked on 16 turbines. Which equation tells you how many more turbines you worked on last week than this week? Use a calculator to find your answer.

   F. $16 \times 16 = 256$

   G. $48 \div 16 = 3$

   H. $48 - 16 = 32$

   J. $48 + 16 = 64$

   K. $16 \times 48 = 768$

   HINT: You are looking for the difference between last week and this week.

Try It Out! ▪ ▪ ▪

Administrative Assistant You are an administrative assistant in a large office. You are preparing materials for a week-long conference. You are creating 400 packets that will be used during the week. Each of the 5 days requires the same number of packets. Which equation tells you how many packets you need each day?

A. $400 + 5 = 405$

B. $400 \div 5 = 80$

C. $400 - 5 = 395$

D. $5 + 400 = 405$

E. $400 \times 5 = 2{,}000$

Step 1 Understand the Problem ▪ ▪ ▪

Complete the *Plan for Successful Solving*.

Plan for Successful Solving		
What am I asked to do?	**What are the facts?**	**How do I find the answer?**
Find the equation that tells you how many packets you need each day.	There are 400 total packets. There are 5 days requiring packets.	The key words *same number* tell you that you are splitting a number into equal-size groups. You must divide to solve this problem.

Step 2 Find and Check Your Answer ▪ ▪ ▪

- You need to find the packets needed each day. You need to divide the number of packets by the number of days. The correct equation will show $400 \div 5 = 80$. Answer B shows this equation.

- Multiply 5 and 80 to check that the quotient shown is correct. $5 \times 80 = 400$.

- **Select the correct answer:** B. $400 \div 5 = 80$
  The equation shows the total number of packets divided by the number of days. Each day 80 packets are required.

Level 2
Applied Mathematics

Skill Support
When trying to decide what the correct operation to use is, it is important to read the question carefully. First make sure you understand what you are being asked. Go through the options, and choose the operation that will help you find the answer. Create and solve the equation. Then reread the question and be sure that your answer makes sense.

On Your Own ■ ■ ■

Read and solve the following problems.

1. **Animal Breeder** One of your dogs has had a litter of puppies. The dog had 9 puppies. You are planning to keep 3 of them and sell the rest. Which expression indicates the number of puppies that will be for sale?

   A. $9 \div 3$

   B. $9 - 3$

   C. $9 + 3$

   D. $3 - 9$

   E. 9×3

2. **Caterer** You are buying strawberries for a wedding you are catering. You need 30 pounds of strawberries. The strawberries cost $3 a pound. Which expression indicates the total cost of the strawberries?

   F. $30 \div 3$

   G. $3 \div 30$

   H. $30 - 3$

   J. $30 + 3$

   K. 30×3

3. **Volunteer Manager** You are organizing a beach clean-up day. You have 90 volunteers. They will be cleaning a total distance of 5 miles. You assign the same number of volunteers to each mile. Which equation indicates the number of volunteers per mile?

   A. $90 \div 5 = 20$

   B. $90 - 5 = 85$

   C. $90 \div 5 = 18$

   D. $90 \times 5 = 450$

   E. $90 + 5 = 95$

4. **Dry Cleaner** A customer has come to pick up her dry cleaning. She owes $32 and gives you $40. Which operation helps you find the correct change?

   F. division

   G. addition

   H. rounding

   J. subtraction

   K. multiplication

5. **Homemaker** You are trying to figure out how much time you spend each day preparing meals. You spend about 5 minutes making breakfast. You spend about 20 minutes making lunch. Finally you spend about 25 minutes fixing dinner. Which operation helps you identify the time you spend preparing meals altogether?

   A. division

   B. addition

   C. multiplication

   D. subtraction

   E. rounding

6. **Taxi Driver** You just dropped a passenger off at the airport. She paid you $31 for the cab fare. She gave you a $5 tip. Which equation indicates the total amount she gave you?

   F. $31 \div 5 = 6$

   G. $31 - 5 = 36$

   H. $31 + 5 = 36$

   J. $31 \times 5 = 155$

   K. $31 - 5 = 26$

7. **Window Washer** You spent 5 hours cleaning windows on a house. The owner paid you $250. Which operation helps you find how much you made per hour?

   A. division

   B. addition

   C. rounding

   D. subtraction

   E. multiplication

8. **Customer Service Representative** You are helping a customer make a deposit into his checking account. He deposits a check for $20. He also deposits $30 in cash. Which equation indicates the total amount of his deposit?

   F. $20 \times 30 = 60$

   G. $30 \times 20 = 600$

   H. $20 + 30 = 50$

   J. $30 - 20 = 10$

   K. $30 + 20 = 60$

9. **Dietician** You are calculating the calories for a serving of 10 shrimp. Each shrimp is 6 calories. Which expression would indicate the total calories for this serving?

   A. $10 \div 6 = 1.7$

   B. $10 - 6 = 4$

   C. $10 + 6 = 16$

   D. $6 + 10 = 16$

   E. $10 \times 6 = 60$

10. **Marketing Director** You are launching a new ad campaign. You hire a freelance marketing consultant to help you plan the campaign. The consultant charges $125 an hour. You agree to hire her for 7 hours of work. Which equation indicates the total money you will owe her for the job?

    F. $125 \div 7 = 18$

    G. $125 \times 7 = 875$

    H. $125 + 7 = 132$

    J. $125 - 7 = 118$

    K. $125 - 7 = 112$

WORKSPACE

Level 2 Performance Assessment ▪ ▪ ▪

These problems are at a Level 2 rating of difficulty. They are similar to problems on a career readiness certificate test. For each question, you can check your answer. To do this, use the answer key. It is located on pp. 267–269 of this book. It explains each answer option. It also shows the lesson that covers that skill. You may refer to that lesson to review the skill.

1. As a veterinarian, you administer rabies vaccinations to animals. You check your schedule for the week. You have 23 such vaccinations a day. You will work 3 days this week. How many vaccinations will you administer this week?

   A. 20   D. 66
   B. 26   E. 69
   C. 59

2. You work as a restaurant server. You are serving 7 tables in your section. Each table seats 4 people. How many total people can you serve at once?

   F. 11   J. 28
   G. 21   K. 32
   H. 24

3. One of your tasks as a police officer is to write traffic tickets. You report the total number of tickets you write each month. You issued 15 tickets this week. There are 4 weeks in this month. If you write the same number of tickets each week, what will the total be?

   A. 15   D. 50
   B. 20   E. 60
   C. 45

4. The 911 call center where you work is understaffed. You worked 16 shifts this month. Each shift was 12 hours. You want to know what you are owed. You calculate the total number of hours you worked. How many total hours did you work?

   F. 28   J. 192
   G. 84   K. 204
   H. 180

5. As a forklift driver in a warehouse, you move heavy items. You have 45 pallets of items to shelve. There are 5 shelves. For safety reasons, each shelf should hold the same amount. Divide the pallets evenly into 5 groups. How many pallets go on each shelf?

   A. 5   D. 40
   B. 8   E. 50
   C. 9

6. You are an acupuncturist. You treat patients by inserting small needles into their skin. A new order of needles is arriving tomorrow. You have one box of needles left for the day. There are 100 needles in the box. The needles can only be used once. Then they are thrown away. You have 10 clients today. You divide the needles evenly. How many needles can you use on each person if they all get the same number of needles?

F. 10　　　　　　J. 100

G. 50　　　　　　K. 110

H. 90

7. It is snack time at the day care center where you work. You give the children crackers as part of their snack. There are 35 crackers in a package. There are 7 children. Each child gets the same number of crackers. How many crackers does each child get?

A. 4　　　　　　D. 28

B. 5　　　　　　E. 35

C. 7

8. You are an art teacher. You have 144 colored pencils for your drawing class students to use. There are 5 students in your class. You divide the pencils evenly. The rest you put on the table for everyone to share. You want to keep track of these remaining pencils so they don't get lost. How many pencils are the remainder?

F. 4　　　　　　J. 28

G. 5　　　　　　K. 144

H. 8

9. You are a barber. A customer tells you how much hair to cut off. What unit of measurement does he use?

A. miles　　　　D. pounds

B. ounces　　　　E. inches

C. gallons

10. As a maintenance worker in an apartment building, you also maintain the pool. Today you add liquid chemicals to the pool water. This keeps the water clean. What unit of measurement do you use to adjust the dose?

F. inches

G. pounds

H. fluid ounces

J. degrees

K. feet

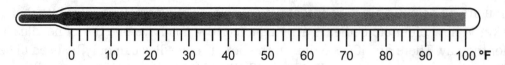

11. As a nurse, you take a patient's temperature when she comes in for an appointment. The patient complains about feeling hot. How many degrees does the thermometer show?

A. 89°F **B.** 90°F **C.** 95°F **D.** 100°F **E.** 105°F

12. A customer places a large order for ground beef at the butcher shop where you work. You use a scale to weigh the meat. He wants 50 pounds. How many pounds does the scale show?

F. 20 **G.** 35 **H.** 40 **J.** 45 **K.** 50

13. You are a farmer. You sell apples at a local farmers' market. You brought these crates of apples shown to the market. So far, the crates shown in color have been sold. What fraction of your fruit has been sold?

A. $\frac{5}{11}$ **B.** $\frac{6}{11}$ **C.** $\frac{1}{2}$ **D.** $\frac{11}{5}$ **E.** $\frac{11}{6}$

14. As a forecasting manager, you make predictions about how well your company will do this year. Based on your research, the company will grow for the next 9 months. The rest of the year will be slow. There are 12 months in a year. What fraction equals $\frac{9}{12}$?

F. $\frac{1}{4}$ **G.** $\frac{1}{3}$ **H.** $\frac{1}{2}$ **J.** $\frac{3}{4}$ **K.** $\frac{5}{6}$

15. You are a restaurant counter attendant. There are 8 slices in a large pizza. You just served 5. You must reheat the pizza when less than half is remaining. What fraction of the pizza is left?

A. $\frac{3}{8}$ **B.** $\frac{5}{8}$ **C.** $\frac{1}{2}$ **D.** $\frac{8}{5}$ **E.** $\frac{8}{3}$

16. You are cooking rice at a restaurant. The recipe calls for 2 cups of rice to 3 cups of water. You are using 9 cups of water. What is an equivalent fraction for 2 to 3 in this case?

F. $\frac{1}{2}$ G. $\frac{3}{5}$ H. $\frac{6}{9}$ J. $\frac{8}{10}$ K. $\frac{10}{12}$

17. You work as a house painter. You are painting the inside of a house. Each gallon of paint covers 350 square feet. You use the same paint for all the walls in the house. The walls are a total of 1,050 square feet. Which operation will help you figure out how many gallons you need?

    A. addition

    B. subtraction

    C. multiplication

    D. division

    E. rounding

18. As a barista, you accept payment and give change for drink orders. A customer orders a $4.50 coffee. He gives you $5.00. Which expression would indicate the correct change you give him?

    F. $5.00 + $4.50

    G. $5.00 – $4.50

    H. $5.00 × $4.50

    J. $5.00 ÷ $4.50

    K. $4.50 – $5.00

19. You are a customer service representative. You answer customer phone calls. A phone call lasts about 6 minutes. You answer 45 calls a day. Which operation would help you find out how many total minutes you spend on the phone?

    A. addition

    B. subtraction

    C. multiplication

    D. division

    E. comparing

20. At the bread factory where you work, you put rolls into boxes to be shipped to stores. It is near the end of your shift. You have 6 more boxes. You have already filled 219 boxes. Which expression would tell you how many total boxes you will fill today?

    F. 219 + 6

    G. 219 – 6

    H. 219 × 6

    J. 219 ÷ 6

    K. 6 ÷ 219

Locating Information ...

L ocating information is an essential skill in the workplace. Information is often presented in graphic formats. These formats include tables and graphs. They also include advertisements, diagrams, and forms. You might need to read a table to find out when an appointment is scheduled. You might need to fill out a form to apply for a job.

Workplace Skills: Basic Skills for the Workplace contains lessons that will help you improve your skills in locating and using information. It will also help you to apply them in the workplace. The questions in the lessons are pulled from real workplace situations. Each lesson includes step-by-step examples of how to perform a skill. You are then given the opportunity to try the skill on your own. You will learn the two-step approach to problem solving. On the next page is an example of a problem.

Level 1

> **Lesson 1:** Understand Signs and Symbols
>
> **Lesson 2:** Read Tables
>
> **Lesson 3:** Read Maps
>
> **Lesson 4:** Use Bar Graphs
>
> **Lesson 5:** Use Line Graphs

Level 2

> **Lesson 6:** Use Circle Graphs
>
> **Lesson 7:** Understand Diagrams
>
> **Lesson 8:** Find Information in Consumer and Business Materials
>
> **Lesson 9:** Use Forms
>
> **Lesson 10:** Find Information in Invoices and Order Forms

Photo: Monty Rakusen/Cultura/Getty Images

Two-Step Approach ■ ■ ■

It is important to learn how to approach locating information problems. You can solve them using two necessary steps. First understand the question and identify important information. Then find and check your answer.

The two-step approach to problem solving is an easy-to-follow model. You can use it to solve workplace problems. It can also be used on a career readiness certificate test.

Here is a problem. You work as a dietician. You are advising a patient to increase the amount of water in her diet. You are using the following bar graph. Which of the foods on the graph has the most water?

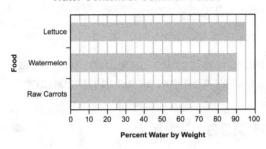

Water Content of Common Foods

Percent Water by Weight

 ## Step 1 Understand the Question ■ ■ ■

Complete the *Plan for Successful Solving.*

Plan for Successful Solving

What am I asked to do?	What are the facts?	How do I find the answer?
Determine what information you are being asked to find. This is usually found in the question.	Identify what information is shown in the graphic.	Determine where within the graphic the answer can be found.
You need to find the food with the most water.	The graph lists several foods. The length of the bar shows the water content of each food.	The longest bar shows the highest water content. Find the food that has the longest bar.

 ## Step 2 Find Your Answer ■ ■ ■

- Review the facts. You need to find the food with the most water. The lengths of the bars tell you how much water is in each food. The longest bar shows the highest water content.

The food with the longest bar is lettuce. Lettuce has the most water.

Skill Support

A **symbol** is something
that stands for
something else. You
may see symbols on
signs. Each symbol
has a meaning.
People use symbols
to communicate.

Signs are used
in the workplace
to communicate
information. Look
at the symbol on a
workplace sign. This
will tell you what it
means. Here are a few
examples of symbols
and their meanings:

- red line = not allowed
- cigarette = smoking
- lightning bolt =
  electricity
- red cross = help,
  first aid
- person in a
  wheelchair =
  handicapped
  accessible

Remember!

Signs have many
different uses. Some
signs indicate location.
They are usually posted
near that location.
Other signs can
indicate danger.

Lesson 1 ...■
Understand Signs and Symbols

*Skill: Identify signs and symbols in the workplace and identify traffic
signs and symbols*

Every day you see many signs and symbols. Signs are used to tell you
things. The exit sign shows you how to leave your office. The stop sign
tells you when to stop your car. A symbol may be a picture, a letter, or a
shape. You need to understand the signs and symbols you see.

In order to understand signs and symbols, you must be able to do
the following:

- Recognize geometric shapes.

- Understand context meaning.

An example of "understand context meaning" is looking at the location of
a sign. The location may give you a clue to its meaning.

Skill Examples ■ ■ ■

EXAMPLE 1 Identify workplace signs.
Identify the meanings of these signs. You may find them in the workplace.

Match the letter of the sign to the meaning. Which sign means:

- no smoking
- caution
- fire exit
- stairs
- handicapped accessible

A.		The first symbol is a person going through a door. This means "exit." The second symbol is a fire.
B.		The cigarette stands for "smoking." A red line through an image means "not allowed."
C.		This symbol is a person in a wheelchair. It means the area is accessible for handicapped people. It can also mean that space is reserved for handicapped people.
D.		The first symbol is a person. The second symbol is a zigzag line. This line is the shape of stairs.
E.		The exclamation point means "important." The background is usually yellow, which means "slow down or caution when in this area."

A. fire exit   **B.** no smoking   **C.** handicapped accessible

D. stairs   **E.** caution

EXAMPLE 2 Identify workplace symbols.

You may have seen these symbols before. They are on the toolbar of a computer. You click on the symbols to perform certain functions.

Match the letter of the symbol to its meaning. Which symbol means:

- open a file
- print a file
- save a file

A.	Click on it when you want to save a file you are working on. It will keep your changes.
B.	Click on it when you want to print a file. This will give you a paper copy.
C.	Folders contain files on the computer. Click on it when you want to open a file.

A. save a file   **B.** print a file   **C.** open a file

EXAMPLE 3 Identify traffic signs.

Identify the meanings of these signs. You may see them while driving. Here are tips for identifying the meanings of signs. Pay attention to their colors and shapes. These give you important information.

Safety Color Codes
- Red: danger, stop
- Yellow: warning, slow
- Green: direction, go
- Black and white: rules

Sign Shapes
- 8 sides: stop
- 5 sides: school zone
- 3-sided triangle: yield
- 4-sided diamond: warning

Match the letter of the sign to its meaning. Which sign means:

- speed limit
- stop
- school crossing

A. STOP	Cars in other directions may have to stop too.
B.	The sign shows people. They are crossing a road.
C. SPEED LIMIT 55	The number shows how fast you can drive on the road.

A. stop   **B.** school crossing   **C.** speed limit

Remember!

The direction of an arrow shows which way to go. This applies to an exit off a highway. It also applies to a curve or turn in the road.

- The arrow points to the right. The road will curve to the right.
- The arrow points to the left. The road will curve to the left.
- The sign below tells you traffic is one-way. This lets you know which way to drive.

Skill Support

Traffic signs are posted on roads. They give important information quickly. This information can be for your safety.

Every state uses traffic signs. Traffic signs are also posted in other countries.

Speed limit signs are one type of traffic sign. In the United States, signs use miles per hour. Countries with the metric system use kilometers per hour.

**Level 1
Locating Information**

Skill Practice ▪ ▪ ▪

Locate information in the signs and symbols. Then answer the questions.

1. Look at the sign in the picture. What does the sign mean?

A. handicapped-accessible parking

B. no parking

C. exit

D. no left turn

E. wet floor

*HINT: Consider the image on the sign.
It is a letter P with a line through it.
Look for context clues. See where the sign is located.*

2. You want to save a computer file. On which symbol should you click?

F.   **J.**

G.   **K.**

H.

HINT: Look at the symbols. Think about what the pictures indicate.

3. You see this sign on the road. What should you do?

A. Drive at least 60 miles per hour.

B. Drive no faster than 60 miles per hour.

C. Drive no farther than 60 miles.

D. Drive at least 60 miles.

E. Take exit number 60.

HINT: Consider the words on the sign. What do they mean?

4. You are an office manager. You need to put a sign on the door to a room where the company only allows top-level managers. Which sign should you use?

F.   **J.**

G.   **K.**

H.

HINT: Read the words on each sign. Think about what those words mean.

Try It Out! ▪ ■ ■

Messenger You work for the Speedy Messenger delivery company. You are delivering a letter to a new client. You are coming up to an intersection. You need to make a left turn at the intersection. You notice there is a sign. You need to be sure that a left turn is allowed. Which sign would indicate that a left turn is not allowed?

A.

B.

C.

D.

E.

Step 1 Understand the Question ▪ ■ ■

Complete the *Plan for Successful Solving*.

Plan for Successful Solving

What am I asked to do?	What are the facts?	How do I find the answer?
Decide if the sign means "no left turn."	There is a sign at the intersection. You need to make a left turn. You need to know if a left turn is allowed.	Look at the pictures on the signs. You need to decide if the sign means "no left turn."

Step 2 Find Your Answer ▪ ■ ■

- Review the facts. You need to know if it is okay to make a left turn. Use the clues to tell you the meaning of the sign.

- Look at the pictures on the signs. Find any arrows that are pointing left.

- You need to find a sign that says "not allowed." A red line through a picture means "not allowed."

- **Select the correct answer: B.**
  You looked at all the clues. You determined the meaning of the signs. You found the sign that means a left turn is not allowed.

Skill Support
In this question, you need to identify the correct sign. The sign says that a left turn is not allowed. Look for the symbol that means "left turn." Then look for the symbol that means "not allowed."

Remember!
You must understand traffic signs. Otherwise, you may cause a car accident. You must understand workplace signs. Otherwise, you may put yourself in danger. If you do not understand a sign, ask another person. You may also look in reference materials. This will reduce the chance of an accident or a mistake.

On Your Own ▪ ▪ ▪

Use the graphics to answer the questions.

1. **Truck Driver** Your truck has broken down. You don't know why. You think it might be the battery. Which symbol means that the battery is dead?

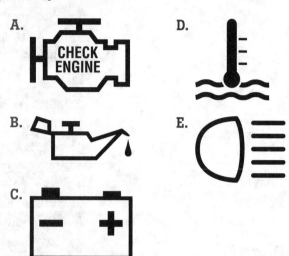

A. CHECK ENGINE

B.

C.

D.

E.

2. **Park Naturalist** You work at a park with trails through the forest. You have found poison ivy on one of the trails. Which sign should you post?

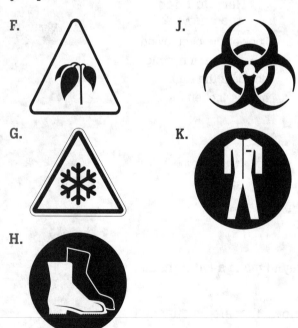

F.

G.

H.

J.

K.

3. **Store Manager** You manage a shop in a mall. The store is located on the second floor. How will this sign help you direct a customer to the store?

    A. It shows where the stairs are.

    B. It shows where the information desk is.

    C. It shows where the mall map is.

    D. It shows where your store is.

    E. It shows where the escalator is.

4. **Delivery Driver** You are delivering a shipment of produce to a factory. You missed your turn for the factory. This sign is on the road. What does the sign mean?

    F. no U-turn

    G. one way

    H. do not enter

    J. reduced speed limit

    K. stop

5. **Mail Carrier** You are driving a mail route that you have never driven before. You see this sign on the road. What does it mean?

    A. An intersection is ahead.

    B. A stop light is ahead.

    C. A rest stop is ahead.

    D. A railroad crossing is ahead.

    E. A post office is ahead.

6. **Store Manager** You are locking the store for the night. Which sign should you put on the door?

F.

J.

G.

K.

H.

7. **Nuclear Station Operator** You inspect the reactor every morning. You have to use safety equipment to protect yourself. Which sign means you should wear glasses?

A.

D.

B.

E.

C.

Wi-Fi here

8. **Computer Network Specialist** You are attending a conference in another city. You need to send documents to your office. What does this sign mean?

F. It shows where you can purchase a laptop.

G. It shows where you can access the Internet.

H. It shows the location of a fax machine.

J. It shows the location of a USPS mail box.

K. It shows the location of a video camera.

9. **Copy Center Operator** A customer asks you to make copies of a sales contract. The pages of the contract are attached by a paper clip. This symbol is on the copier. What does it mean?

A. Do not use paper clips in the copier.

B. Only one page may be copied at a time.

C. Copies with paper clips should be placed in a separate tray.

D. Only stapled papers can be used.

E. The sales contract cannot be copied.

10. **Bailiff** You are required to enforce the rules of the courtroom. This sign is posted on the wall. What does it mean?

F. The phone is out of order.

G. The emergency phone is behind the sign.

H. Cell phones are not allowed.

J. No phones are available in the courtroom.

K. Phones should not be used while driving.

Remember!

Do the following when reading a table for the first time:

- Read from the left to the right.
- Then read from the top to the bottom.

Once you have read the whole table, it will be easier to find specific information.

Skill Support

It is important to read tables closely and carefully. Here are some tips for reading tables.

- First look at the **title** of the table. It tells you the main idea of the table.
- Look at a table's columns. A **column** is a vertical section—it goes up and down. The column heading tells you what information you will find in it.
- Then look at the table's rows. A **row** is a horizontal section—it goes from left to right. The row shows you the data.
- Compare the columns and rows to find the information you need.

Lesson 2
Read Tables

Skill: Find information in tables

Tables are used to organize information. This helps make information easier to read. The title of a table gives the main idea. The columns and rows give details. Consider the example below. A stock clerk may use a table called "Inventory Count." The columns list the items. They also show the number of items the store has in stock. The rows show the items being counted.

Inventory Count

Item	Number in Stock
Chairs	62
Sofas	25
Beds	20

There are other ways to use tables. A manager may create a schedule entitled "Weekly Schedule." The columns show the days of the week. The rows show the employees' names.

In order to find information in a table, you must be able to:

- Compare and order numbers.
- Identify the main idea.
- Recognize and recall details.

Skill Examples

EXAMPLE 1 Locate information in a table.

A pet store owner made this table. She will use it to decide how many animals to keep in her store. How many of each type of animal has she sold in January?

- First look at the title of the table. It tells you the main idea of the table. This table is about animal sales.

Animals Sold at Dogma Pet Store

Type of Animal	Number Sold in January
Cats	10
Dogs	6
Fish	14
Lizards	2

- Look at the headings of the columns. Columns go up and down. They are vertical. Columns tell you what details you will find. The left column tells you the types of animals. The right column tells you the number of animals sold.

- Look at the rows. Rows go across. They are horizontal. The rows identify the specific types of animals sold. The store sells cats, dogs, fish, and lizards.

- Read the table. How many of each type of animal were sold? Look at both the column and the row. Look at the first item in the first column. Now look at the item in the column next to it. Then move to the next row, and so on.

The table says that the store sold 10 cats, 6 dogs, 14 fish, and 2 lizards.

EXAMPLE 2 Locate information in a table without numbers.

You are the manager of Sunrise Café. You want to find who works the morning shift on Friday. To do this, you must read the table.

- Look at the table's left column. This column tells you the day of the week.

- Now look at the second column. This is the schedule for the morning shift. The column heading tells you this important information.

- Read the heading for the third column. This is the schedule for the afternoon shift.

- To answer the question, read the table. Look at the "Friday" row. Find where the row meets the "Morning Shift" column.

Work Schedule

Day	Morning Shift	Afternoon Shift
Monday	Beth	Ali
Tuesday	Karim	Jason
Wednesday	Jason	Karim
Thursday	Julia	Beth
Friday	Ali	Julia

Ali works the morning shift on Friday.

EXAMPLE 3 Compare information in a table.

You want to find the lowest golf score at the tournament. Read the table. Which golfer had the lowest score?

- Look at the column headings. Look at the right column. This column tells the score for each golfer.

- The lowest score is the least number in the right column. The numbers are 96, 83, 97, and 88. The least number is 83.

- Next locate the name of the golfer in the left column of the same row. The golfer with a score of 83 is Darren.

Charity Golf Tournament

Player	Golf Score
Alyssa	96
Darren	83
Miguel	97
Lena	88

Darren had the lowest score.

Remember!

Some tables have numbers and words. Some only have words. Work schedules can list names, days, and hours.

Repair logs may not use numbers. They may only list items that were repaired. They may also list the names of the repair people.

Skill Support

Some questions ask you to find the greatest amount of something. They may say *highest, largest,* or *most.* Look for the greatest number in the table. Some questions ask you to find the least amount of something. They may say *smallest, fewest,* or *lowest.* Look for the least number in the table.

Level 1
Locating Information

Skill Practice ▪ ▪ ▪

Locate information in the tables. Then answer the questions.

1. You sell ice cream. There are five flavors at your store. One of the flavors is mint. How many gallons of mint did you sell last month?

   A. 11 gallons

   B. 12 gallons

   C. 13 gallons

   D. 20 gallons

   E. 21 gallons

   Ice Cream Sales: Scoops Ice Cream Parlor

Flavor	Number of Gallons Sold Last Month
Chocolate	12
Vanilla	13
Mint	20
Strawberry	11
Coffee	21

   HINT: Look at the left column. Find mint. The left column shows the flavor. The right column shows the numbers of gallons sold.

2. Look at the Ice Cream Sales table again. Which flavor sold the most?

   F. chocolate   G. coffee   H. mint   J. strawberry   K. vanilla

   HINT: You are looking for the flavor that has the highest number of gallons sold. High numbers mean more gallons. Low numbers mean fewer gallons.

3. You work in a museum. Your duty is to assign staff to exhibits. You need to know how many people visit an exhibit. How many people visit the penguins each month?

   A. 153   D. 800

   B. 250   E. 880

   C. 490

   Number of Visitors Natural History Museum

Exhibit	Visitors per Month
Dinosaurs	153
Whales	490
Tigers	250
Penguins	880
Bears	800

   HINT: Find the row labeled "Penguins." Then identify the visitors per month in the right column.

4. You work in an automobile repair shop. A customer calls about a 1991 Volvo. She wants to know who repaired it. Use the vehicle repair log to answer the question.

   F. Abe   J. Marie

   G. Bob   K. Stephanie

   H. George

   Vehicle Repair Log, Reliable Auto Repairs

Vehicle	Repaired By
1991 Volvo	George
2004 Jeep	Stephanie
2010 Honda	Abe
1995 Toyota	George
2000 Chrysler	Marie
1999 Dodge	Bob

   HINT: Look at the column headings. The left column identifies vehicles that were repaired. The right column identifies who repaired the vehicle.

Try It Out! ■ ■ ■

Farm Manager You need to order seeds for next season. This table shows the number of acres for each crop. Which seed will you need the most of?

Planting Plan for Next Season

Crop	Acres to Plant
Corn	70
Hay	14
Rice	62
Soybeans	77
Wheat	76

A. corn   **B.** hay   **C.** rice   **D.** soybeans   **E.** wheat

 Step 1 ## Understand the Question ■ ■ ■

Complete the *Plan for Successful Solving.*

Plan for Successful Solving

What am I asked to do?	What are the facts?	How do I find the answer?
Find the seed you will need the most of.	You will plant 70 acres of corn. You will plant 14 acres of hay. You will plant 62 acres of rice. You will plant 77 acres of soybeans. You will plant 76 acres of wheat.	You must find the greatest number in the "Acres to Plant" column. Then you must find the crop in that row.

 Step 2 ## Find Your Answer ■ ■ ■

- Look for the crop with the most acres. You will need more seeds of this crop.

- Remember high numbers mean more acres. Low numbers mean fewer acres.

- Select the crop with the most acres. Look at the table to be sure you have selected the row with the highest number.

- **Select the correct answer: D.** soybeans
  The highest number is 77. The seed you will need the most of is soybeans.

On Your Own ▪ ▪ ▪

Use the graphics to answer the questions.

Hunting Injuries 2009–2011

Year	Game Sought	Injury	Cause of Injury
2009	Turkey	Large gunshot wound	Could not tell what was in front of him
2009	Pheasant	Small shotgun wounds	Did not see victim
2009	Deer	Fall from hunting bench	No safety harness
2009	Pheasant	Small shotgun wounds	Did not see victim
2009	Deer	Fall from hunting bench	No safety harness
2010	Geese	Small shotgun wounds	Victim in line of fire
2010	Coyote, squirrel	Fall from hunting bench	Alcohol
2010	Deer	Fall from hunting bench	No safety harness
2011	Deer	Heart attack	Natural causes

1. **Forest Ranger** You work in a state forest. This is a record of hunting accidents in your forest. What injury occurred and what game was sought in 2011?

   A. small shotgun wounds while hunting for pheasant

   B. fall from hunting bench while hunting for deer

   C. large gunshot wound while hunting for turkeys

   D. small shotgun wounds while hunting for geese

   E. heart attack while hunting for deer

2. **Forest Technician** You work in a state forest. You keep track of hunting accidents. What is the main idea of this table?

   F. to record types of animals hunted each year

   G. to record number of injuries each year

   H. to record dangerous accidents each year

   J. to record injuries and causes of injuries each year

   K. to record unsafe hunting behaviors each year

Pearl's Pizza Place

	Small	Medium	Large
	10"	12"	14"
Slices	6	8	10
Cheese Pizza	$5.75	$10.00	$13.00
Extra Cheese	$1.00	$1.25	$1.50
Each Extra Regular Topping	$0.50	$0.75	$1.00

3. **Cashier** You work at Pearl's Pizza Place. You use this table to figure out how much customers owe. What is the main idea of the table?

   A. types of toppings

   B. sizes of pizzas

   C. prices of pizzas

   D. number of slices per pizza

   E. sizes and prices of pizzas

4. **Food Server** A customer orders a large pizza. He wants to know how much extra cheese will cost. What do you say?

   F. $0.50

   G. $0.75

   H. $1.00

   J. $1.25

   K. $1.50

5. **Waiter** A customer wants a medium pizza. How many slices does she get?

   A. 6

   B. 8

   C. 10

   D. 12

   E. 14

Train Schedules from Philadelphia to New York

Depart	Arrive	Route	Train
Mon 3:30 P.M.	Mon 4:45 P.M.	Acela Express	2168
Mon 3:56 P.M.	Mon 5:20 P.M.	Northeast Regional	94
Mon 4:35 P.M.	Mon 5:45 P.M.	Acela Express	2170
Mon 5:00 P.M.	Mon 6:31 P.M.	Northeast Regional	148
Mon 5:18 P.M.	Mon 6:48 P.M.	Keystone	652
Mon 5:30 P.M.	Mon 6:45 P.M.	Acela Express	2172
Mon 5:55 P.M.	Mon 7:19 P.M.	Northeast Regional	178
Mon 6:30 P.M.	Mon 7:45 P.M.	Acela Express	2122
Mon 6:50 P.M.	Mon 8:12 P.M.	Keystone	654
Mon 7:02 P.M.	Mon 8:38 P.M.	Northeast Regional	196

6. Conductor You work on the Philadelphia-to-New York train. You use this table to share information with travelers. What is the main idea of the table?

F. routes

G. departure times

H. arrival times

J. train numbers

K. routes and times of trains

7. Railroad Switch Operator You operate railroad track switches. There is a problem on a track from Philadelphia to New York. The train left at 4:35 p.m. Which train number is it?

A. 94

B. 196

C. 2168

D. 2170

E. 2172

Nutritional Information for Fast-Food Sandwiches

Food Item	Calories	Protein (g)	Fat (g)
Hamburger	428	28	19
Cheeseburger	470	31	23
Fish Sandwich	344	33	10
Chicken Sandwich	378	32	12
Ham Sandwich	451	30	21

g = gram

8. **Food Service Worker** You wait on customers in a fast-food restaurant. You answer questions from customers about the food you serve. This table has information about different sandwiches. What is the main idea of the table?

F. nutritional information

G. calorie information

H. fat information

J. protein information

K. types of sandwiches served

Glamour U Hair Salon Services

	Stylist	Master Stylist
Women's Cut	$40	$55
Men's Cut	$30	$35
Facial Waxing	$10	$15
Color Services		
One Process (Touch-up)	$50	$55
Gloss	$20	$20
Highlights (partial)	$65	$70
Highlights (full)	$95	$105
Extensions	Call	Call

9. **Receptionist** You work at Glamour U Hair Salon. You greet customers. You also share information from this table. What is the main idea of this table?

A. prices of services at the salon

B. cut and waxing services

C. prices of different stylists

D. services available for men

E. color services

10. **Hairdresser** A customer calls about haircuts. He wants a master stylist. How much is a men's cut?

F. $10   G. $30   H. $35   J. $40   K. $55

Skill Support

Below is a list of the major features found on a map.

- Map title: This tells you what is on the map.
- A **map key** shows what the symbols on the map mean.
- A **compass rose** shows north, south, east, and west. These are the cardinal directions. There are other directions halfway between each cardinal direction. These directions are northeast, southeast, southwest, and northwest.
- Most maps are drawn to scale. The **scale** shows distances on the map.

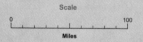

Remember!

Symbols represent objects and places. On a map, they may look different from real life. For example, squares may represent buildings. Cups may represent cafés. The key identifies what the symbols mean.

Basic Skills for the Workplace

Lesson 3
Read Maps

Skill: Use a map to find information

A map is a drawing of an area. There are many different types of maps. There are road maps and street maps. There are also floor plans and political maps. A map gives information about where things are. You can use maps for directions. Maps show you north, south, east, and west. Maps use symbols. Maps are usually drawn to scale.

In order to use maps, you must be able to do the following:

- Understand signs and symbols.
- Recognize the directions north, south, east, and west.

Skill Examples

EXAMPLE 1 Understand the symbols in a map key.

This is a map of a part of a city. What can you learn about the city from the map?

- First look at the map title. The title says this is a map of Midtown District.
- Now look at the map key. The key lists symbols that match information on the map. The symbols show what places can be found in the district.
- Look at the compass rose on the map. The compass shows direction. N is for north. E is for east. S is for south. W is for west.

The map tells you general information. For example, there is an airport in the district. The map also tells you specific information. For example, the post office is east of the mall.

EXAMPLE 2

Identify the directions north, south, east, and west on a map.

A truck driver uses this map to plan his route. He is on Fairwood Avenue. He must go to Fleet Street and then to Route 1. The compass rose shows him the directions. In which directions should he go?

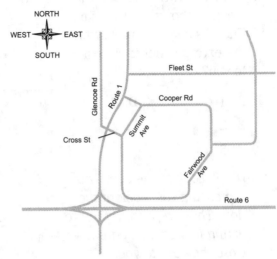

- Look at the compass. Look at Fleet Street. Look at Fairwood Avenue. Fleet Street is north of Fairwood Avenue. Fairwood Avenue is south of Fleet Street. The driver must go north.

- Next he must go to Route 1. Look at the map and the compass. Route 1 is left of Fleet Street. On the compass, left means west. The driver must go west.

The driver must go north on Fairwood Avenue to Fleet Street. Then he must go west on Fleet Street to Route 1.

EXAMPLE 3 Locate information on a map.

Identify where you are on the map. Decide which direction to take to get to River Road.

- Maps show relative location. This map shows your location.

- Look at the flag. It says, "YOU ARE HERE." This shows where you are on the map.

- What is the name of the street you are on? You are on Market Street.

- Now find River Road on the map.

- Look at where you are on Market Street. Look at River Road. Look at the compass. Market Street is east of River Road. River Road is west of Market Street.

To get to River Road from Market Street, you need to go west. Before going west, you need to go south to Highland Avenue.

Remember!

Road maps are a common type of map. They are very useful. They help travelers learn where places are. Road maps help travelers find cities and towns. **Street maps** show the streets in a city or district. **Floor plans** show the layout of a building. They show rooms and exits.

Skill Support

You can use a map to plan how to get somewhere. First locate where you are on the map. Next locate where you want to go. Then follow the roads that lead there. There may be multiple routes. The fastest is usually the route that covers the shortest distance.

Remember!

The directions on a compass are not always written out. Sometimes they are abbreviated. It is important to remember the abbreviations for directions.

- N = North
- S = South
- E = East
- W = West
- NW = Northwest
- NE = Northeast
- SW = Southwest
- SE = Southeast

Skill Support

Some maps come in hard copy. You see these maps on paper. Others come in digital format. You see these maps on a computer or other digital device. With hard-copy maps you can trace routes with a pencil. With digital maps you can run your finger along the screen.

Skill Practice ...

Locate information in the maps. Then answer the questions.

1. You work at the store in the location shown on the map. There is a small fire. Which fire extinguisher is closest to you?

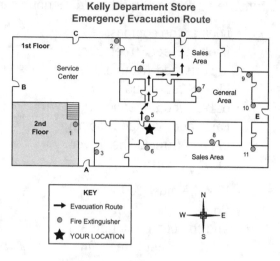

A. 1	**D.** 8
B. 3	**E.** 11
C. 5	

HINT: Look at the star. This represents you. Look at the dots. These represent the fire extinguishers. Compare how close they are to you.

2. The arrows indicate an emergency evacuation route. They show you where to go in case of an emergency. Which exit is the emergency exit?

F. Exit A   **G.** Exit B   **H.** Exit C   **J.** Exit D   **K.** Exit E

HINT: Look at the arrows. Which exit do they point toward?

3. You work for a floral shop. Your job is to deliver flowers. The map shows your neighborhood. You begin your route in the Garden District. You finish it in Uptown. In which direction are you going?

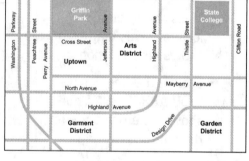

A. north	**D.** northwest
B. south	**E.** southwest
C. northeast	

HINT: Look at the compass. Then find the Garden District and Uptown on the map. Identify the direction by looking at the compass.

4. You begin in the Garment District. You stop in the Arts District. Which road is the most direct?

F. Jefferson Avenue	**J.** Design Drive
G. Cross Street	**K.** Washington Parkway
H. Thistle Street	

HINT: You will want to travel from south to north.

Try It Out!

Receptionist You work at a dentist's office. It is in Medical Village. A new patient lives in Holiday Apartments. She calls for directions to the office. Which subway line do you tell her to take?

A. 1 Line

B. 10 Line

C. 25 Line

D. 30 Line

E. 40 Line

City Subway Map

Medical Village

Holiday Apartments

Subway Lines
- 1 Line
- 10 Line
- 25 Line
- 30 Line
- 40 Line

Step 1 **Understand the Question** ■ ■ ■

Complete the *Plan for Successful Solving*.

Plan for Successful Solving

What am I asked to do?	What are the facts?	How do I find the answer?
Find the subway line that goes from Holiday Apartments to Medical Village.	The subway lines are called the 1 Line, 10 Line, 25 Line, 30 Line, and 40 Line.	The 10 line stops at both Holiday Apartments and Medical Village.

Step 2 **Find Your Answer** ■ ■ ■

- Find Holiday Apartments on the map. Identify the lines that pass through this location. The 10 and 1 Lines pass through it.

- Trace the lines. Which line also passes through Medical Village? The 10 Line passes through both Holiday Apartments and Medical Village.

- Before selecting an answer, read the question again. Be sure your answer makes sense.

- **Select the correct answer: B.** 10 Line
  You used the map. You found that the 10 Line stops at Holiday Apartments. It also stops at Medical Village. The patient should take the 10 Line. It goes from her home to the office.

Remember!

This question asks you to plan a route. First find where you want to start on the map. Next find where you want to stop. Then plan your route. What is the most direct way to get where you want to go?

Skill Support

There are many different types of maps.

- Geographical maps show natural features. They might show lakes or rivers.
- Directional maps show roads and streets or sailing routes.
- Informational maps show information. For example, they might show birthrates.

Even maps of the same type may look different. Labels, symbols, and colors vary. Read the maps closely to be sure you understand them.

Level 1
Locating Information

On Your Own ▪ ▪ ▪

Use the graphics to answer the questions.

White House and West Mall, Washington, D.C.

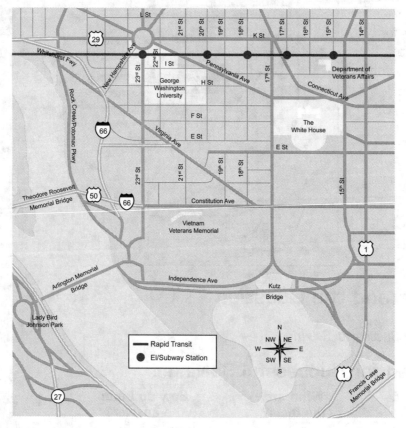

1. **White House Intern** You drive from the White House to Lady Bird Johnson Park. You must cross a bridge. Which bridge is closest to the park?

    A. Francis Case Memorial Bridge

    B. Kutz Bridge

    C. Arlington Memorial Bridge

    D. Theodore Roosevelt Memorial Bridge

    E. Vietnam Veterans Memorial

2. **News Reporter** You just finished an interview at the White House. Now you must cover an event at the Vietnam Veterans Memorial. Which direction is the memorial?

    F. east

    G. southeast

    H. west

    J. southwest

    K. south

Art Museum Floor Plan

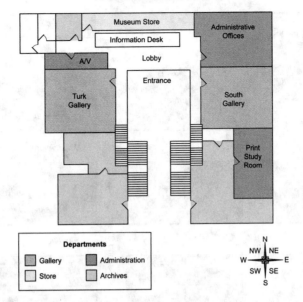

3. **Copy Writer** You are writing an article about a local artist. You have a meeting with her in the Print Study Room. Where is this room located?

   A. next to the A/V room

   B. next to the Turk Gallery

   C. next to the Museum Store

   D. next to the Administrative Offices

   E. next to the South Gallery

4. **Network Repair Person** You will check the Internet connections in the museum. You will start with the administration department. Which room(s) will you work in?

   F. Turk Gallery, South Gallery, and Print Study Room

   G. Museum Store

   H. A/V Room, Administrative Offices, and Print Study Room

   J. Information Desk

   K. Archives

5. **Artist** The museum will hang your work in the Turk Gallery. You go to the gallery to help. On which side of the building is the gallery?

   A. north

   B. south

   C. east

   D. west

   E. northeast

Fairview

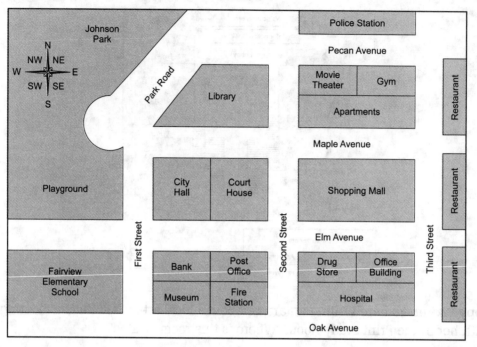

6. **Brick Layer** You are repairing the west wall of the shopping mall. You must drop off supplies. Which street is next to the west wall of the shopping mall?

F. Elm Avenue

G. Maple Avenue

H. First Street

J. Second Street

K. Third Street

7. **Surveyor** You report on all north-south streets in Fairview. Which of the following streets will you report on?

A. First Street

B. Elm Avenue

C. Maple Avenue

D. Oak Avenue

E. Pecan Avenue

Office Floor Plan

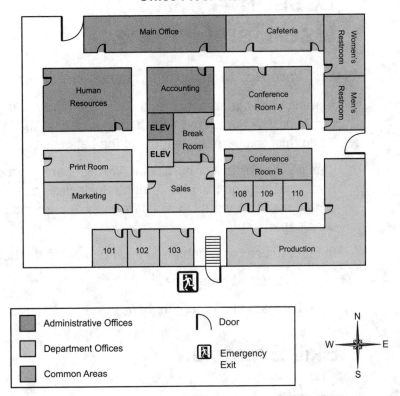

8. **Mail Sorter** You sort mail in the Main Office. Then you hand deliver it. You leave the Main Office and walk east to the end of the hall. Then you walk south to the end of the hall and enter the room to deliver the mail. Which room are you in?

F. Accounting

G. Human Resources

H. Sales

J. Marketing

K. Production

9. **Secretary** You work for the CEO. You have been asked to invite clients to a meeting in Conference Room A. You give directions to the clients. Which outside door is the closest to Conference Room A?

A. northwest corner

B. northeast corner

C. south side

D. east side

E. north side

10. **Marketing Agent** You stop at the Main Office for a meeting. You ask for directions to Marketing. Where is it?

F. next door to the Main Office

G. between the Main Office and Human Resources

H. between Accounting and Sales

J. between Room 101 and the Print Room

K. between Accounting and Production

Remember!

A **graph** represents information. It usually shows information in a picture. It can show a lot of information in a small space. This is why people use graphs to show data. Types of graphs include:

- bar graphs
- line graphs
- circle graphs

Skill Support

A **bar graph** uses bars to represent information. When reading a bar graph, follow these steps:

- Look at the graph title. It tells what the graph is about.
- Look at the labels on the graph. The labels are found on the *x-* and *y-*axes. The **x-axis** runs across. The **y-axis** runs up and down. These tell you what information you will find.
- Look at the lengths of the bars.
- Compare the bars to gain information.

Lesson 4 ...
Use Bar Graphs

Skill: Understand and use bar graphs to find information

A graph shows information in a picture format. A bar graph compares numbers. The bars stand for different amounts. You can compare amounts. To do this, compare the lengths of the bars.

Bars can be vertical or horizontal. Vertical bars go from bottom to top. Horizontal bars go from left to right. Businesses use graphs. For example, a store manager wants to compare sales. A bar graph can show sales for each department.

In order to use bar graphs, you must be able to do the following:

- Understand graph basics.
- Compare and order numbers.

Skill Examples ■ ■ ■

EXAMPLE 1 Locate information on a vertical bar graph.
A manager of a baseball stadium made this graph. He needs to decide how many workers to assign to the gates. Which gate needs the least amount of workers based on the number of people entering?

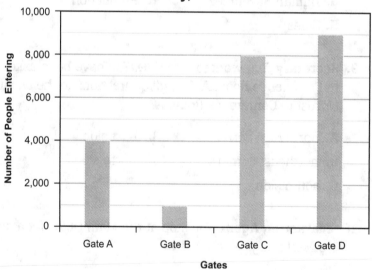

- Look at the title. It tells you what information you will find. The bars show information about the entrance gates of the ballpark.
- Next look from the top of each bar over to the vertical scale, or range of numbers, on the left. This is the *y-*axis. The scale markers are 2,000, 4,000, and so on.

- The *x*-axis (or horizontal axis) runs across the bottom of the graph. The *x*-axis represents the gates. Each bar is for one gate. The gates are labeled A, B, C, and D.

- The graph shows general information. Gate B has the shortest bar. The fewest people used Gate B. Gates C and D have the tallest bars. The greatest number of people used gates C and D.

- The graph also shows specific information. Look at the bar for Gate A. The top of the bar is at 4,000. This means 4,000 people entered Gate A.

The fewest number of people enter the park at Gate B. The least number of workers should be assigned to Gate B.

EXAMPLE 2 Compare information on a horizontal bar graph.
The graph shows the number of pillows made. The supervisor needs to know which pillow type the factory makes least often.

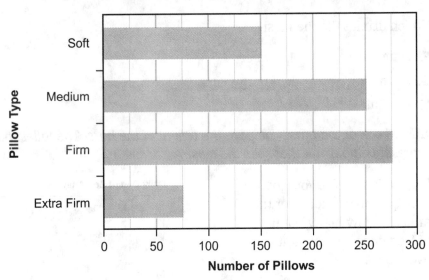

Pillows Made Daily at SleepMore, Inc.

- The *y*-axis (or vertical axis) runs along the left side of the graph. The *y*-axis represents the types of pillows. Each bar is for one type of pillow. The types of pillows are Soft, Medium, Firm, and Extra Firm.

- Next look from the right side of each bar down to the horizontal scale at the bottom. This is the *x*-axis. The scale will tell you the number of pillows made daily. The scale markers are 50, 100, and so on. The point halfway between 0 and 50 is 25.

- The pillow that is made the least often will have the shortest bar. Compare the four bars.

- The bar for "Extra Firm" is the shortest bar.

Extra Firm pillows are made least often.

Information in a bar graph can be shown vertically or horizontally. In the examples below, the information is easy to understand both ways.

Below is a vertical bar graph. To help understand it, look at the top end of the bar. Then look at the category at the bottom.

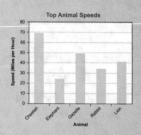

Below is a horizontal bar graph. To help understand it, look at the right end of the bar. Then look down to see the value.

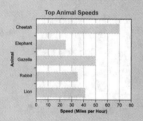

Skill Support

The bars in the graph stand for different amounts. Compare the lengths of the bars. The longest bar is the highest number. The shortest bar is the lowest number.

Skill Practice

Locate information in the graphs. Then answer the questions.

1. You work in a school cafeteria. You track sales of drinks. Look at the graph. How many bottles of water are sold daily?

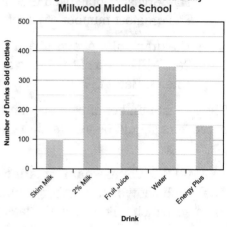

   A. 100   D. 350

   B. 150   E. 400

   C. 200

   HINT: Look at the bar for "Water." Find the top of the bar. Follow the line to the scale on the left. If the line is between two numbers, figure out the number that is halfway. This number tells you how many were sold.

2. Which drink sells the most?

   F. skim milk   J. water

   G. 2% milk   K. Energy Plus

   H. fruit juice

   HINT: Look at the bars. Compare the height of the bars. The tallest bar represents the drink that sells the most.

3. You work at a zoo. Your job is to help prepare meals for the animals. How many pounds of food does an elephant eat every day?

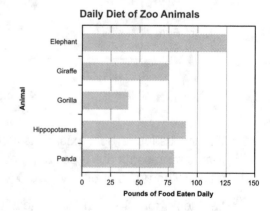

   A. 100

   B 110

   C. 125

   D. 145

   E. 150

   HINT: Find the bar for elephants. Follow it to the end and match it to the number on the x-axis.

4. Which animal eats the least amount of food each day?

   F. elephant   G. giraffe   H. gorilla   J. hippopotamus   K. panda

   HINT: Compare the lengths of the bars. The shortest bar represents the least amount of food.

Try It Out!

Truck Driver You drive a semitruck. The truck carries products for an appliance manufacturer. You live in Dallas, Texas. You use the bar graph to help plan your trips from home. You can drive to the cities on the graph. Which city is the closest to Dallas?

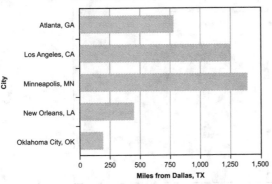

Distances from Dallas, TX

Atlanta, GA
Los Angeles, CA
Minneapolis, MN
New Orleans, LA
Oklahoma City, OK

City

0   250   500   750   1,000   1,250   1,500
Miles from Dallas, TX

A. Atlanta, GA

B. Los Angeles, CA

C. Minneapolis, MN

D. New Orleans, LA

E. Oklahoma City, OK

Step 1 — Understand the Question ▪ ▪ ▪

Complete the *Plan for Successful Solving*.

Plan for Successful Solving

What am I asked to do?	What are the facts?	How do I find the answer?
Find the city that is closest to Dallas.	The cities shown on the graph are on the y-axis. The distances on the graph are on the x-axis.	The shortest bar shows the shortest distance. You must find the shortest bar.

Step 2 — Find Your Answer ▪ ▪ ▪

- Remember to find the city closest to Dallas.

- Long bars show long distances. Short bars show short distances. You are looking for the city with the shortest bar.

- Select the answer that names the city closest to Dallas.

- **Select the correct answer:** **E.** Oklahoma City, OK
  You read the bar graph. You compared the lengths of the bars. The shortest bar is Oklahoma City. Oklahoma City is closest to Dallas.

Skill Support

Try to rule out incorrect answer choices. This will help you with multiple-choice questions. Look at the *Try It Out!* example. You need to find the closest city to Dallas. That city will be the shortest distance. The shortest distance is the shortest bar. You can rule out answers B and C. These are the longest bars.

Remember!

The amounts are often shown in increments. Tick marks may show increments of any amount. They may be unlabeled. Measure the bar to the nearest number. Do this even if it is not labeled. For example, a bar graph has amounts in increments of two. One bar falls halfway between the ticks labeled "6" and "8." This bar should be measured as 7.

On Your Own ▪ ■ ▪

Use the graphics to answer the questions.

Amount of Fat in Select Foods

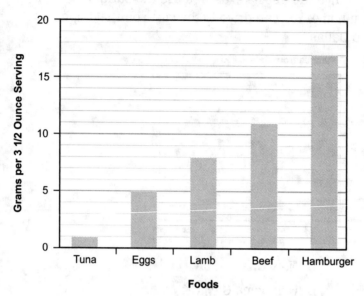

1. Dietary Aide You plan a low-fat menu. Which food has the lowest amount of fat?

A. tuna

B. eggs

C. lamb

D. beef

E. hamburger

2. Cook You make a dish with beef. How much fat is in a serving of beef?

F. 1 gram

G. 5 grams

H. 8 grams

J. 11 grams

K. 17 grams

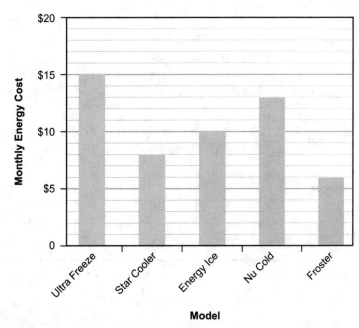

Home Freezer Electricity Costs

3. **Energy Efficiency Engineer** You review the product line. Which model is most costly to run?

A. Ultra Freeze

B. Star Cooler

C. Energy Ice

D. Nu Cold

E. Froster

4. **Energy Engineer** You review energy use in freezers. You like the Froster. How much does it cost to run per month?

F. $6

G. $8

H. $10

J. $13

K. $15

5. **Energy Manager** You review your product line. You study this graph. What does the *x*-axis show?

A. the price of home freezers

B. the monthly energy cost

C. the popularity of the freezers

D. the model name of the freezers

E. the type of electricity used

Bike Rentals—March

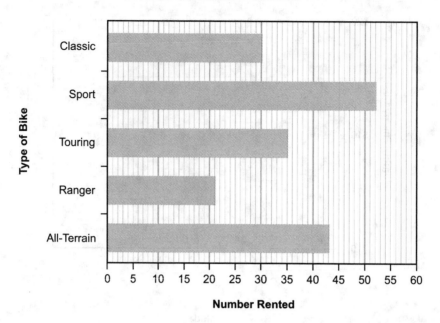

6. **Tour Guide** You lead bicycle tours. Your clients rent bikes. Which style was rented most?

    F. Classic

    G. Sport

    H. Touring

    J. Ranger

    K. All-Terrain

7. **Activity Aide** You handle bike rentals. How many Rangers did you rent in March?

    A. 21

    B. 30

    C. 35

    D. 43

    E. 52

On-Time Flights at Windy City Airfield

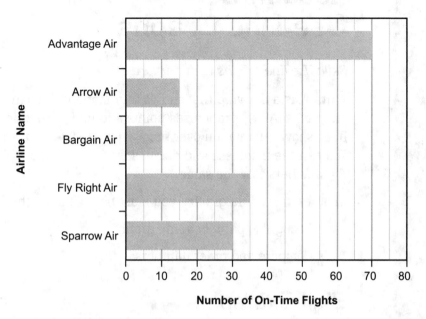

8. **Aircraft Maintenance Supervisor** You work for Sparrow Air. You inspect every flight before departure. How many on-time flights did you inspect?

   F. 10

   G. 15

   H. 30

   J. 35

   K. 70

9. **Counter Clerk** Bargain Air increased its number of on-time flights. You want to update the graph. How do you change the bar?

   A. Delete it.

   B. Shorten it.

   C. Lengthen it.

   D. Keep it the same length.

   E. Change the color.

10. **Air Traffic Controller** You work for Windy City Airfield. You direct all flights. Which airline had the most on-time flights?

   F. Advantage Air

   G. Arrow Air

   H. Bargain Air

   J. Fly Right Air

   K. Sparrow Air

Remember!

Line graphs have a
lot in common with
other graphs. They are
a visual way to show
data. They help you
find information.

Skill Support

A **line graph** uses
points and lines to
represent information.

It is important to
identify the *y*-axis
and the *x*-axis. The
y-axis runs along the
left side of the graph. It
is vertical. The *x*-axis
runs along the bottom
of the graph. It is
horizontal. The **labels**
of each axis explain
what the numbers and
words represent.

Lesson 5
Use Line Graphs

Skill: Use line graphs to find information

A graph is a drawing that shows information. You can compare numbers
on graphs. A line graph uses points and lines on a grid. The points and
lines show information over time. They are useful in showing trends.
You can see increases and decreases in the numbers. You can also see if
the numbers stay the same.

In order to use line graphs, you must be able to do the following:

- Recognize parts of a line graph.

- Compare and order numbers.

Skill Examples

EXAMPLE 1 Identify and use the parts of a line graph.
A gear manufacturer made this graph. How many errors were there
in September?

- First look at the title. It
tells you what information
is in the graph. This graph
shows the production
errors at ABC Gears.

- The *y*-axis is on the left of
the graph. This line goes
from low to high. Read
the label for this axis.
It shows the number of
errors.

- The *x*-axis is at the
bottom of the graph. It
goes from left to right.
Look at the label for this
axis. It shows the month.

Production Errors at ABC Gears

- The points on a line
graph show exact
numbers. Look at the point above
"June." It lines up with "50" on the
y-axis. There were 50 errors in June.

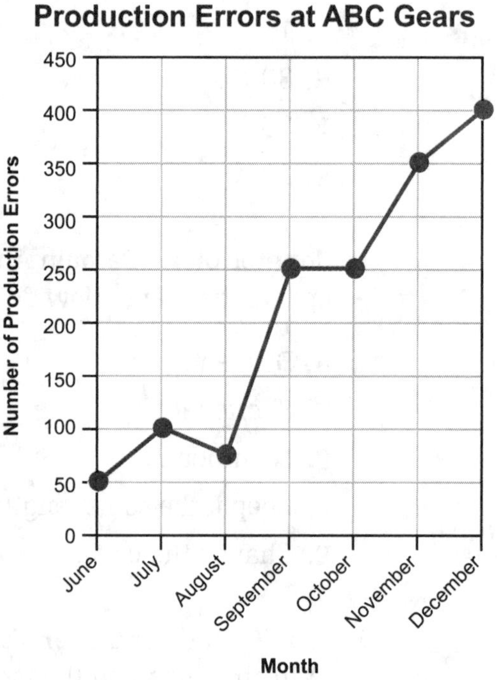

The point above "September" lines up with "250" on the *y*-axis.
There were 250 errors in September.

EXAMPLE 2 Compare points on a line graph.

A coffee shop owner created this graph. Look at the graph. Identify whether sales increased during this period.

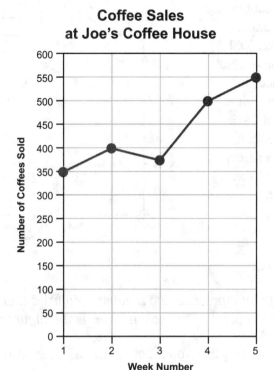

Coffee Sales at Joe's Coffee House

- Look at the title. The line shows coffee sales.

- The *y*-axis shows the number of coffees sold. The *x*-axis shows the week number.

- Look at the point above Week 1. Look at the *y*-axis. In Week 1, 350 coffees were sold.

- Look at the point above Week 2. Look at the *y*-axis. In Week 2, 400 coffees were sold.

- Look at the line between these points. It goes up from left to right. This means sales increased between Week 1 and Week 2.

- Look at the point above Week 3. About 375 coffees were sold. Look at the line between Week 2 and Week 3. It goes down from left to right. Sales decreased in this period.

- Look at the points above Weeks 3, 4, and 5. Look at the lines between Weeks 3, 4, and 5. The lines go up from left to right.

Sales increased during this period.

Remember!

Line graphs show information over time. Points represent numbers. You can compare points to see changes in numbers over time. If the change forms a pattern, it is called a **trend.** The trend can go up. It can go down. It can stay mostly flat. A trend can tell you what is likely to happen in the future.

Skill Support

Line graphs use points on a **grid**. A grid is made of lines that intersect. The lines come from the *y*-axis and *x*-axis. Points on the grid show information. The graph shows a line drawn from point to point. To read a line graph, find the information line. Then read the labels on the *x*-axis and *y*-axis.

Skill Practice ▪▪▪

Locate information in the graphs. Then answer the questions.

1. You are an Occupational Safety and Health Administration (OSHA) inspector. You evaluate the safety records of companies. You must decide if Dash Bros. Construction has improved safety. What year had the most injuries?

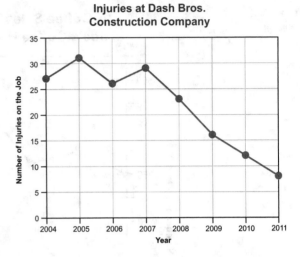

A. 2004   D. 2007

B. 2005   E. 2008

C. 2006

HINT: *Each point represents the number of injuries that year. Compare the height of the points. The most injuries is the highest point.*

2. Look at the graph again. About how many injuries occurred in 2007?

F. 12   G. 23   H. 26   J. 29   K. 31

HINT: *Find the point above 2007. If a point does not fall on a grid line, you have to estimate the number.*

3. A company is trying to reduce costs. The company hires Clark Consultants. The line graph shows monthly office supply savings. Which month had the greatest savings?

A. January   D. April

B. February   E. May

C. March

HINT: *The greatest savings is the highest point on the graph. Look for the highest point on the graph.*

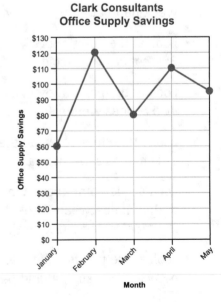

4. In April, how much did the company save?

F. $60   G. $80   H. $95   J. $110   K. $120

HINT: *Locate April on the x-axis. Then find the point on the line.*

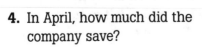

Try It Out! ▪ ▪ ▪

Retail Manager You are a manager at a sports store. You need to complete a report. This line graph shows recent sales. Which month had the highest sales of soccer balls?

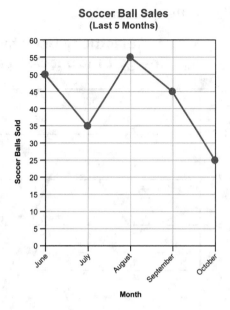

Soccer Ball Sales
(Last 5 Months)

A. June

B. July

C. August

D. September

E. October

Step 1 Understand the Question ▪ ▪ ▪

Complete the *Plan for Successful Solving*.

Plan for Successful Solving

What am I asked to do?	What are the facts?	How do I find the answer?
Find the month with the highest sales of soccer balls.	The *x*-axis shows the month. The *y*-axis shows the number of soccer balls sold.	The key word is *highest*. It tells you that you are looking for the highest sales. You must find the highest point on the line graph.

Step 2 Find Your Answer ▪ ▪ ▪

- Remember you are looking for the highest sales.

- Review the facts. The x-axis shows the month. The y-axis shows the number of soccer balls sold.

- The highest points represent the highest sales. The lowest points represent the lowest sales. Find the highest point.

- The highest point is above August.

- **Select the correct answer:** C. August
  You read the line graph. You found the highest point. The highest point represents the highest sales.

Line graphs can help you make predictions. Look at the *Try It Out!* example. Soccer ball sales went down from August to September. Sales also went down from September to October. This shows a trend, or pattern. Sales went down in these months. Based on this, you may predict that sales will decrease from October to November in the future.

Skill Support

The points on a graph represent numbers. They indicate the total for that time period. You can compare points to see changes in numbers. The highest point on the graph is usually the highest number. The lowest point is usually the lowest number. Follow the line from left to right. If it slants down, the amount decreased. If it slants up, the amount increased.

Level 1
Locating Information

On Your Own ▪ ▪ ▪

Use the graphics to answer the questions.

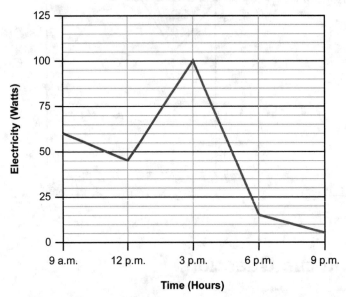

Electricity Used by Energy-Efficient Computers

1. **Computer Support Specialist** You work at Carson's Data Entry. You installed new energy-efficient computers. You check this graph to see how well they work. When do the computers use the least energy?

   A. 9 a.m.

   B. 12 p.m.

   C. 3 p.m.

   D. 6 p.m.

   E. 9 p.m.

2. **Energy Auditor** You analyze energy usage. How much electricity do the new computers use at 3 p.m.?

   F. 5 watts

   G. 15 watts

   H. 45 watts

   J. 100 watts

   K. 125 watts

Workplace Injuries per Month

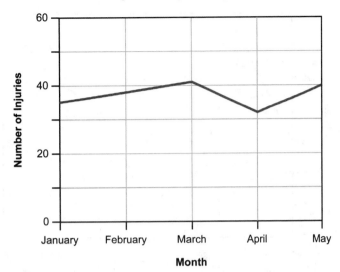

3. **Safety Specialist** You work for Allen Wrench Manufacturing. You are investigating workplace injuries. What does this graph show?

   A. how many people got hurt each year

   B. how many months the factory has been operating

   C. how many workplace injuries happened in March

   D. how many workplace injuries happened each month

   E. the months when there were no workplace injuries

4. **Health and Safety Manager** You are working on strategies to improve workplace safety, and you are using this graph as a reference. Look at the y-axis. What is being measured?

   F. workplace injuries per month

   G. months

   H. January

   J. number of injuries

   K. May

5. **Safety Consultant** You are writing a report on workplace safety. How many injuries occurred in April?

   A. 0

   B. 25

   C. 32

   D. 40

   E. 48

My Reading Graph

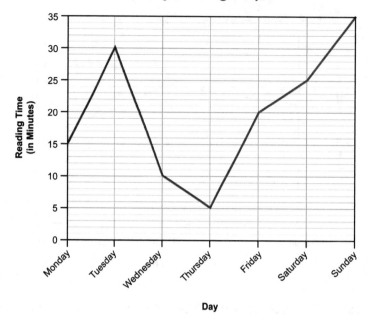

6. Instructional Aide This graph measures how long your student read each day. He is supposed to read 15 minutes a day. What days did he read less?

F. Tuesday and Wednesday

G. Wednesday and Thursday

H. Thursday and Friday

J. Saturday and Sunday

K. Sunday and Monday

7. Teacher You work in a third-grade classroom. You are helping a student chart his reading times. What is the title of this graph?

A. Reading Time

B. My Reading Graph

C. (in Minutes)

D. Day

E. Sunday

Nesting Pairs* of Bald Eagles in the United States

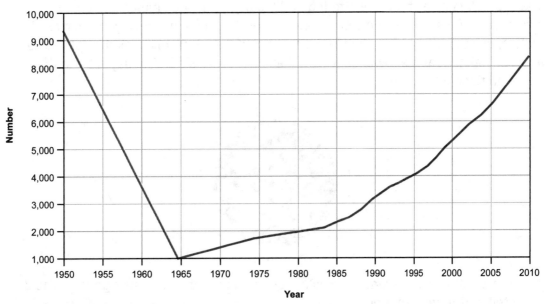

*A nesting pair is two birds that are raising baby birds together.

8. **Forest Technician** You work for the forestry service. You track wildlife. You read this graph about bald eagles. What is the title of the graph?

   F. Nesting Pairs of Bald Eagles in the United States

   G. in the United States

   H. Number

   J. Nesting Pairs of Bald Eagles

   K. Year

9. **Wildlife Technician** You keep track of the number of animals in the wild. Read the label on the *y*-axis. What is being measured?

   A. bald eagles in the United States

   B. 1980

   C. year

   D. 3,000

   E. number of pairs of bald eagles

10. **Conservationist** You track the status of bald eagles to make sure they are not endangered. Which of the following years had the lowest number of eagles?

    F. 1950

    G. 1990

    H. 1995

    J. 2005

    K. 2010

Level 1 Performance Assessment ▪ ■ ▪

These problems are at a Level 1 rating of difficulty. They are similar to problems on a career readiness certificate test. For each question, you can check your answer. To do this, use the answer key. It is located on pp. 269–271 of this book. It explains each answer option. It also shows the lesson that covers that skill. You may refer to that lesson to review the skill.

1. You are returning to work as a cook after a bathroom break. This sign is on the door in the bathroom. What does it mean?

   A. Wash your hands.

   B. Turn off the water.

   C. Caution: hot water.

   D. Running water is available.

   E. Turn on the water.

2. As a taxicab driver, you drive people to different destinations. You pick up a rider. He needs to go the opposite way. You drive to the end of the block. You see this sign there. What does this sign mean?

   F. no right turn

   G. one way

   H. no U-turn

   J. U-turn allowed

   K. no turn on a red light

3. You are a computer engineer. You see this symbol on a button on your computer. What does the button do?

   A. It turns on the computer.

   B. It turns on the printer.

   C. It turns up the volume.

   D. It turns down the volume.

   E. It opens the display menu.

Annual Spending in United States

Age	Small Appliances	Laundry and Cleaning Supplies	Clothing	Pets, Toys, Hobbies, and Playground Equipment	Reading Materials
Under 25	$49	$83	$1,351	$380	$48
25–34	$85	$150	$1,965	$696	$79

4. You work as a survey researcher. You are a conducting a survey for a marketing company. The company wants to know about the products people buy. You use this table for information in your interviews. What is the main idea of this table?

   F. how much money is spent on clothing each year

   G. how much money is spent on reading materials each year

   H. how much money is spent on small appliances each year

   J. how much money is spent by people ages 25–34 each year

   K. how much money people from different age groups spend on certain products each year

5. You are interviewing people under 25. You want to know what they buy. You use this table as research for the interviews. You look at items they spend the most money on. According to the table, which category does this group spend the most on?

   A. small appliances

   B. clothing

   C. pets, toys, hobbies, and playground equipment

   D. laundry and cleaning supplies

   E. reading materials

Top Five Countries by Population (Millions)

Country	Population
China	1,347
India	1,210
United States	313
Indonesia	238
Brazil	192

6. You are a reporter. You are doing a story about population sizes. You refer to this table. Which country has the second highest population?

   F. China

   G. India

   H. United States

   J. Indonesia

   K. Brazil

Forecast

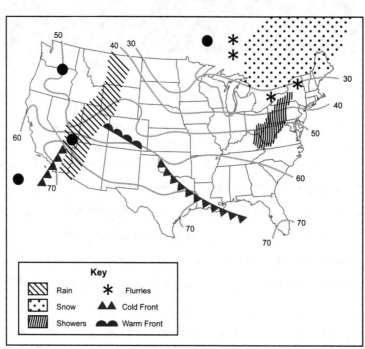

7. You are a meteorologist. You give weather reports on TV. You study this incoming weather forecast. You are looking for areas with bad weather. According to the map key, what do the polka dots mean?

   A. flurries

   B. rain

   C. showers

   D. warm front

   E. snow

Montana

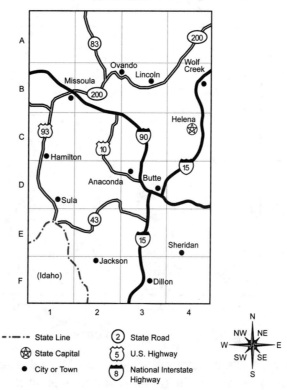

- – – - State Line
- ⊛ State Capital
- ● City or Town
- ② State Road
- ⑤ U.S. Highway
- ⑧ National Interstate Highway

Compass: N, NW, NE, W, E, SW, SE, S

8. As a long–haul driver, your route is through Montana. You are driving on State Road 200. You will be dropping off products in Missoula. You have just passed Lincoln. Which direction is Missoula from where you are now?

   F. east

   G. west

   H. north

   J. northwest

   K. southeast

9. Your next stop is Helena. You read the map to find out how to get there. What is the closest road that goes by Helena?

   A. 10

   B. 15

   C. 43

   D. 83

   E. 90

Percentage of Fat in Select Foods

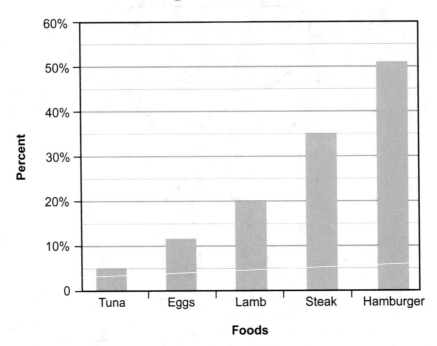

10. As a dietician, you have a client who should eat less fat. You share this table with her. You explain how to read the table. What label is on the *x*-axis?

    F. Percent

    G. Percentage of Fat in Select Foods

    H. Foods

    J. Hamburger

    K. 60%

11. You create a menu for your client. This table helps you decide what she should eat. You study the table. According to the table, how much fat is in steak?

    A. 5%

    B. 12%

    C. 20%

    D. 35%

    E. 51%

12. You need to design a new meal for your client. It has to be very low in fat. Which item has the least amount of fat?

    F. eggs

    G. hamburger

    H. tuna

    J. lamb

    K. steak

US Government Spending 1940–2010

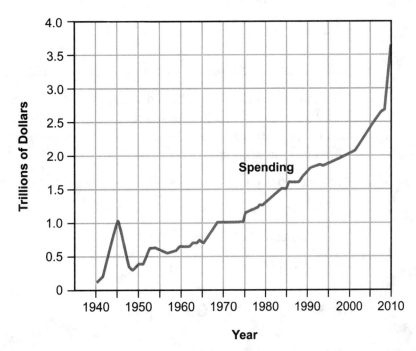

13. You are a newspaper reporter. You are writing an article about changes in government spending. You come across this line graph in your research. What is the title of the graph?

    A. Year

    B. US Government Spending 1940–2010

    C. Trillions of Dollars

    D. Spending

    E. 1940–2010

14. You are giving historical information in the article. You look at the year 1970. How much money did the government spend that year?

    F. $1 trillion

    G. $1.5 trillion

    H. $2 trillion

    J. $2.5 trillion

    K. $3 trillion

15. You write about trends in government spending. Look at the graph. Which of the following years had the biggest increase in spending?

    A. 1940–1945

    B. 1955–1960

    C. 1970–1975

    D. 1980–1985

    E. 1995–2000

Remember!

A **circle graph** shows an entire quantity divided into sections. The sections are called **segments**. Each segment of the circle graph shows an amount. The amounts are parts of the whole. The whole graph represents the total of what is being measured.

Skill Support

It is important to read circle graphs carefully. Here are some things to look for when reading a circle graph:

- First look at the title. It tells you what information is in the graph.

- Look at the **key**. It shows you what the different segments represent.

- Look at the labels for each segment. The labels show the exact amount of the whole that each segment represents.

- Use the key and labels to find general and specific information on the graph.

Lesson 6 ▪ ▪ ▪
Use Circle Graphs

Skill: Locate and interpret information in a circle graph

A circle graph shows a whole divided into parts. Each part of the circle is called a segment. Each segment has its own value. In many cases, values on circle graphs are percents of a whole. You can compare values, or amounts, on graphs.

In order to use circle graphs, you must be able to do the following:

- Understand graph basics.

- Compare and order numbers.

- Understand fractions.

Skill Examples ▪ ▪ ▪

EXAMPLE 1 Identify the parts of a circle graph.
A teacher made this graph to get information about her students. The data are the grades her students received on a recent test. There are 25 students in the class. Which is the largest segment in the graph?

- First look at the title. It tells you what information is in the graph. This graph shows student test scores.

- Look at the key on the right side. These patterns stand for different grades.

- Look at the labels around the graph. The labels show the exact portions of the whole that each segment represents. In this graph, the labels are 1, 2, 4, 8, and 10.

- The graph tells you general information. For example, more students got Bs than Fs. This is easy to see. The B segment is much larger than the F segment.

- The graph also tells you specific information. For example, look at the label of the B segment. This tells you 10 students earned Bs.

The largest segment in the graph is labeled 10. It has a white background and straight lines.

EXAMPLE 2 Read information on a circle graph.

The circle graph is made of sections, or segments. Segments represent data. This graph shows sales of three different shampoos at a salon. Which shampoo is the second most popular?

Sales of Salon Shampoos

Key
- Shampoo 1
- Shampoo 2
- Shampoo 3

25%
30%
45%

- You can see that the segment with vertical lines is larger than the other two segments. Look at the key. The vertical lines represent Shampoo 2.

- There are labels next to the segments that show percentages. Shampoo 2 was 45% of sales. This is the largest percentage. Shampoo 2 is the most popular.

- Which shampoo is the second most popular? The other two segments look similar in size. The labels show which sold more.

- Shampoo 3 was 30% of sales. Shampoo 1 was 25% of sales.

Shampoo 3 is the second most popular shampoo.

EXAMPLE 3 Compare pieces of information in a circle graph.

This graph shows sales at a sporting goods store. The store sells football, soccer, baseball, basketball, and hockey equipment. The owner wants to compare sales of different equipment. Which areas have the same percentage of sales?

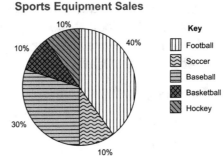

Sports Equipment Sales

Key
- Football
- Soccer
- Baseball
- Basketball
- Hockey

10%
10%
40%
30%
10%

- The segments of the graph with vertical and horizontal lines are the largest. They show sales for football and baseball equipment. These are the most popular categories.

- Look at the labels. Football equipment makes up 40% of the sales. Baseball equipment makes up 30%. Football equipment sales are greater than baseball equipment sales.

- The key shows that diagonal lines represent hockey, crossed lines represent basketball, and wavy lines represent soccer. These segments are the same size. They are all 10%.

Hockey, soccer, and basketball equipment have the same percentage of sales.

Skill Practice

Locate information in the graphs. Then answer the questions.

1. You are a lightbulb manufacturer. You've been in business since 2007. You want to see in which year you made the smallest percentage of profits. In which year did you have the lowest profits?

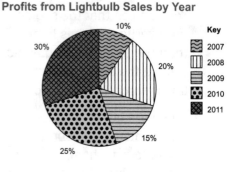

Profits from Lightbulb Sales by Year

   A. 2007   **D.** 2010

   B. 2008   **E.** 2011

   C. 2009

   HINT: *Look at the segments in the circle graph. Compare the sizes of the segments. The smallest segment represents the lowest profits.*

2. Look at the graph again. What percentage of profits was made in 2009?

   F. 10   **G.** 15   **H.** 20   **J.** 25   **K.** 30

   HINT: *Find the pattern of the segment that represents 2009 in the key.*

3. You are a medical assistant. The doctor wants to stock up on vaccines for next year. She asks you to find out the percentage for each vaccine administered last year. You look at the graph. Which vaccine was used the second most often?

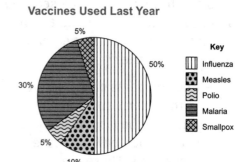

Vaccines Used Last Year

   A. influenza

   B. measles

   C. polio

   D. malaria

   E. smallpox

   HINT: *Compare the size of the segments. Identify the largest segment. Then identify the second largest.*

4. What percentage of the vaccines was for influenza?

   F. 5%   **G.** 10%   **H.** 20%   **J.** 30%   **K.** 50%

   HINT: *Locate influenza on the key. Identify the pattern. Find that pattern in the graph.*

Try It Out!

Store Manager You are a manager at an office supply store. You need to know which supplies earned the least profit. Which type of supply earned the smallest share of profits?

Office Supply Profits

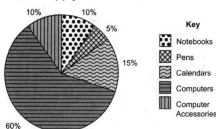

10%   10%
        5%

                    15%

60%

Key
- ⊡ Notebooks
- ⊠ Pens
- ▨ Calendars
- ▦ Computers
- ▥ Computer Accessories

A. notebooks

B. pens

C. calendars

D. computers

E. computer accessories

 Step 1 ## Understand the Question ■ ■ ■

Complete the *Plan for Successful Solving.*

Plan for Successful Solving

What am I asked to do?	What are the facts?	How do I find the answer?
Find the supply that made the lowest share of the profits.	The graph shows profits from sales of notebooks, pens, calendars, computers, and computer accessories.	Look for the lowest percentage of profit. Of the percentages, 5% is the lowest amount.

Step 2 ## Find Your Answer ■ ■ ■

- Remember to look for the lowest percentage of the profits.

- The large segments represent higher profits, and the smaller segments represent lower profits. You are looking for the smallest segment.

- **Select the correct answer: B.** pens
  The smallest segment represents the lowest profits. Therefore, pens made the lowest share of profits for the store.

Remember!

This question asks you to find the smallest amount on the graph. Look for the smallest segment of the circle. Then match the pattern to the label on the key.

Skill Support

A circle graph is made up of parts that equal a whole. No segment will be larger than 100%. The whole will equal 100%.

For example, add up the percentages on the graph in the *Try It Out!* section.
60 + 10 + 10 + 5 + 15 = 100

On Your Own ■ ■ ■

Use the graphics to answer the questions.

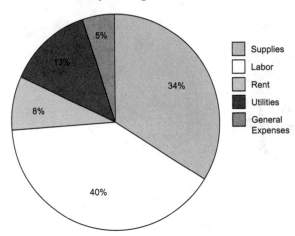

Annual Operating Costs

Supplies · Labor · Rent · Utilities · General Expenses

5% · 13% · 8% · 34% · 40%

1. **Chef** Part of your job involves purchasing supplies and food. You review the annual budget. How much of the annual operating costs is budgeted for supplies?

   A. 5%

   B. 8%

   C. 13%

   D. 34%

   E. 40%

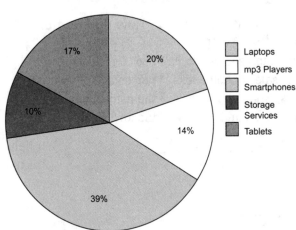

Annual Sales

Laptops · mp3 Players · Smartphones · Storage Services · Tablets

17% · 20% · 10% · 14% · 39%

2. **Computer Programmer** You work for a company that designs laptops. What does the graph tell you about laptop sales?

   F. Laptops are the highest selling item.

   G. Laptops are the lowest selling item.

   H. Laptop sales are lower than tablet sales.

   J. Laptop sales are higher than storage services sales.

   K. Laptop sales are equal to MP3 player sales.

Monthly Expenses

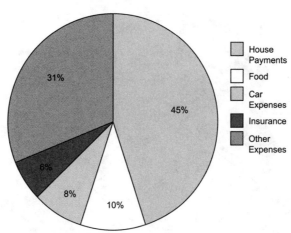

3. **Personal Financial Adviser** You advise a family on their finances. You review what they spend their money on every month. What is the title of the graph?

   A. Food

   B. Insurance

   C. Car Expenses

   D. Monthly Expenses

   E. Other Expenses

4. **Financial Consultant** Your clients are a newly married couple. They want to map out a budget. What percentage of their monthly expenses is insurance?

   F. 6%

   G. 8%

   H. 10%

   J. 31%

   K. 45%

5. **Financial Counselor** You advise a single homeowner. You help him manage his finances. On what does he spend the greatest percentage of his monthly budget?

   A. house payments

   B. food

   C. car expenses

   D. insurance

   E. other expenses

Construction Costs

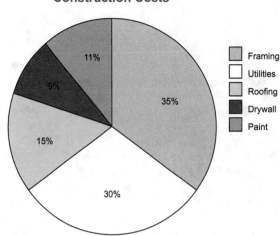

Framing
Utilities
Roofing
Drywall
Paint

6. **Cost Estimator** You are estimating the cost of constructing a new building. You review the costs of a previous building project. The graph shows the percentage of the total project costs for each segment. Look at the graph. Which segment of the previous project cost the most?

F. framing
G. utilities
H. roofing
J. drywall
K. paint

7. **Painter** You work for a home builder who is building a new house. The graph shows the percentage of the total costs for each segment of a previous house construction project. What percentage of the total project is the painting segment?

A. 9%
B. 11%
C. 15%
D. 30%
E. 35%

Major Manufacturing Sectors

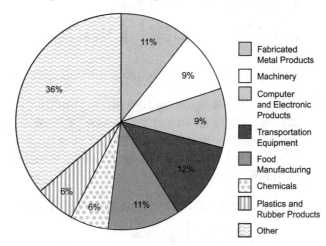

11% 9% 36% 9% 12% 6% 6% 11%

- Fabricated Metal Products
- Machinery
- Computer and Electronic Products
- Transportation Equipment
- Food Manufacturing
- Chemicals
- Plastics and Rubber Products
- Other

8. **Maintenance Worker** You are looking for work in manufacturing. You want to find the largest manufacturing sectors. Based on the graph, which of the following is true?

   F. Fabricated metal products has the highest percentage of manufacturing.

   G. Chemical manufacturing has a higher percentage than food manufacturing.

   H. Fabricated metal products has a higher percentage of manufacturing than plastics and rubber products manufacturing.

   J. Plastics and rubber products manufacturing has a higher percentage than food manufacturing.

   K. Other manufacturing and chemical manufacturing have the two highest percentages.

9. **Factory Technician** You want to be certified to fix equipment for the largest manufacturing sector. Look at the graph. Which sector listed below is the largest?

   A. fabricated metal products

   B. machinery

   C. computer and electronic products

   D. transportation equipment

   E. chemicals

10. **Factory Manager** You manage a computer factory. You want to know how the computer and electronics products sector compares to other manufacturing sectors. Based on the graph, which of the following is true?

    F. Your sector is larger than the food manufacturing sector.

    G. Your sector is larger than the fabricated metal products sector.

    H. Your sector is smaller than the plastics and rubber products sector.

    J. Your sector is smaller than the transportation equipment sector.

    K. Your sector is smaller than the chemicals sector.

Remember!

A **diagram** is a drawing that represents information. It shows relationships between parts. It can show the order in which things occur. It can also give specific information about when things will occur.

Skill Support

A **time line** is a diagram that shows information over time. The time frame can be years, months, days, or hours. A time line could be a plan for starting your own business. It would be a step-by-step tool you can look at regularly. You can check off dates when you have completed each step.

Lesson 7 ...
Understand Diagrams

Skill: Use diagrams to show order of events, processes, and schedules

A diagram is a drawing that shows information. It gives the relationship of different parts. Diagrams can be presented in many different formats. Time lines show important events over time. Flowcharts show steps taken in a process. Schedules identify when events occur. These are all types of diagrams.

In order to use diagrams, you must be able to do the following:

- Understand sequence.

- Understand time order.

- Read time with a clock and calendar.

Skill Examples ▪ ▪ ▪

EXAMPLE 1 Understand the structure and content of time lines.
The marketing team for Health & Wellness Gym made this time line. When did the first gym location open?

- First look at the title. It tells you what information is in the time line. This time line shows the major events in the gym's history.

- Look at the years on the left side. They show you when each major event occurred.

- Look at the labels on the right. The labels show what happened in that year on the time line.

- The time line shows you general information. One example of general information is that Health & Wellness Gym grew over time.

**Major Event History
of Health & Wellness Gym**

2002	Gym opens first location on January 21.
2003	
2004	Membership reaches 200.
2005	Membership doubles in size.
2006	First location adds swimming pool.
2007	
2008	
2009	Yoga classes begin.
2010	Health & Wellness adds two new locations.
2011	
2012	First location doubles in size.

- The time line also tells you specific information. One example of specific information is when the first gym location opened.

The first gym location opened on January 21, 2002.

EXAMPLE 2 Understand that flowcharts show a sequence of steps to complete a task.

A bagel shop sells breakfast sandwiches. The manager is teaching the cooks how to make them. He creates this flowchart to outline the process. The customer orders eggs and cheese on a sesame bagel. What step does the cook skip for this order?

- The flowchart shows general information. For example, the first step is always toasting the bagel the customer orders. The final step is always serving the sandwich.

- The flowchart also shows specific information. A new cook follows the steps in the flowchart to make the sandwich.

- The cook toasts the bagel and scrambles the eggs. The customer wants cheese, so the cook melts it, as in Step 4. The customer does not want bacon.

How to Make Breakfast Sandwiches at Good Morning Bagel Shop

Step 1 — Toast the bagel the customer requests.

Step 2 — Ask what the customer wants on it.

Step 3 — Scramble eggs.

Step 4 — Does the customer want cheese?

Yes: Melt cheese on top of the eggs. | No: Skip step 4.

Step 5 — Does the customer want bacon?

Yes: Fry bacon and put on top of eggs. | No: Skip step 5.

Step 6 — Put ingredients on toasted bagel.

Step 7 — Serve.

The cook skips Step 5.

EXAMPLE 3 Understand that schedules show when events occur.

A calendar can serve as a schedule. A yoga studio uses this calendar. It shows members' birthdays. Members get coupons for a free class on their birthdays. When should the studio send Jane A. a free coupon?

- The schedule shows general information. For example, it shows the sequence in which coupons should go out. Lizzie L.'s birthday is before Lucia G.'s birthday. This tells you that Lizzie L. should get her coupon before Lucia G.

March						
Sunday	Monday	Tuesday	Wednesday	Thursday	Friday	Saturday
		1	2	3	4 Jane A.	5
6	7	8	9	10 Keisha R.	11 José M.	12
13	14	15	16	17	18	19
20	21	22 Lizzie L.	23	24	25	26
27	28	29	30 Lucia G.	31		

- The schedule also shows specific information. Find Jane A.'s birthday on the calendar. Her birthday coupon should be mailed three days before her birthday.

The studio should send Jane A. a coupon by March 1.

Remember!
Diagrams use images to simplify information. They present both specific information and general information. Make sure to read a diagram completely before identifying specific or general information. You should understand the diagram before obtaining information from it. If you do not, you may not get correct information.

Skill Support
A **flowchart** is a diagram of a sequence of actions. A flowchart may be used to show how to do something. An example of a flowchart would be the steps in processing an order.

A **schedule** shows when events occur. It can also show a plan for carrying out a process. Examples include train schedules, bus schedules, and work schedules.

Flowcharts are helpful
when learning a new
task. Flowcharts "flow"
from one step in a
process to another.
They show how to
complete a task. The
first step should start
a process, and the
last part should end
a process.

Skill Support

When reading a time
line, flowchart, or
schedule, be sure to
follow the correct order.
Most time lines move
from left to right. They
go from earliest to
latest. Most flowcharts
move from Step 1, to
Step 2, to Step 3, and
so on. Schedules are
placed in a specific
order. The things listed
first are expected to
happen first. The things
listed last are expected
to happen last.

Skill Practice ▪ ▪ ▪

Locate information in the diagrams. Then answer the questions.

1. You are a teaching assistant in a history class. Students are learning about the presidents in the early 1900s. You create a time line to show what years they came into office. Which president is the earliest on the time line?

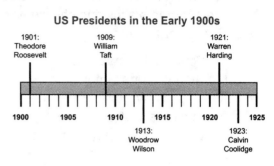

A. Theodore Roosevelt

B. William Taft

C. Woodrow Wilson

D. Warren Harding

E. Calvin Coolidge

HINT: *Look at the dates on the time line. From left to right, they go from earliest to latest. The president on the far left served the earliest term.*

2. In what year did Woodrow Wilson begin his term?

F. 1901   G. 1909   H. 1913   J. 1921   K. 1923

HINT: *Find the mark that represents Woodrow Wilson.*

3. You are a manicurist. Which client do you see for the third appointment on Wednesday morning?

A. Padma

B. Sally

C. Roberta

D. Kyra

E. Lin

HINT: *The third appointment would be the third person on the list.*

Appointments	
8:00 a.m.	Padma
9:00 a.m.	Sally
10:00 a.m.	Roberta
11:00 a.m.	Kyra
12:00 p.m.	Lin

4. What time does Kyra's appointment take place?

F. 8 a.m.   G. 9 a.m.   H. 10 a.m.   J. 11 a.m.   K. 12 p.m.

HINT: *Look for Kyra's name on the schedule.*

Try It Out! ■ ■ ■

Store Assistant You are nursery worker at a garden center. You use this flowchart as a guide in completing each sale. At what step do you put soil in the pot?

A. Step 1

B. Step 2

C. Step 3

D. Step 4

E. Step 5

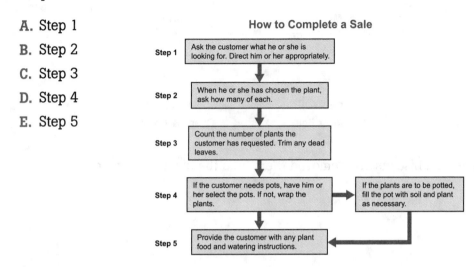

How to Complete a Sale

Step 1 — Ask the customer what he or she is looking for. Direct him or her appropriately.

Step 2 — When he or she has chosen the plant, ask how many of each.

Step 3 — Count the number of plants the customer has requested. Trim any dead leaves.

Step 4 — If the customer needs pots, have him or her select the pots. If not, wrap the plants. → If the plants are to be potted, fill the pot with soil and plant as necessary.

Step 5 — Provide the customer with any plant food and watering instructions.

 Step 1 — Understand the Question ■ ■ ■

Complete the *Plan for Successful Solving.*

Plan for Successful Solving

What am I asked to do?	What are the facts?	How do I find the answer?
Find the step in which you put soil in the pot.	The steps are listed on the left side of the flowchart. They are labeled 1, 2, 3, 4, 5.	You fill the pot after trimming the dead leaves and before providing plant food.

 Step 2 — Find Your Answer ■ ■ ■

- Filling the pot with soil happens somewhere in between the first and last steps. Look for the step during which this happens.

- Once you have located when this happens, count the steps to this information. Filling the pot with soil happens in Step 4.

- **Select the correct answer: D. Step 4**
  You read the flowchart and found the information you needed. You counted the steps to find when in the process this step happens.

On Your Own ▪ ▪ ▪

Use the graphics to answer the questions.

Biscuit Baking Equipment Flowchart

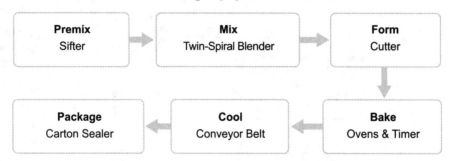

1. **Baker** You just baked the biscuits and removed them from the ovens. What step comes next?

   A. premixing

   B. mixing

   C. forming

   D. cooling

   E. packaging

2. **Dough Mixer** You have just mixed a batch of dough. Your boss asks you to fill in for an absent employee and form the dough. What piece of equipment will you use?

   F. sifter

   G. twin–spiral blender

   H. cutter

   J. conveyor belt

   K. carton sealer

Printing Time Line

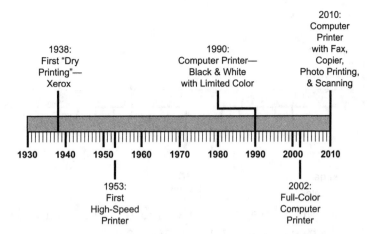

3. Printer You must purchase a new printer for your company. You want the most modern printer. In what year was the last printer on the time line launched?

A. 1938

B. 1953

C. 1990

D. 2002

E. 2010

Food Prep Schedule

Time	Specialty	Extra Prep
6 A.M.	Tamales	Mix Masa
7 A.M.	Empanadas	Make Dough
8 A.M.	Adobos	Mix Marinade
9 A.M.	Fajitas	Make Tortillas
10 A.M.	Enchiladas	Make Green Sauce

4. Cook During your morning prep, you start to mix the marinade for adobos. You check the clock to see if you are on schedule. What time should it be?

F. 6 a.m.   G. 7 a.m.   H. 8 a.m.   J. 9 a.m.   K. 10 a.m.

5. Prep Cook The head cook asks you to help prepare tamales. You check the schedule. What extra prep work is needed to make tamales?

A. Make green sauce.

B. Make tortillas.

C. Mix the marinade.

D. Make the dough.

E. Mix masa.

Architectural Time Line

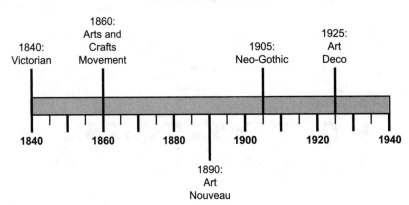

6. **Architecture Teacher** You plan to teach architectural eras. You will cover eras from 1840 to 1940. Which era is earliest in that time span?

F. Victorian

G. Arts and Crafts

H. Art Nouveau

J. Neo-Gothic

K. Art Deco

7. **Architect** A client requests a home designed in the Arts and Crafts style. You study houses built in the era. What year did the movement begin?

A. 1840

B. 1860

C. 1890

D. 1905

E. 1925

Network Flowchart

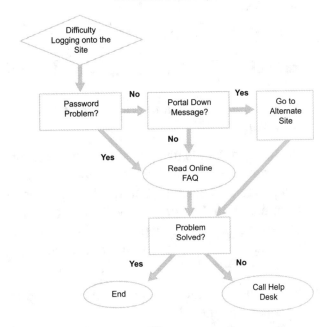

8. **Communications Engineer** You have trouble logging on to your computer. After you check your password, which is correct, you find the portal is down. What step do you take now?

   F. Go to alternate site.
   G. Read online FAQ.
   H. Call help desk.
   J. End flowchart.
   K. Log on again.

9. **Network Security Specialist** You work at the help desk. When should users call?

   A. before going to the alternate site
   B. as soon as they have difficulty logging on
   C. after noting that the problem is solved
   D. while reading the Online FAQ
   E. after following the steps and noting that the problem is not solved

Auto Production Schedule

Month:	June	July	August	September	October
# Cars Assembled	1,803	1,510	986	1,100	1,405

10. **Statistician** You have been hired to monitor productivity of factory workers. Which month has the lowest productivity?

    F. June
    G. July
    H. August
    J. September
    K. October

Skill Support

An **advertisement** is a notice or announcement that promotes a product, service, or event. The following features are typically found in advertisements.

- A logo or title: This shows the name of the company.
- Products and/or services offered: The company may offer a variety of products and services.
- Website address: You can use this to get more information.
- Contact information: This makes it easy for customers to e-mail, phone, or write the business.

Remember!

It is important to read nutritional facts thoroughly. Be sure to look at the "Servings per Container" figure. This tells you how many servings are in the package. In Example 1, there are two servings per box. If one person ate the entire package, the figures would then be double.

Lesson 8 ...
Find Information in Consumer and Business Materials

Skill: Find information in product information materials, advertisements, and want ads

Business materials give consumers information about people or companies. Product information materials explain how to use a product. They may also describe details of the product. Advertisements provide information to the public. This information is often about a product or service that has been improved or is on sale. Want advertisements provide information about something that is sought. This may be a job opening or a service needed. Read these materials carefully.

In order to find information in consumer and business materials, you must be able to do the following:

- Identify the main idea.
- Identify details.

Skill Examples ■ ■ ■

EXAMPLE 1 Find information in product information materials.
A food label is an example of product information material. First look at the title, "Nutrition Facts." It tells you what information is on the label. This label contains nutrition facts for a frozen dinner. How many milligrams of sodium are in a serving?

- Look at the second line. It says there are two servings per container.
- The left column,"Amount per Serving," tells you that each figure shown is for one serving of the frozen dinner.
- Look at the right column. It is titled "% Daily Value." This is the percentage that each item makes up of your recommended daily intake of that item.
- The label shows you general information. For example, the dinner contains a higher percentage of calcium than of iron.
- The label also tells you specific information. For example, it tells you how much sodium is in a serving.

Nutrition Facts

Serving Size 1 cup (228g)	
Servings per Container 2	
Amount per Serving	
Calories 280	**Calories from Fat** 120
	% Daily Value*
Total Fat 13g	20%
Saturated Fat 5g	25%
Trans Fat 2g	
Cholesterol 2mg	10%
Sodium 660mg	28%
Total Carbohydrate 31g	10%
Dietary Fiber 3g	12%
Sugars 5g	
Protein 5g	
Vitamin A 4% * Vitamin C 2%	
Calcium 15% * Iron 4 %	

*Percent Daily Values are based on a 2,000-calorie diet. Your daily values may be higher or lower depending on your calorie needs.

g = gram, mg = milligram

There are 660 milligrams of sodium in a serving.

EXAMPLE 2 Find information in advertisements.

Advertisements display the products or services of companies. They usually show contact information. What is the phone number listed in this advertisement?

- First look at the ad's logo or title. This advertisement is for Unlimited Technology Professionals, or UTP.

- The advertisement states what the company offers. This company provides information technology (or IT) professionals to other businesses.

- Most companies have websites. The final line of this advertisement shows UTP's website address. This can be used to find more information about the company.

- Advertisements usually show how to contact a company. Look at UTP's phone number and e-mail address. This makes it easy for customers to get in touch with the business. They may have questions, want to place an order, or use the company's services.

The phone number listed is 123-555-0167.

EXAMPLE 3 Find information in want ads.

Want ads are usually brief and to the point. This want ad shows that an office needs to hire a cleaning crew. The ad includes job requirements, job duties, and contact information. It also specifies when to call to apply. When should an applicant call?

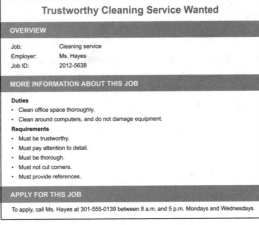

- Look for job requirements. This job requires a trustworthy, detailed, and thorough person. References are also required.

- Look for job duties. The service must clean the office thoroughly and not damage the computer equipment.

- Look for contact information. The person to contact in this want ad is Ms. Hayes.

- The phone number to call is 301-555-0139.

- Look for further instructions. This ad specifies when to call Ms. Hayes.

To apply, an applicant should call between 8 a.m. and 5 p.m. on Mondays and Wednesdays.

Skill Support

Many products come with instructional materials. They tell the consumer how to use the product. Sometimes they tell the consumer how to put the product together. They may warn the customer of dangers involved in using the product. You must read the instructions carefully. If you do not, you may not get the product to work properly. You could also cause injury to yourself or the product.

Remember!

Consumer and business materials tell you about a product or a service. They may tell you what is desirable about a product or service. They can also give contact information for companies or individuals.

Skill Practice • • • ▪ ▪

Find information in the consumer or business materials. Then answer the questions.

1. You are a caterer. You need to set up an outdoor awning. You have the materials and instructions. What is your first step?

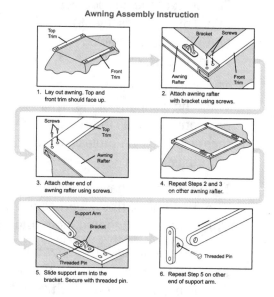

Awning Assembly Instruction

A. Lay out awning with top and front trim facing up.

B. Attach the awning rafter to the top trim using screws.

C. Slide the support arm into the bracket.

D. Secure the support arm with a threaded pin.

E. Attach the awning rafter to the front trim using screws.

HINT: Look at steps 1–6 in the instructions. You need information in Step 1. Locate Step 1. Read the instructions.

2. Look at the illustrations. The support arm, bracket, and threaded pin are needed in one step. Which step is this?

F. Step 1   G. Step 2   H. Step 3   J. Step 4   K. Step 5

HINT: Look at the illustrations. Find the illustration that requires these three materials.

3. You see this advertisement and decide to buy a Blanket by Ro. You want one in yellow. Which line tells you this may be possible?

A. Blankets by Ro

B. Hand-woven and only $30 each!

C. Get yours today at www.blanketsbyro.net

D. Cold in the wintertime?

E. Different colors available!

HINT: Look for a line that refers to colors.

> **Blankets by Ro**
>
> *Cold in the wintertime?*
>
> **Order a Blanket by Ro!**
>
> *The softest blankets you'll ever cozy up to.*
>
> Hand-woven and only $30 each!
> Visit our website for color options!
> Different colors available!
>
> **Get yours today at www.blanketsbyro.net**

4. How much money does a Blanket by Ro cost?

F. $10   G. $15   H. $20   J. $25   K. $30

HINT: Look for the price in the advertisement.

Try It Out!

Photographer You are looking for work as a photographer's assistant. You see this want ad. Which item do you NOT need to have?

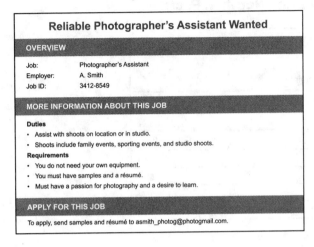

Reliable Photographer's Assistant Wanted

OVERVIEW

Job:	Photographer's Assistant
Employer:	A. Smith
Job ID:	3412-8549

MORE INFORMATION ABOUT THIS JOB

Duties
- Assist with shoots on location or in studio.
- Shoots include family events, sporting events, and studio shoots.

Requirements
- You do not need your own equipment.
- You must have samples and a résumé.
- Must have a passion for photography and a desire to learn.

APPLY FOR THIS JOB

To apply, send samples and résumé to asmith_photog@photogmail.com.

A. your own equipment

B. samples

C. résumé

D. flexible schedule

E. knowledge of the equipment

 ## Step 1 Understand the Question

Complete the *Plan for Successful Solving.*

Plan for Successful Solving

What am I asked to do?	What are the facts?	How do I find the answer?
Find the item that is not a requirement.	does not need own equipment needs to send samples needs to send résumé	The key words *not need* tells you something is not required. You must find what it is.

 ## Step 2 Find Your Answer

- Read carefully for what you do NOT need to have.

- The first sentence under "Requirements" is about equipment. Look for the part that is not a requirement.

- **Select the correct answer: A.** your own equipment
  You read the want ad. You identified the one thing that was not needed.

Remember!
It is very important to read a want advertisement correctly. It may list what is required and what is *not* required. You must make sure you understand the ad. You must follow the instructions in the ad. If you do not, it may reflect poorly on you.

On Your Own ▪ ▪ ▪

Use the graphics to answer the questions.

Energy Drink Nutrition Facts

Nutrition Facts

Serving Size 8 fl oz (240ml)
Servings per Container 4

Amount per Serving	
Calories 50	
	% Daily Value*
Total Fat 0g	**0%**
Sodium 110mg	**5%**
Potassium 30mg	**1%**
Total Carbohydrate 14g	**5%**
Sugars 14g	
Protein 0g	

Not a significant source of Calories from Fat, Saturated Fat, Cholesterol, Dietary Fiber, Vitamin A, Vitamin C, Calcium, Iron

*Percent Daily Values are based on a 2,000-calorie diet.

g = gram   mg = milligram

1. **Coach** You work as a children's basketball coach at a local recreational center. You give your players nutritional advice. A player is drinking an energy drink. You read the label with him. How many grams of sugars are in one serving of this drink?

   A. 0

   B. 14

   C. 30

   D. 50

   E. 110

2. **Assistant Coach** One of your players is drinking this energy drink. She wants to know if she should drink it all. How many servings are in this drink?

   F. 4

   G. 8

   H. 14

   J. 30

   K. 50

Mailroom Clerk Wanted

OVERVIEW

Location:	Denver, CO	Company Name:	Bankers-R-US	Department:	Mailroom
Job Category:	Full-Time, Weekdays, and some Saturdays (no Sundays)				

MORE INFORMATION ABOUT THIS JOB

Duties
- Manage incoming mail on established time schedule
- Manage outgoing mail on established time schedule
- Receive and sort mail for delivery

Requirements
- Good reading and oral English skills
- Able to meet deadlines
- Able to lift 50 pounds
- Well organized
- Previous experience working in a mailroom or office

---

3. **Mail Clerk** You are applying for a job with Bankers-R-US. You want to make sure the work schedule is not a problem for you. Read the job advertisement. What days must applicants be able to work?

   A. weekdays and some Sundays

   B. weekdays only

   C. weekdays and some Saturdays

   D. weekends only

   E. some Saturdays

4. **Mail Sorter** You want to apply for this job at Bankers-R-US. Before applying, you check the job responsibilities. What is one duty you will have if you get this job?

   F. speak and read English

   G. lift 50 pounds

   H. be well organized

   J. receive and sort mail for delivery

   K. meet deadlines

5. **Billing Clerk** You use a calculator to check billing data and prepare invoices at work. Your calculator must solve value-of-money calculations. Read this advertisement for calculators. Which calculator is best for your job?

   A. Graphing

   B. Printing

   C. Basic

   D. Scientific

   E. Financial

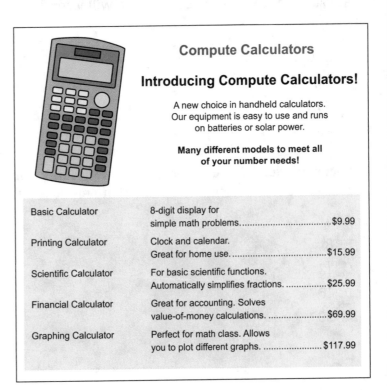

Compute Calculators

Introducing Compute Calculators!

A new choice in handheld calculators. Our equipment is easy to use and runs on batteries or solar power.

Many different models to meet all of your number needs!

Basic Calculator	8-digit display for simple math problems.	$9.99
Printing Calculator	Clock and calendar. Great for home use.	$15.99
Scientific Calculator	For basic scientific functions. Automatically simplifies fractions.	$25.99
Financial Calculator	Great for accounting. Solves value-of-money calculations.	$69.99
Graphing Calculator	Perfect for math class. Allows you to plot different graphs.	$117.99

All-in-One Security Camera Systems

Welcome to Secure-U!

Our all-in-one security camera systems include everything you need for your home or commercial security needs. Because our system is a 20-Channel System, you can upgrade to include up to 16 more cameras! Check out our packages and pricing below.

Our camera systems include:

- 22-inch TV monitor
- 4 infrared security cameras
- Built-in computer hard drive
- Professional grade images

Basic Security
includes 4 cameras $950.00

Upgrades Security
includes 8 cameras $1,600.00

Professional Security
includes 12 cameras $2,200.00

Elite Security
includes 16 cameras $3,000.00

Superstar Security
includes 20 cameras $3,600.00

Visit us online at **www.allspy.com** or call us toll free at
1 (800) 555-STOP to purchase your security camera system now!

6. **Security Guard** You are upgrading the security system at the building where you work. You read this advertisement for all-in-one security camera systems. You need a system with 12 cameras. How much will it cost?

    F. $950

    G. $1,600

    H. $2,200

    J. $3,000

    K. $3,600

7. **Security Agent** You are researching new security camera systems at work. You read this advertisement. How many channels does this camera system have?

    A. 4

    B. 8

    C. 12

    D. 16

    E. 20

Insurance Sales Agent Wanted

OVERVIEW

Job Title: Insurance Sales Agent

Company: Healthy Safe, Inc.

Job ID: HS220011

MORE INFORMATION ABOUT THIS JOB

Duties
- Cold-call possible new customers
- Contact existing clients to add on business
- Maintain an organized filing system
- Achieve monthly and yearly sales quotas

Requirements
- Previous sales experience
- Proven ability to work independently
- Professional attitude in person
- Professional attitude on the telephone

APPLY FOR THIS JOB

If interested in this opportunity, please e-mail your résumé/cover letter. Note job title and ID#HS220011 in subject line. Send to: R_Lyon@healthysafe.com. For more information, please visit our website at www.healthysafe.com. Or, call us at 1 (888) 555-4567.

8. **Insurance Sales Agent** You are looking for a job in sales. You decide to apply for an insurance sales agent job with Healthy Safe. What is one of the requirements for this job?

F. filing experience

G. achieving monthly sales quotas

H. achieving yearly sales quotas

J. cold-calling experience

K. previous sales experience

9. **Insurance Broker** You read this advertisement for an insurance sales agent. If you get this job, what will be one of your duties?

A. be able to work independently

B. previous sales experience

C. have a professional attitude in person

D. cold-call possible new customers

E. have a professional attitude on the telephone

10. **Sales Representative** You have finished filling out an application for this job. You are ready to submit it. How do you submit the application?

F. Go to www.healthysafe.com.

G. Send it to job ID#HS220011.

H. E-mail it to R_Lyon@healthysafe.com.

J. Call 1 (888) 555-4567.

K. Write job title in subject line.

Remember!

You will fill out many **forms** in your lifetime. Forms ask you for information. You will complete forms when you do the following:

* Apply for a job (this form is called a **job application**).
* Start a new job.
* Enroll in school.
* Apply for licenses.
* Rent or buy a home.
* Order items.
* Go to a doctor's office for the first time.

Skill Support

When filling out any type of form, you need to complete it properly. Some forms have only a few questions. Most forms have several questions, however. Read the entire form first before you start filling it out. You will also need to make sure the information is readable. Be sure to print clearly or type. When you fill out a form by hand, do not use cursive.

Lesson 9 ...
Use Forms

Skill: Follow directions to recognize and use different kinds of business forms

A form is a document that has blank spaces for you to fill in with information. Some forms are electronic, and some are paper. To fill out a form, write or type your information in the blank spaces. An employer might ask for a job application. When you register for a course, you fill out a form. Other types of forms include checklists and employee records. There are also order forms and invoices.

In order to use forms, you must be able to do the following:

* Identify the main idea and details.
* Use tables and charts.

Skill Examples ...

EXAMPLE 1 **Understand that forms are documents with blank spaces that must be filled in.**
To apply for a job, often you will need to fill out a job application. A job application may have several sections. The first section usually asks for personal information. This includes your name and contact information. What do you write on the bottom of this form?

* Read the form to find out what information is requested. This form asks for your name. It also asks for your street address, city, state, and ZIP code.

Job Application

Name: _____
Street Address: _____
_____
City: _____ State: _____ ZIP Code: _____

* You will need to write your information in the blank spaces. Write your first and last name in the blank space next to "Name."

* Write your building number and street name next to "Street Address." You do not write the city and state here.

Job Application

Name: Natalie Jones
Street Address: 1539 Elm Street
_____
City: Richmond   State: VA   ZIP Code: 23229

* The bottom line asks for your city, state, and ZIP code.

Write your city, state, and ZIP code on the bottom line.

EXAMPLE 2 Follow directions to fill out simple forms.

When you fill out a job application, you are usually asked to give your job history. This includes other jobs you have had. It may include the dates for those jobs. It may ask for the names of your current or former employers. What should you write on the "Phone Number" line of this form?

- To fill out a job history form, write your most recent job first. Next to "Job," write your job title.

- Next to "Employer," write the name of the company you worked for.

Job History
Provide the following information about the last job you held.

Job: _____

Employer: _____

Dates Employed: _____

Phone Number: _____

- Often a job application will ask for the dates you were employed. This means the date you started working at that job and the date you stopped. If you do not know the exact date, write the month and year instead.

Job History
Provide the following information about the last job you held.

Job: _Teacher_____

Employer: _Red Fox Middle School____

Dates Employed: _September 2006 – May 2010_

Phone Number: _(313) 555-0193_____

- The "Phone Number" line is asking for your employer's phone number. Include the area code.

Write your employer's phone number on the "Phone Number" line.

EXAMPLE 3 Recognize and use different kinds of forms.

You just took a job in another town. You need to lease a new apartment. To apply for a lease, you will need to fill out all of the boxes in the form. What do you write on the "Current Landlord's Phone" line?

- First write your name in the blank space.

- Next to "DOB," write your date of birth. *DOB* is an abbreviation for "date of birth."

Lease Application

Name: _____ DOB: _____

Current Address: _____

City: _____ State: _____ ZIP Code: _____

Current Landlord: _____

Current Landlord's Phone: _____

- After "Current Address," "City," "State," and "ZIP Code," write your current building number, street, city, state, and ZIP code. You can write the two-letter abbreviation for the state instead of the full name.

Lease Application

Name: _Jamal Robinson____ DOB: _4/15/1985____

Current Address: _157 Green St._____

City: _Johnston____ State: _MD_ ZIP Code: _21301_

Current Landlord: _Hector Martinez____

Current Landlord's Phone: _301-555-4653____

- Next to "Current Landlord," write the name of your current landlord.

- The last line, "Current Landlord's Phone," is for the phone number for your present landlord.

Write the phone number for your current landlord on the "Current Landlord's Phone" line.

Skill Support

Follow these steps when you fill out any kind of form:

- Read the whole form before you start to write.
- Look for headings to see if there are different parts of the form.
- Look for any abbreviations. Make sure you know what they mean.
- Use a dictionary to look up words you do not know.

Remember!

To fill out a form, write information in the blank spaces. Different types of forms ask for different information. On a job application, include your contact information. You will also include information about your previous jobs.

Level 2
Locating Information

Remember!

Forms are one way that businesses gather and organize information about consumers. Some forms are short and ask only a few questions. Other forms are long. Longer forms are usually divided into sections. All the questions in a particular section ask for one kind of information.

Skill Support

When you are filling out a form, think about the information you need to include. Try to fill in each section of the form. If a section does not apply to you, insert "N/A." This stands for "not applicable." This will let the person reviewing the form know you looked at this section but did not need to fill it in.

Skill Practice ▪ ▪ ▪

Locate information in the forms. Then answer the questions.

1. What should you write next to the highlighted words?

   A. 882 Ventura Blvd., Los Angeles, CA

   B. Los Angeles, CA

   C. 882

   D. Ventura Blvd.

   E. 882 Ventura Blvd.

   Name: _____
   Street Address: _____
   _____ Apartment: _____
   City: _____ State: ___ ZIP Code: ___
   Phone Number: _____

   HINT: *The street address does not include the city and state.*

2. You are filling out this application for a job at a lumber yard. At your last job, you were a delivery driver. Where would you write that information on the form?

   F. Line 1

   G. Line 2

   H. Line 3

   J. Line 4

   K. Line 5

   1. Job: _____
   2. Employer: _____
   3. Dates Employed: _____
   4. Phone Number: _____
   5. Address: _____

   HINT: *Look for the place on the form that refers to a job.*

3. You are applying for a lease on an apartment. What information do you need to fill out this form?

   A. your current landlord's address

   B. your current landlord's name and phone number

   C. your current landlord's city and ZIP code

   D. your current landlord's job history

   E. your current landlord's date of birth

   Lease Application
   Name: _____ DOB: _____
   Current Address: _____
   City: _____ State: ___ ZIP Code: ___
   Current Landlord: _____
   Current Landlord's Phone: _____

   HINT: *Only look for information asked for on the form.*

4. You are a landlord. You are reviewing an application for a lease on an apartment. What is the applicant's name?

   F. Hector Martinez

   G. Hector Green

   H. Jamal Robinson

   J. Jamal Johnston

   K. Jamal Green

   Lease Application
   Name: _Jamal Robinson_ DOB: _4/15/1985_
   Current Address: _157 Green St._
   City: _Johnston_ State: _MD_ ZIP Code: _21301_
   Current Landlord: _Hector Martinez_
   Current Landlord's Phone: _301-555-4653_

   HINT: *The applicant is the person who filled out the form.*

Try It Out! ▪ ▪ ▪

Clothing Store Manager You work at Edith's Dresses. One of your jobs is hiring employees. You are looking for a store clerk. Min Lee turned in a job application yesterday. According to the job application, she previously worked as a store clerk. How long did Min Lee work at Quick Feet Shoes?

A. 1 month

B. 10 months

C. 1 year

D. 1 year and 10 months

E. 2 years

Name: ___Min Lee_____

Employment History

Job: ___Store clerk_____

Employer: ___Quick Feet Shoes_____

Dates Employed: ___January 2011–January 2012___

Phone Number: ___(410) 555-6789_____

Job: ___Shop assistant_____

Employer: ___Great Notes Music Store_____

Dates Employed: ___April 2010–January 2011_____

Phone Number: ___(410) 555-1209_____

 Step 1

Understand the Question ▪ ▪ ▪

Complete the *Plan for Successful Solving.*

Plan for Successful Solving

What am I asked to do?	What are the facts?	How do I find the answer?
Find how long Min Lee worked at Quick Feet Shoes.	Min Lee worked at Quick Feet Shoes from January 2011 to January 2012.	Look at the dates employed. Then you can find how long she was employed at Quick Feet Shoes.

 Step 2

Find Your Answer ▪ ▪ ▪

- You need to find the length of employment. How long did Min Lee work at Quick Feet Shoes?

- Look at the dates employed. Min Lee began working at Quick Feet Shoes in January 2011. She stopped working there in January 2012. She worked at the job for one year.

- **Select the correct answer:** C. 1 year
  You looked at the job application form. You found the dates employed. Then you found how long Min Lee was employed at Quick Feet Shoes.

Skill Support

This question asks you to locate information on a form. You need to find where the form lists the dates of previous employment. Then figure out how long that employment lasted.

Remember!

When filling out a form, be honest. Do not say you worked somewhere or did something you did not do. Do not say you received or sent materials that you did not. When you sign a form, you are saying that the information in the form is true. If the information is not true, there may be harsh consequences.

Level 2
Locating Information

On Your Own ▪ ■ ▪

Use the graphics to answer the questions.

Vacation Request Form

Employees should submit vacation requests to their supervisors as far in advance as possible of the requested vacation (at least 30 calendar days in advance). Requests will be evaluated based on various factors, including anticipated workload and staffing considerations.

If this vacation request will be for more than 10 days you must contact the Human Resources Department.

All leave (vacation and sick time are not considered leave) requests MUST go through Human Resources.

Employee Name: _____

Vacation start date: _____

Returning to work date: _____

Total time off: _____ day(s)

Signature of employee: _____ Date: _____

··

Authorization

Request Approved: _____

Supervisor: _____ Title: _____

Project #: _____

Request denied (Specify Reason): _____

Any denial of vacation must be sent to HRA Human Resources before the employee is notified.

---

1. **Telemarketer** You have worked for eight months without any time off. You are planning a three-week vacation in May. What does this form tell you?

   A. You need to keep vacations under 10 days.

   B. Your vacation request is rejected.

   C. You cannot submit your request until 30 days before your vacation.

   D. You don't need to fill out the request form.

   E. You need to contact the Human Resources Department.

2. **Machine Operator** You would like to request a vacation. You have made sure there are enough people to cover for you and that the vacation is short. Where do you write the length of your vacation?

   F. after "Returning to work date"

   G. after "Total time off"

   H. after "Title"

   J. after "Vacation start date"

   K. after "Date"

Job Application

(1) First Name: __April__ Middle Initial: __M.__ Last Name: __Smith__

(2) Street Address: __155 Elm Street__ (3) City/State/Zip: __River City, TN 11111__

(4) Home Phone: __888-555-1212__ (5) Cell Phone: __888-555-9999__

(6) Have you worked for us before? ☐ yes ☒ no If yes, when? _____

(7) Position you are applying for: __data entry__ (8) Date you can start: __immediately__

(9) ☒ full-time ☐ part-time

(10) Education—List the last high school, college, or other educational institution you attended and the diploma or degree you received.

____associate's degree, ABC Community College____

(11) Previous employment—List employer, position, and dates:

____data entry for XYZ Data Information from April 1 to December 31____

(12) The information on this form is true and correct.

Signature: __April M. Smith__ Date: __1/15__

---

3. **Data Entry Operator** You are trying to find a job in the computer information field. You fill out the application form. According to the application form, what is your educational experience?

   A. full-time
   B. part-time
   C. associate's degree
   D. XYZ Data Information
   E. data entry

4. **Data Entry Manager** You are looking at an application that someone sent in. What specific previous work experience does the applicant have?

   F. full-time
   G. part-time
   H. from April 1
   J. data entry for XYZ Data Information
   K. associate's degree from ABC Community College

5. **Data Information Manager** You work at a company that lays people off for the winter. You want everyone to reapply when the season starts up. You look at the application from April Smith. According to her application, when can she start?

   A. immediately
   B. April 1
   C. December 31
   D. full-time
   E. part-time

Library Card Application

Brown County Public Library
123 Main St., Smalltown, CT 06601
phone: 888-555-1221   fax: 888-555-9988

Date ___September 5___   I.D. Provided ___Student ID 1234___

SS# _____

Name ___Stone___   ___William___   ___R.___
        (Last)   (First)   (Middle)

Local Address ___11 Cedar Street___

City, State, Zip ___New England City, CT 06601___

Home Phone ___888-555-3456___   E-mail ___bills@xmail.com___

D.O.B __12_ / _6_ / _2000_

Circle: (Male) Female

___Bill Stone___
Signature of Applicant

___Bill Stone___
(Print Name)

___Stephen Stone___
Signature of Parent or Guardian
(if under 14)

___9/5___
Date

---

6. **Librarian** A 12-year-old boy turned in the library card application. What is the boy's parent's or guardian's name?

   F. Bill Stone

   G. William Stone

   H. Student ID 1234

   J. Stephen Stone

   K. Stone William

7. **Library Assistant** A library patron has a book that was due three days ago. You need to call him and ask him to bring the book in. You look at his library card application. What is his telephone number?

   A. 888-555-1221

   B. 888-555-9988

   C. Student ID 1234

   D. 888-555-3456

   E. bills@xmail.com

Farm Labor Contractor and Workers Agreement

Rate of Pay—For this job, you will be paid at the following rate (rate per hour or piece work)	$10.00

Employment Conditions	(Dates):	(Approximately)	Your working hours and days are as follows:	5 days per week, Monday through Friday
Agreement begins on	July 31	And ends on August 15		

Your place of employment will be: Darby Farm, Clifton, OK	Special conditions, if any:

Equipment and clothing

A. Equipment and clothing required for this job (Employer must list):	heavy waterproof boots

B. Equipment and clothing provided each worker including PPE (Personal Protective Equipment). (Employer must list):

☐ Necessary equipment and clothing may be purchased or borrowed from the employer. The price and/or conditions for obtaining equipment and clothing are as follows:

Labor dispute

☒ There is no labor dispute at the work site	☐ There is a labor dispute at the work site

Owner of Operations	Phone Number
Name Juan Sanchez	888-355-9876

Address 5 Main Street	City John Otis City	State OK	Zip 73004

8. **Farm Labor Contractor** You are hiring a group of workers to harvest crops for farms. You fill out the form. According to the form, what equipment or clothing will your workers need?

   F. gloves

   G. hats

   H. heavy shirts

   J. heavy waterproof boots

   K. personal protective equipment

9. **Farm Worker** You have just been hired to harvest tomatoes at a farm. You are reviewing the agreement. You want to know how much you will be making on this job. According to the agreement, how much per hour will you earn?

   A. $3

   B. $5

   C. $10

   D. $15

   E. $31

10. **Farm Manager** The owner of the farm has asked you to hire a new worker to help with the harvest. According to the agreement, how long will the new worker be on the job?

   F. one day

   G. two days

   H. one week

   J. two weeks

   K. one year

Skill Support

An **invoice** is a form that a business uses as a bill for goods or services. Most invoices are filled out by the business and sent to the customer. Invoices often have the following features:

- business name
- contact information
- date and due date
- invoice number
- name of customer or client
- list of products or services, number of products or services, and cost of each
- total due

Remember!

You will fill out many forms in life. You fill out forms when you apply for a job, enroll in school, or apply for a license. You must make sure you fill out forms correctly. Some forms only ask for a little information, while others ask for a lot.

Lesson 10 ...
Find Information in Invoices and Order Forms

Skill: Find information in invoices and order forms

Invoices are forms you might use at work. They are used to bill for goods or services. You might also use an order form. Order forms are used to purchase goods or services. An electrician fills out an invoice after finishing a repair. An office manager fills out an order form to get supplies.

When you use invoices and order forms, you must be able to:

- Read tables and charts.
- Understand consumer and business materials.
- Understand addition and multiplication facts.
- Read time with a calendar.

Skill Examples ■ ■

EXAMPLE 1 Identify the parts of an invoice.

An invoice is a common type of form. This form may have several parts. What is the total amount due on the invoice from the animal hospital?

- The name, address, and phone number of the business are at the top. This tells you where to send the money or call if you have questions.

- The next section has two dates. The invoice date is 5/24. This is the date when the invoice was created. The due date is when the payment is due. This is a month later on 6/24.

> **Falls Avenue Animal Hospital**
> 208 S. Falls Ave.
> Portland, OR 97212
> (909) 555-5569
> www.fallsavenueanimalhospital.com
>
> Invoice #92582   Date: 5/24
>   Due Date: 6/24
>
> To: Hidden Elm Farm
>
> For: Farm animal vaccinations
>   10 vaccines @ $20.00 each $200.00
>
>   Farm animal checkups
>   10 checkups @ $50.00 each $500.00
>
> Total due: $700.00

- The invoice number allows the company to keep track of all its invoices. This invoice number is listed as 92582.

- The next section shows the name of the customer, Hidden Elm Farm.

- The next section lists services and their costs. It says how much one vaccination or checkup costs and that 10 of each were provided.

- The total due shows the amount the customer owes. This number is reached by adding all the charges together.

The total due for this invoice is $700.

EXAMPLE 2 Understand the parts of an order form.

When you want to purchase items online or through the mail, you often use an order form. What is the cost of shipping in the following order form?

- The company name is at the top. The contact information is listed below.

- A product will often have an item description and item number.

Everlast Lab Equipment
1500 Main St.
Springfield, IL 62701
(800) 555-1138
www.everlastlabequipment.com

Item Description	Item Number	Size/Color	Item Price	Quantity	Line Total
Glass beaker	224	100ml	$2.50	15	$37.50
Safety goggles	29	Blue	$7.00	25	$175.00
				Subtotal:	$212.50
				Shipping:	$8.50
				Total:	$221.00

The two item numbers on this invoice are 224 and 29.

- Sometimes you will have to give more information about the item. This order form has an additional column for size and color of the products. The size of the glass beaker is 100 ml, or 100 milliliters.

- To calculate the line total, look for each item's price. You also need to look at the quantity (how many) you are ordering. To get the line total, multiply the item price by the quantity.

- When you add all the line totals together, you get the subtotal. You will need to add shipping to the subtotal to get the total.

The cost of shipping for the order is $8.50.

EXAMPLE 3 Add missing information to an order form.

You have to say how you will pay for an order. You also have to identify where the order should be sent. This is called the billing and shipping information.

- The billing section asks where to send the bill for the order and how you will pay for it.

Bill To:
Name: _____
Address: _____

Credit Card Number:
_____

Expiration Date: _____

Ship To:
Name: _____
Address: _____
_____

- Sometimes the shipping and billing address will be the same. Other times, they will be different. The shipping information is where the order will ship.

Imagine you buy a present for your friend. You want to ship it to your friend's house. His address is 435 Point Road, Millersville, AK 55515. Where should you write this information on the order form?

- You bought the present, so the cost will be billed to your address.

- The package will ship to your friend. This is the "Ship To" address.

You should write his address in the "Ship To" section.

Order forms are used to order goods and services. Order forms are often filled in by the customer and given to the business. Order forms are also used for Internet orders, as many people place orders online. Order forms typically have the following features:

- name of company and contact information
- item description
- item number
- additional information
- item price
- item quantity
- total price for items
- additional charges (e.g., taxes and shipping)
- total price for order
- billing information
- shipping information

Skill Practice ...

Locate information in the forms. Then answer the questions.

1. What is the total amount due?

A. $6.00   **D.** $60.00

B. $10.00   **E.** $110.00

C. $50.00

HINT: Remember that the total due is reached by adding all the charges together. This is the amount that the customer owes.

Warming Comfort Natural Health Suppliers
900 Fifth Street
Elyria, OH 44035
(800) 555-3125
www.warmingcomfort.com

Invoice #10003   Date: 12/20
                                                  Due Date: 1/20

To: Holistic Health Clinic

For: Dandelion Herbal Tea
        10 pounds @ $6.00 per pound.................................$60.00

        Dried Lavender
        5 pounds @ $10.00 per pound..............................$50.00

Total due:...$110.00

2. Look at the invoice again. When is the payment due?

F. January 20   **J.** December 20

G. January 21   **K.** December 21

H. October 3

HINT: You are looking for a date on the invoice. Look for the date that tells when the payment is due.

3. You work at a sporting goods store. You received this order today. How many medium team jerseys were ordered?

Fair Ball Sporting Goods Order Form

Item Description	Item Number	Size/Color	Item Price	Quantity	Line Total
Team jersey	105	Medium	$22.00	10	$220.00
Team jersey	105	Large	$23.00	6	$138.00
				Subtotal:	
				Shipping:	
				Tax:	
				Total:	

A. 2   **D.** 16

B. 6   **E.** 105

C. 10

HINT: Study the order form. The Quantity column tells you "how many."

4. Look at the order form again. The cost of the jerseys is $358 before shipping. Where do you write this number on the order form?

F. below the words "Item Price"

G. next to the word "Total"

H. next to the word "Shipping"

J. next to the word "Subtotal"

K. below the word "Quantity"

HINT: You want the price of the jerseys without the shipping cost.

Try It Out! ▪ ▪ ▪

Groundskeeper You work at Pruners Landscaping. You are in charge of reviewing invoices. Last week Pruners Landscaping worked at the University Art Museum. You have identified the total cost as $972.00, including taxes. Where do you write this number on the invoice?

A. next to "Invoice #"

B. next to "Pruning hedges"

C. next to "Total Due"

D. next to "Subtotal"

E. next to "Due Date"

Invoice #11780   Date: 5/29
                                                    Due Date: 7/29

To: University Art Museum

For: Planting rose bushes
        6 bushes @ $120.00 each $720.00

        Pruning hedges $100.00

        General maintenance
        4 hours @ $20.00/hour..$80.00

                                    Subtotal: ...._____
                                    State tax: ...._____
                                    Total Due: ...._____

Skill Support

Total cost represents the total of all the charges. It will include the cost of taxes. It will also include any shipping rates.

The subtotal is only the cost of items or services you are purchasing. It does not include additional charges.

Step 1 — Understand the Question ▪ ▪ ▪

Complete the *Plan for Successful Solving.*

Plan for Successful Solving

What am I asked to do?	What are the facts?	How do I find the answer?
Find where to write the total cost on the invoice.	You need to fill in $972 on the invoice. This represents the total cost. The total cost represents the "Total Due" section of the invoice.	Look at the information on the invoice. You need to find the section for total due.

Remember!

Filling out an invoice correctly is important. Mistakes in invoices may cause a customer to be overcharged or undercharged. Mistakes may also cause confusion in a company's records. Filling out an order form is also important for customers. Mistakes in order forms may cause errors in the items ordered. They may cause payment errors. They may also cause shipping errors.

Step 2 — Find Your Answer ▪ ▪ ▪

- You are billing for a total of $972. You must find the section for total cost.

- The total cost is written next to "Total Due."

- **Select the correct answer: C.** next to "Total Due"
  You reviewed the information on the invoice. You needed to find where to place the total cost. You found the section "Total Due" to write in the total cost.

On Your Own ■ ■ ■

Use the graphics to answer the questions.

ABC Mechanics			REPAIR ORDER

123 Main St.
Your Town, NY
(555) 555-5555

Sold to:
US Railroad Co.
545 Main St.
Your Town, NY

Invoice Number	536524
Invoice Date	Sept. 5
Our Order Number	726278
Your Order Number	1892727

Quantity	Description	Item Price	Amount
4	Brake Shoe	$ 19.00	$ 76.00
6	Labor to install shoes (hours)	$ 44.00	$ 264.00
		Subtotal	$ 340.00
		Tax	$ 20.00
		Total	$ 360.00

1. **Railroad Brakeman** You prepare a budget for future work on brake shoes. For the invoice, you base the cost on the parts and the number of hours worked. How many hours did it take to install the brake shoes?

   A. 4
   B. 6
   C. 19
   D. 20
   E. 44

2. **Photographer** You are looking through invoices to see how many prints to make of a photograph. Where can you find the number of 4" × 6" prints?

   F. the Photo Number column
   G. the Item Price column
   H. the Totals column
   J. the Total Photos column
   K. the Total Due box

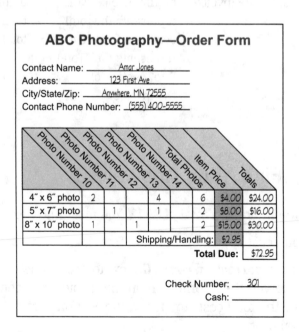

ABC Photography—Order Form

Contact Name: _____Amar Jones_____
Address: _____123 First Ave_____
City/State/Zip: _____Anywhere, MN 72555_____
Contact Phone Number: _____(555) 400-5555_____

	Photo Number 10	Photo Number 11	Photo Number 12	Photo Number 13	Photo Number 14	Total Photos	Item Price	Totals
4" x 6" photo	2			4		6	$4.00	$24.00
5" x 7" photo		1		1		2	$8.00	$16.00
8" x 10" photo	1		1			2	$15.00	$30.00
					Shipping/Handling:		$2.95	
						Total Due:		$72.95

Check Number: _____301_____
Cash: _____

Invoice

Invoiced To:
Aime Alvador

Ship To:
Aime Alvador

Invoice Number	291
Invoice Date	Nov 29
P/O Number	6546456
ABN:	555555555

Dr. Z's Computer

Description	Quantity	Price	Extended Price
350mz CPU	1	$204.33	$204.33
Motherboard 1MB	1	$126.00	$126.00
16MB RAM	1	$25.20	$25.20
Cables	1	$168.00	$168.00
17" Monitor	1	$324.00	$324.00
Mouse	1	$7.95	$7.95
		Total Items	$855.48
		Labor/Shipping	0.00
		GST @ 10.00%	$85.55
		Total Invoice	$941.03

Terms: C.O.D.

Delivery: Pick-Up

3. Computer Repairperson You made computer repairs for a customer. You send this invoice. What total are you owed for the repairs?

A. $204.33   **B.** $324.80   **C.** $463.22   **D.** $855.48   **E.** $941.03

ABC Motorsports Order Form

Shipping Information:
Name: _Jiao Wu_
Address: _100 Future Dr._
City & State: _YourTown, AL_   Zip Code: _46555_
Phone Number: _(555) 305 - 1555_
E-mail address: _jiaow@mail.com_

Quantity (Example: 1)	Description (from our online product pages)	Color Choices (Example: red/blue)	Price (on Website)
1	Helmet	black/white	$49.99

Current shipping rates

Shipping: _$5.00_
Total: _$54.99_

Please make checks payable to **ABC Motorsports.**

4. Salesperson A customer has sent this form in, along with a check. Which line should be the same as the check amount?

F. the Quantity column

G. the Description column

H. the Color Choices column

J. the Total line

K. the Shipping line

5. Delivery Driver You ride a motorcycle. You need to order a new helmet. Where do you indicate what product you are ordering?

A. in the Description column

B. in the Price column

C. in the Quantity column

D. on the Shipping line

E. on the Total line

A&B Nursery | **INVOICE**

123 Main St.
Your Town, NY
(555) 555-5555

CUSTOMER:
JS Gardening
545 Main St.
Your Town, NY

Invoice Number	536524
Invoice Date	Sept. 5
Our Order Number	726278
Your Order Number	1892727

Quantity	Description	Item Price	Amount
4	White Spruce 5'	109.00	436.00
2	Eastern White Pine 15'	445.00	890.00
6	Japanese Red Pine 6'	119.00	714.00
		Subtotal	2,040.00
		Tax	102.00
		Total	$ 2,142.00

6. Landscaper You ordered trees for a job. You received this invoice. How much do you have to pay the nursery?

   F. $436   **G.** $714   **H.** $890   **J.** $2,040   **K.** $2,142

Police Supply

ORDER / QUOTATION FORM

Billing Address	Shipping Address (if different)
Agency/Company:	Agency/Company:
Name:	Name:
Address:	Address:
City/State/Zip:	City/State/Zip:
Phone:	Phone:
Fax:	Fax:
E-Mail:	E-Mail:

Quantity	Item Number	Description	Item Price	Amount
8	BV2056	Bulletproof Vest	$425.00	$3,400
20	FL3233	Duty LED Flashlight	$99.00	$1,900
100	BDS050	Button Down Duty Shirt	$18.00	$1,800

Method of Payment (Check one)

☐ Check or Money Order Enclosed
☐ Credit Card

Card Number _ _ _ _ _ _ _ _ _ _ _ _ _ _ _ _ _

Exp _ _/_ _   CID _____

Subtotal	$7,100
CA Sales Tax (7.75%)	$500.25
Shipping	$100.00
Total	$7,750.25

Notes: _____

Authorized Signature: _____ Date: _____

7. Police Officer You are ordering bulletproof vests for your department. Where did you indicate the number of vests you want?

   A. in the Item Number column   **D.** in the Amount column

   B. in the Item Price column   **E.** in the Description column

   C. in the Quantity column

Locating Information   Basic Skills for the Workplace

```
School Builders, Inc.          INVOICE
123 Anywhere St.
Olympia, WA 98501         Invoice Number: 1
555-555-5555              Date: January 6, 2003
Fax: 555-555-5556

Bill To:                  Billing Period:
City High School          August 2002
```

Activity	Description	Amount
	Completed to date	$10,000.00
	Billed to date	00.00
	Contract amount due to date	$10,000.00
	Subtotal	$10,000.00
	Sales Tax 8%	800.00
	Less Deposit (5% of $10,000)	(500.00)
	Total Due this billing	$10,300.00

```
Make all checks payable to: School Builders, Inc.

Thank you for your business!
```

8. **School Administrator** You are reviewing an invoice for work on a new school. You want to know how much has been paid to the builder already. Where on the invoice can you find this information?

   F. the Total Due box

   G. the Subtotal box

   H. the Less Deposit box

   J. the Activity column

   K. the Description column

9. **Superintendent** You need to approve the payment of this invoice. How much does the school owe for this invoice?

   A. $300

   B. $500

   C. $800

   D. $10,000

   E. $10,300

10. **School Principal** This invoice is in your mailbox when you arrive at school today. To whom is the invoice billed?

    F. you

    G. the school board

    H. City High School

    J. Invoice #1

    K. School Builders, Inc.

Level 2 Performance Assessment ▪ ▪ ▪

These problems are at a Level 2 rating of difficulty. They are similar to problems on a career readiness certificate test. For each question, you can check your answer. To do this, use the answer key. It is located on pp. 272–273 of this book. It explains each answer option. It also shows the lesson that covers that skill. You may refer to that lesson to review the skill.

Adult Marital Status in the United States

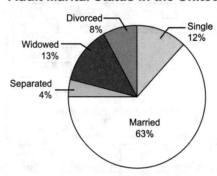

1. You are a marriage and family counselor. You are giving a lecture at a conference on marriage. You use this graph in your research. What do all the segments in the graph indicate?

   A. size of adult population

   B. marital status percents

   C. married people

   D. separated people

   E. divorced people

2. A person at your lecture asks about the number of divorced people in the United States. You refer to this graph. According to the graph, what percentage of US adults are divorced?

   F. 4%

   G. 8%

   H. 12%

   J. 13%

   K. 63%

3. In your lecture, you compare the information in the graph. You talk about which status is most represented. Which marital status represents the greatest percentage of US adults?

   A. divorced

   B. widowed

   C. separated

   D. married

   E. single

US Civil War Events

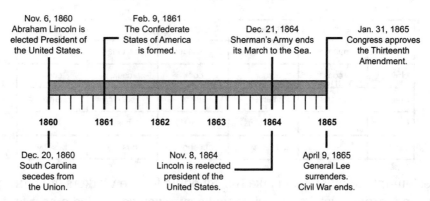

4. You are a history teacher. You are going to be teaching a unit on the American Civil War. Which of these events happened last?

F. Abraham Lincoln is elected president of the United States.

G. The Confederate States of America is formed.

H. South Carolina secedes from the Union.

J. The 13th Amendment is approved.

K. Sherman's March to the Sea ends.

Sequence for Shipment Packing

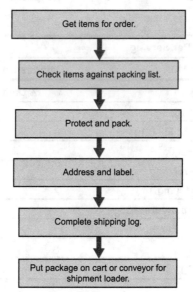

5. You work as a packer in a warehouse. You have just checked the items against the packing list. You look at the flowchart. What step comes next?

A. Get items for order.

B. Protect and pack.

C. Address and label.

D. Put on cart or conveyor.

E. Complete shipping log.

Pizza Pad Workers' Shifts

	4–5 P.M.	5–6 P.M.	6–7 P.M.	7–8 P.M.	8–9 P.M.
Soledad	manager	manager	manager	manager	manager
Linh	cook	cook	cook	cook	cook
Phil	server	server	server	server	server
Clay			host	host	host
Jameel		busboy	busboy	busboy	busboy

6. As a restaurant manager, you make the schedule for the workers. It is 6:15 p.m. Your host has not arrived yet. You check to make sure you scheduled a host for the night. What time is Clay supposed to start work?

   F. 4 p.m.

   G. 5 p.m.

   H. 6 p.m.

   J. 7 p.m.

   K. 8 p.m.

Nutrition Facts

Serving Size 1 cup (30g)

Amount Per Serving	
Calories 110	**Calories from Fat** 4
	% Daily Value*
Total Fat 1g	2%
Saturated Fat 0.1g	1%
Trans Fat 0g	
Cholesterol 0mg	0%
Sodium 160mg	7%
Total Carbohydrate 25g	8%
Dietary Fiber 1g	5%
Sugars 2g	
Protein 1g	

g = gram

7. You are a dietician. You are showing your client how to read nutrition labels. This is a label for one of her favorite cereals. Your client needs to eat more protein. How much protein is in a serving of this cereal?

   A. 0 grams

   B. 0.1 grams

   C. 1 gram

   D. 2 grams

   E. 25 grams

Take advantage of our credit card!

Put all your credit charges on one card.

You will enjoy an APR (annual percentage rate)
as low as 2.9%* on transferred balances
for one year.

Monthly payments must be made to keep this low rate.

See how much you save!

* 1. Rate of 3% for one year on transfers of $4,000 or more.
2. Rate of 4% for one year on transfers of $3,500 or less.
3. Rate for new purchases is 14%.
4. Rate for cash advances is 20%.
5. If you miss a payment, rate jumps to 24%.

*Call 1-800-555-CARD today
to get your new credit card!*

8. You are a contractor. You need a new business credit card to buy construction materials. You get this advertisement in the mail. You have a balance on another card already. What is the annual percentage rate for a balance transfer of $3,500?

F. 3%   J. 20%

G. 4%   K. 24%

H. 14%

Social Worker, County Health and Human Services. Full-time position. Occasional weekend shifts required. Requires bachelor's degree in social work. Minimum two years' previous experience. To apply, e-mail résumé to jobs@TCHHS.gov. No phone calls or in-person applicants, please. You may mail a résumé to PO Box 180, Capital Town, 87711.

---

9. You are a social worker. You see this want ad. You want to apply for the job. What should you do to apply?

A. call or e-mail

B. call or visit in person

C. e-mail or visit in person

D. mail or call

E. e-mail or mail

Child Care Registration Form

One form must be completed for each child.

Section 1: Child

(1) Child's full name _____ (2) Child's nickname _____

(3) ☐ male ☐ female

(4) Birth date _____ (5) Language spoken at home _____

Section 2: Emergency Contacts (other than parents)

(6) Contact #1 name _____ Relationship to child _____

    Employer _____

    Work schedule _____

    Work phone _____ Home phone _____ Cell phone _____

(7) Contact #2 name _____ Relationship to child _____

    Employer _____

    Work schedule _____

    Work phone _____ Home phone _____ Cell phone _____

Section 3: Medical Information

(8) Child's doctor _____ Phone _____

(9) Is child current on all vaccinations? ☐ yes ☐ no Attach vaccination record.

(10) Food or other allergies _____

(11) Illnesses, prescriptions, or medical conditions _____

Section 4: Other

(12) Please give any other information that will be helpful for caring for your child.

_____

(13) Parent's signature _____ (14) Date _____

---

10. You work at the Elm Day Care Center. A new parent comes to the center. You give him this form. The form needs to be signed before a child is enrolled. Who should sign the form?

    F. child

    G. child's parent

    H. contact #1

    J. contact #2

    K. child's doctor

11. Some children have food allergies. You need to know what allergies this new child may have. What line would you read to learn about allergies?

    A. 8   **B.** 9   **C.** 10   **D.** 11   **E.** 12

12. The new parent has filled out the form and is bringing his child in tomorrow. He hands you the form, and you check it over. It is missing an attachment. According to the directions in Section 3, what should be attached to the form?

    F. contact information

    G. vaccination record

    H. parent signature

    J. medical history

    K. doctor information

Patty's Bakery

1779 Main Street / 555-1212
Special Thanksgiving pie order form

- Place your order no later than noon on Monday, November 21.
- Pick up orders at the bakery by 5 p.m. on Wednesday, November 23. We're closed on Thanksgiving!
- Each 10-inch pie serves 8 people.
- Pay by cash, check or credit card when you place the order.

Type of Pie	Quantity	Price per Pie	Total
Apple	3	$12.50	$37.50
Cherry	1	$13.00	$13.00
Pecan	5	$15.00	$75.00
Pumpkin	6	$12.50	$75.00
Sweet Potato	2	$14.00	$28.00
		Subtotal	
		8% Sales Tax	
		Total	

Name: _____

Phone Number: _____

Date Ordered: _____

Payment Information (credit card number): _____

13. You work the front counter at Patty's Bakery. A customer is checking on an order for holiday pies. You review this order form. How many apple pies did she order?

A. 1

B. 2

C. 3

D. 5

E. 6

14. You figure out how much the customer owes for her pies. Where do you put the total amount before tax?

F. Quantity

G. Payment Information

H. 8% Sales Tax

J. Total

K. Subtotal

15. Special orders for Thanksgiving can be ordered no later than November 21. You write down the date of the order. Where on the form do you write when an order is placed?

A. Date Ordered

B. Quantity

C. Name

D. Phone Number

E. Payment Information

Answer Key ■ ■ ■
Reading for Information

Level 1

Lesson 1 (pp. 4–11)
Skill Practice:

  1. A   2. G

On Your Own:

1. B	3. C	5. C	7. B	9. C
2. J	4. J	6. H	8. F	10. G

Lesson 2 (pp. 12–19)
Skill Practice:

  1. B   2. J

On Your Own:

1. D	3. E	5. E	7. E	9. E
2. J	4. G	6. H	8. F	10. J

Lesson 3 (pp. 20–27)
Skill Practice:

  1. B   2. J

On Your Own:

1. E	3. E	5. D	7. D	9. B
2. F	4. G	6. F	8. F	10. H

Lesson 4 (pp. 28–35)
Skill Practice:

  1. C   2. K

On Your Own:

1. C	3. B	5. E	7. B	9. C
2. F	4. F	6. K	8. K	10. J

Lesson 5 (pp. 36–43)
Skill Practice:

  1. B   2. G

On Your Own:

1. E	3. C	5. D	7. A	9. D
2. G	4. F	6. H	8. G	10. H

Level 1 Performance Assessment (pp. 44–49)

1. Determine the main idea of the e-mail from the subject line. *(Lesson 1)*

   A. Incorrect: Accounting Department is the sender.

   B. **Correct:** The subject line and first sentence contain the main idea.

   C. Incorrect: This is a detail, not a main idea.

   D. Incorrect: This is a detail, not a main idea.

   E. Incorrect: This is not the main idea of the whole message, but the second paragraph.

2. Determine the main idea of the second paragraph by finding the most important idea. *(Lesson 1)*

   F. **Correct:** The most important idea is following steps to clock in.

   G. Incorrect: Placing your finger on the touchpad is a detail.

   H. Incorrect: Holding for 15 seconds is a detail.

   J. Incorrect: The computer scanning is a detail.

   K. Incorrect: This is a detail, not the main idea.

3. Determine the main idea in the third paragraph by finding the most important idea. *(Lesson 1)*

   A. **Correct:** Clocking out at breaks and at the end of a shift is the most important idea.

   B. Incorrect: This sentence is not in the third paragraph.

   C. Incorrect: This sentence is not in the third paragraph.

   D. Incorrect: This sentence is not in the third paragraph.

   E. Incorrect: Forgetting to clock out is not the main idea.

4. Check the headings and numbered list to see what to do first in case of injury. *(Lesson 2)*

   F. Incorrect: Your supervisor needs to fill the form out before you sign it.

   G. Incorrect: You must report the injury before going to the medical center.

   H. **Correct:** Reporting the injury is the first thing to do.

   J. Incorrect: Using sick time for the first three days is a supporting detail for a different idea.

   K. Incorrect: Contacting human resources is not what you should do first in case of injury.

5. Find the detail that provides a fact about medical payment. *(Lesson 2)*

   A. Incorrect: This does not refer to medical payment.

   B. **Correct:** This statement refers to an act or law that provides for medical payment.

   C. Incorrect: This does not refer to medical payment.

   D. Incorrect: Using sick days or vacation time is an instruction, not a fact.

   E. Incorrect: Reporting the injury does not refer to medical payment.

6. Find the detail that says what could happen if you do not report your injury right away. *(Lesson 2)*

   F. Incorrect: This statement does not provide a reason.

   G. Incorrect: This statement is not a reason for reporting the injury.

   H. **Correct:** It may be hard to get payment if you do not report the injury immediately.

   J. Incorrect: This statement is a detail about when payment kicks in.

   K. Incorrect: This statement is not a reason for reporting the injury.

7. Find the word that is a synonym for *chop*. *(Lesson 3)*

   A. Incorrect: *Mix* does not mean the same thing as *chop*.

   B. **Correct:** *Dice* is the same as *cut* or *chop*.

   C. Incorrect: *Add* does not mean the same thing as *chop*.

   D. Incorrect: *Pour* does not mean the same thing as *chop*.

   E. Incorrect: *Serve* does not mean the same thing as *chop*.

8. Look at the letters in the abbreviation to see what word it is short for. *(Lesson 3)*

   F. Incorrect: *Tsp.* is not short for *tablespoon*.

   G. Incorrect: *Tsp.* is not short for *cup*.

   H. Incorrect: *Tsp.* is not short for *ounce*.

   J. **Correct:** *Tsp.* is short for *teaspoon*.

   K. Incorrect: *Tsp.* is not short for *dash*.

9. Find the word that is the antonym for *combine*. *(Lesson 3)*

   A. Incorrect: *Mix* does not mean the opposite of *combine*.

   B. Incorrect: *Add* does not mean the opposite of *combine*.

   C. Incorrect: *Pour* does not mean the opposite of *combine*.

   D. Incorrect: *Chop* does not mean the opposite of *combine*.

   E. **Correct:** *Separate* means the opposite of *combine*.

10. Use the context clues *show* and *prove* to find the meaning of *verify*. *(Lesson 4)*

    F. **Correct:** *Verify* means "show or confirm."

    G. Incorrect: *Verify* does not mean "review."

    H. Incorrect: *Verify* does not mean "test."

    J. Incorrect: *Verify* does not mean "disprove."

    K. Incorrect: *Verify* does not mean "decide."

11. Use the context clue *beginning* to find the meaning of *prior*. *(Lesson 4)*

    A. Incorrect: *Prior* does not mean "after."

    B. **Correct:** *Prior* means "before."

    C. Incorrect: *Prior* does not mean "during."

    D. Incorrect: *Prior* does not mean "beginning."

    E. Incorrect: *Prior* does not mean "ending."

12. Use the context clues to find the meaning of *in-service day*. *(Lesson 4)*

    F. Incorrect: Only teachers will have training.

    G. Incorrect: Only teachers will have training.

    H. **Correct:** Teachers will follow the training schedule, and students will have no classes.

    J. Incorrect: Teachers will follow the training schedule.

    K. Incorrect: Students will have no classes, and teachers will follow the training schedule.

13. The activities are in chronological order. See which one falls right after lunch. *(Lesson 5)*

    A. Incorrect: First Aid does not happen right after lunch.

    B. Incorrect: The Staff Meeting does not happen right after lunch.

    C. Incorrect: Improving Communication with Parents does not happen right after lunch.

    D. **Correct:** Materials Overview happens right after lunch.

    E. Incorrect: New Standards Training does not happen right after lunch.

14. Find the second step in the instructions by looking for the next step after the first one. *(Lesson 5)*

    F. Incorrect: A preaudit interview is the first step.

    G. Correct: The second step is to get an explanation of the payroll format.

    H. Incorrect: Studying the printouts is the third step.

    J. Incorrect: Testing employees is part of the third step.

    K. Incorrect: Understanding all payroll records is part of the introduction.

15. Find the word that is used to show what happens last. *(Lesson 5)*

    A. Correct: *Finally* is used to show what happens last.

    B. Incorrect: *Then* is used in the middle of instructions.

    C. Incorrect: *First* is used to show what comes at the beginning.

    D. Incorrect: *Steps* tells you there is more than one thing to do.

    E. Incorrect: *Next* is used in the middle of instructions.

Reading for Information

Level 2

Lesson 6 (pp. 50–57)
Skill Practice:

    1. C   2. F

On Your Own:

1. E	3. B	5. D	7. A	9. A
2. H	4. F	6. K	8. H	10. K

Lesson 7 (pp. 58–65)
Skill Practice:

    1. E   2. H

On Your Own:

1. E	3. D	5. B	7. B	9. E
2. F	4. H	6. J	8. G	10. F

Lesson 8 (pp. 66–73)
Skill Practice:

    1. A   2. G

On Your Own:

1. D	3. B	5. A	7. D	9. E
2. H	4. H	6. G	8. H	10. F

Lesson 9 (pp. 74–81)
Skill Practice:

    1. C   2. H

On Your Own:

1. C	3. A	5. E	7. B	9. A
2. G	4. G	6. H	8. J	10. K

Lesson 10 (pp. 82–89)
Skill Practice:

    1. D   2. H   3. A

On Your Own:

1. C	3. A	5. D	7. C	9. D
2. K	4. G	6. G	8. J	10. K

Level 2 Performance Assessment (pp. 90–95)

1. Use context clues like *system* and *computer* to determine the meaning of *server*. *(Lesson 6)*

    A. Incorrect: In this case, *server* is not a person who brings food or drink.

    B. Incorrect: In this case, *server* is not a tennis player.

    C. Correct: In this case, *server* is the main computer in a network.

    D. Incorrect: In this case, *server* is not a person who serves legal papers.

    E. Incorrect: In this case, *server* is not a wide fork or spoon.

2. Find the meaning of *running* as it is used in the memo. *(Lesson 6)*

    F. Incorrect: In this case, *running* does not mean "moving quickly by foot."

    G. Correct: In this case, *running* means "performing."

    H. Incorrect: In this case, *running* does not mean "escaping."

    J. Incorrect: In this case, *running* does not mean "flowing."

    K. Incorrect: In this case, *running* does not mean "occurring over and over."

3. Use the context clues of *test, monitor,* and *problems* to determine the meaning of *bugs*. *(Lesson 6)*

    A. Incorrect: In this case, *bugs* does not mean "small insects."

    B. Incorrect: In this case, *bugs* does not mean "nonspecific sicknesses."

    C. Correct: In this case, *bugs* means "defects or flaws."

    D. Incorrect: In this case, *bugs* does not mean "hidden listening devices."

    E. Incorrect: In this case, *bugs* does not mean "germs."

4. Find which signal word forms a cause-and-effect relationship. *(Lesson 7)*

   F. **Correct:** The word *so* signals a cause-and-effect relationship.

   G. Incorrect: This sentence does not use a cause-and-effect signal word.

   H. Incorrect: This sentence does not use a cause-and-effect signal word.

   J. Incorrect: This sentence does not use a cause-and-effect signal word.

   K. Incorrect: This sentence does not use a cause-and-effect signal word.

5. Find the scenario that shows an action causing another action to happen. *(Lesson 7)*

   A. Incorrect: There is only one action in this scenario.

   B. Incorrect: There is no cause-and-effect relationship stated.

   C. Incorrect: This is an instruction, not a cause-and-effect relationship.

   D. **Correct:** This statement shows an action causing another action.

   E. Incorrect: This is a statement of fact.

6. Find which signal word forms a cause-and-effect relationship. *(Lesson 7)*

   F. Incorrect: This sentence does not use a cause-and-effect signal word.

   G. Incorrect: This sentence does not use a cause-and-effect signal word.

   H. **Correct:** The word *therefore* signals a cause-and-effect relationship.

   J. Incorrect: This sentence does not use a cause-and-effect signal word.

   K. Incorrect: This sentence does not use a cause-and-effect signal word.

7. Look for the word that signals a contrast between rakes and pin brushes. *(Lesson 8)*

   A. Incorrect: *Different* is not used for rakes and pin brushes.

   B. Incorrect: *Good* is not a contrast signal word.

   C. Incorrect: *Both* is a comparison signal word.

   D. Incorrect: *Used* is not a contrast signal word.

   E. **Correct:** *Unlike* signals a contrast between rakes and pin brushes.

8. Look for a signal word telling you whether the clinical trials are set up the same or different. *(Lesson 8)*

   F. **Correct:** The use of the word *similar* explains that the trials should be set up the same.

   G. Incorrect: This statement does not provide enough information about all clinical trials.

   H. Incorrect: This statement talks about just one detail of clinical trials.

   J. Incorrect: This statement talks about only one part of a clinical trial.

   K. Incorrect: This statement refers only to the control group, not the entire trial.

9. Look for the signal word that shows a comparison. *(Lesson 8)*

   A. Incorrect: *Any* does not signal a comparison or contrast.

   B. Incorrect: *Must* signals an instruction.

   C. **Correct:** *Best* signals a comparison.

   D. Incorrect: *All* does not signal a comparison or contrast.

   E. Incorrect: *Also* does not signal a comparison or contrast.

10. Use the context of the workplace to define the word *benefits*. *(Lesson 9)*

    F. Incorrect: *Benefits* does not commonly mean "help" in the workplace.

    G. Incorrect: *Benefits* does not commonly mean "aid" in the workplace.

    H. **Correct:** *Benefits* refers to "payments" received for work.

    J. Incorrect: *Benefits* does not commonly mean "kind deeds" in the workplace.

    K. Incorrect: *Benefits* does not commonly mean "events to raise money" in the workplace.

11. Use the content to decide what the term *compensation* is referring to. *(Lesson 9)*

    A. **Correct:** *Compensation* refers to salary, insurance, and other benefits.

    B. Incorrect: *Compensation* does not refer to reimbursement for injuries.

    C. Incorrect: *Compensation* does not refer to medical coverage alone.

    D. Incorrect: *Compensation* does not refer to basic life insurance alone.

    E. Incorrect: *Compensation* does not refer to family insurance coverage.

12. Determine the correct definition of *schedule* in this scenario. *(Lesson 9)*

   F. Incorrect: *Schedule* does not mean "to register" in this passage.

   G. Incorrect: *Schedule* does not mean "to list" in this passage.

   H. **Correct:** In this scenario *schedule* means "to plan for a certain time."

   J. Incorrect: *Schedule* does not mean "to enroll" in this passage.

   K. Incorrect: *Schedule* does not mean "to create a timetable" in this passage.

13. Identify the information that is actually stated in the e-mail. *(Lesson 10)*

   A. Incorrect: This is not actually stated.

   B. **Correct:** The e-mail clearly states construction will be complete August 15.

   C. Incorrect: This statement is implied but not stated.

   D. Incorrect: This is not stated anywhere in the e-mail.

   E. Incorrect: The e-mail does not say what parts of the bathrooms are not yet done.

14. Use the stated information to give you clues about what is left unstated. *(Lesson 10)*

   F. Incorrect: This is stated information.

   G. Incorrect: This is stated in the e-mail.

   H. **Correct:** The e-mail does not directly state that there will be no permanent power before August 30.

   J. Incorrect: This information is stated in the e-mail.

   K. Incorrect: This information is stated in the e-mail.

15. Draw conclusions that are not specifically stated, based on information in the e-mail. *(Lesson 10)*

   A. Incorrect: This is stated in the e-mail.

   B. **Correct:** You can infer that staff should not enter the building before August 15.

   C. Incorrect: The construction crew will not sign off on the project until August 30.

   D. Incorrect: There is no indication that the bathrooms are the most difficult part of construction.

   E. Incorrect: This is a statement from the e-mail.

Answer Key ■ ■ ■

Applied Mathematics

Level 1

Lesson 1 (pp. 98–103)
Skill Practice:

   1. A   2. J   3. A   4. J

On Your Own:

   1. C   3. A   5. C   7. D   9. E
   2. G   4. F   6. H   8. J   10. J

Lesson 2 (pp. 104–109)
Skill Practice:

   1. B   2. H   3. B   4. H

On Your Own:

   1. C   3. D   5. B   7. A   9. A
   2. G   4. K   6. F   8. K   10. H

Lesson 3 (pp. 110–115)
Skill Practice:

   1. B   2. H   3. A   4. G

On Your Own:

   1. C   3. C   5. E   7. A   9. D
   2. G   4. F   6. F   8. F   10. G

Lesson 4 (pp. 116–121)
Skill Practice:

   1. E   2. G   3. D   4. G

On Your Own:

   1. B   3. E   5. E   7. C   9. B
   2. G   4. H   6. K   8. G   10. K

Lesson 5 (pp. 122–127)
Skill Practice:

   1. C   2. K   3. E   4. J

On Your Own:

   1. A   3. B   5. D   7. B   9. C
   2. G   4. F   6. J   8. G   10. J

Level 1 Performance Assessment (pp. 128–131)
1. Round 27 to the nearest ten. *(Lesson 1)*

   A. Incorrect: 10 is too low.

   B. Incorrect: 25 is not rounded to the nearest ten.

   C. **Correct:** 27 to the nearest ten is 30.

   D. Incorrect: 40 is too high.

   E. Incorrect: 100 is too high.

2. Put the weights in order from least to greatest. *(Lesson 1)*

 F. Incorrect: 165 is greater than 146.

 G. **Correct:** 78 is the least, and 165 is the greatest.

 H. Incorrect: 146 is not the least.

 J. Incorrect: 146 is not the least.

 K. Incorrect: 165 is not the least.

3. Round 183 to the nearest hundred. *(Lesson 1)*

 A. Incorrect: 100 is too low.

 B. Incorrect: 150 is not rounded to the nearest hundred.

 C. Incorrect: 180 is rounded to the nearest ten.

 D. Incorrect: 190 is not rounded to the nearest hundred.

 E. **Correct:** 183 rounds up. 200 is the nearest hundred.

4. Determine the largest monthly expense. *(Lesson 1)*

 F. Incorrect: $99 is the lowest expense.

 G. Incorrect: $245 is $305 less than $550.

 H. Incorrect: $450 is $100 less than $550.

 J. Incorrect: $534 is $16 less than $550.

 K. **Correct:** $550 is the largest expense.

5. Add the number of tables to find the total. *(Lesson 2)*

 A. Incorrect: Subtracted 7 from 12 instead of added.

 B. Incorrect: 7 is one of the addends, not the sum.

 C. Incorrect: 12 is one of the addends, not the sum.

 D. Incorrect: Added incorrectly. $7 + 12 \neq 18$.

 E. **Correct:** $7 + 12 = 19$.

6. Add the number of miles to find the total. *(Lesson 2)*

 F. Incorrect: Added the ones column incorrectly.

 G. Incorrect: Added the ones column incorrectly.

 H. **Correct:** $53 + 65 = 118$.

 J. Incorrect: Added the tens column incorrectly.

 K. Incorrect: Added the tens column incorrectly.

7. Add the number of shirts to find the total. *(Lesson 2)*

 A. Incorrect: Forgot to regroup the 1.

 B. Incorrect: Added the ones incorrectly.

 C. Incorrect: Added the ones incorrectly.

 D. **Correct:** $12 + 14 + 7 = 33$.

 E. Incorrect: Regrouped 2 instead of 1.

8. Add the number of computers to find the total. *(Lesson 2)*

 F. Incorrect: Added the ones column incorrectly.

 G. **Correct:** $11 + 2 + 5 = 18$.

 H. Incorrect: Added the ones column incorrectly.

 J. Incorrect: Added the ones column incorrectly and regrouped unnecessarily.

 K. Incorrect: Regrouped when not needed.

9. Subtract the number of shingles used from the total in the bundle. *(Lesson 3)*

 A. Incorrect: Subtracted the ones column incorrectly.

 B. **Correct:** $100 - 65 = 35$.

 C. Incorrect: Subtracted the tens and ones columns incorrectly.

 D. Incorrect: Forgot about carrying the 1 from the hundreds column.

 E. Incorrect: Added rather than subtracted.

10. Subtract the number of students who got As from the total number of students. *(Lesson 3)*

 F. Incorrect: Subtracted the ones column incorrectly.

 G. Incorrect: Subtracted the ones column incorrectly.

 H. **Correct:** $20 - 13 = 7$.

 J. Incorrect: Forgot about carrying the 1 from the tens place.

 K. Incorrect: Added instead of subtracted.

11. Subtract the number of bags of gravel inventoried this month from last month's inventory. *(Lesson 3)*

 A. Incorrect: Subtracted the tens column incorrectly.

 B. Incorrect: Subtracted the ones column incorrectly.

 C. **Correct:** $58 - 22 = 36$.

 D. Incorrect: Subtracted the ones column incorrectly.

 E. Incorrect: Added instead of subtracted.

12. Subtract the number of doughnuts sold from the number you started with. *(Lesson 3)*

 F. Incorrect: Carried from the thousands place unnecessarily.

 G. **Correct:** $2,800 - 1,600 = 1,200$.

 H. Incorrect: Subtracted the hundreds column incorrectly.

 J. Incorrect: 1,600 is the number being subtracted, not the answer.

 K. Incorrect: Subtracted the hundreds column incorrectly.

13. Subtract the cost of the sandwich from $10. *(Lesson 4)*

    A. Incorrect: This is $1 too little.

    B. Incorrect: This is 86 cents too little.

    C. Incorrect: This is 1 cent too little.

    D. Correct: $10 − $4.19 = $5.81.

    E. Incorrect: Added rather than subtracted.

14. Add the two image sizes together. *(Lesson 4)*

    F. Incorrect: Did not regroup 1 to the ones column.

    G. Incorrect: Added the tenths column incorrectly.

    H. Correct: 2.6 + 4.5 = 7.1.

    J. Incorrect: Added the tenths column incorrectly.

    K. Incorrect: Added the ones column incorrectly.

15. Subtract the price of the parking ticket from $50. *(Lesson 4)*

    A. Incorrect: Subtracted the tens column incorrectly.

    B. Incorrect: Subtracted the tenths and hundredths columns incorrectly.

    C. Correct: $50 − $32.50 = $17.50.

    D. Incorrect: Subtracted the ones column incorrectly.

    E. Incorrect: Did not regroup 1 to the ones column.

16. Subtract the amount of dye from the total size of the bottle. *(Lesson 4)*

    F. Incorrect: Subtracted the tenths column incorrectly.

    G. Incorrect: Subtracted the tenths column incorrectly.

    H. Incorrect: Subtracted the hundredths column incorrectly.

    J. Correct: 2.5 − 1.25 = 1.25.

    K. Incorrect: Subtracted the ones column incorrectly.

17. Look at the numbers the hour and minute hands are pointing to. *(Lesson 5)*

    A. Incorrect. 2:10 is when both the hour and minute hands are on the 2.

    B. Incorrect: 2:20 is when the hour hand is on the 2 and the minute hand is on the 4.

    C. Incorrect: 2:40 is when the hour hand is on the 2 and the minute hand is on the 8.

    D. Correct: 4:10. The hour hand is on the 4 and the minute hand is on the 2.

    E. Incorrect: 4:40 is when the hour hand is on the 4 and the minute hand is on the 8.

18. Read the digits on the digital clock. *(Lesson 5)*

    F. Incorrect: 3:34 is not the number shown on the clock.

    G. Incorrect: 3:44 is not the number shown on the clock.

    H. Incorrect: 4:34 is not the number shown on the clock.

    J. Correct: 4:43 is the number shown on the clock.

    K. Incorrect: 4:44 is not the number shown on the clock.

19. Read the dates and corresponding days on the monthly calendar to find February 3. *(Lesson 5)*

    A. Incorrect: February 2, 9, 16, and 23 are Mondays.

    B. Correct: February 3 is a Tuesday.

    C. Incorrect: February 4, 11, 18, and 25 are Wednesdays.

    D. Incorrect: February 5, 12, 19, and 26 are Thursdays.

    E. Incorrect: February 6, 13, 20, and 27 are Fridays.

20. Look for the column marked Tuesday and count down the rows. *(Lesson 5)*

    F. Incorrect: 8:00 a.m. is the first time slot.

    G. Correct: 9:00 a.m. is the second time slot.

    H. Incorrect: 10:00 a.m. is the third time slot.

    J. Incorrect: 11:00 a.m. is the fourth time slot.

    K. Incorrect: 12:00 p.m. is the fifth time slot.

Applied Mathematics

Level 2

Lesson 6 (pp. 132–137)
Skill Practice:

1. C	2. K	3. D	4. H

On Your Own:

1. D	3. A	5. B	7. E	9. A
2. H	4. K	6. J	8. G	10. G

Lesson 7 (pp. 138–143)
Skill Practice:

1. B	2. H	3. C	4. K

On Your Own:

1. B	3. C	5. A	7. D	9. B
2. H	4. J	6. J	8. K	10. J

Lesson 8 (pp. 144–149)
Skill Practice:

1. D   2. J   3. A   4. G

On Your Own:

1. E   3. B   5. C   7. C   9. E
2. H   4. H   6. H   8. K   10. G

Lesson 9 (pp. 150–155)
Skill Practice:

1. C   2. J   3. B   4. J

On Your Own:

1. D   3. E   5. A   7. A   9. C
2. G   4. H   6. G   8. K   10. J

Lesson 10 (pp. 156–161)
Skill Practice:

1. E   2. F   3. C   4. H

On Your Own:

1. B   3. C   5. B   7. A   9. E
2. K   4. J   6. H   8. H   10. G

Level 2 Performance Assessment (pp. 162–165)

1. Multiply the number of vaccinations a day by the number of days worked. *(Lesson 6)*

   A. Incorrect: Subtracted instead of multiplied.

   B. Incorrect: Added instead of multiplied.

   C. Incorrect: Incorrectly multiplied the tens column.

   D. Incorrect: Incorrectly multiplied the ones column.

   E. **Correct:** 23 × 3 = 69. In the ones column, 3 × 3 is 9. In the tens column, 2 × 3 is 6.

2. Multiply the number of tables by the number of seats at each table. *(Lesson 6)*

   F. Incorrect: Added instead of multiplied.

   G. Incorrect: Multiplied 7 × 3 instead of 7 × 4.

   H. Incorrect: Multiplied 6 × 4 instead of 7 × 4.

   J. **Correct:** 7 × 4 = 28. 4 groups of 7 is 28.

   K. Incorrect: Multiplied 8 × 4 instead of 7 × 4.

3. Multiply the number of traffic tickets by the number of weeks in the month. *(Lesson 6)*

   A. Incorrect: 15 is a factor.

   B. Incorrect: Forgot to multiply the tens column.

   C. Incorrect: Multiplied 15 × 3 instead of 15 × 4.

   D. Incorrect: Incorrectly regrouped in the tens column.

   E. **Correct:** 15 × 4 = 60. 4 groups of 15 is 60.

4. Multiply the number of hours in a shift by the number of shifts worked. *(Lesson 6)*

   F. Incorrect: Added instead of multiplied.

   G. Incorrect: Multiplied 12 × 7 instead of 12 × 16.

   H. Incorrect: Multiplied 12 × 15 instead of 12 × 16.

   J. **Correct:** 12 × 16 = 192. 16 groups of 12 is 192.

   K. Incorrect: Multiplied 12 × 17 instead of 12 × 16.

5. Divide the number of pallets by the number of shelves. *(Lesson 7)*

   A. Incorrect: 5 is the divisor.

   B. Incorrect: Divided incorrectly. 45 ÷ 5 ≠ 8.

   C. **Correct:** 45 ÷ 5 = 9. 45 split into 5 groups is 9 in each group.

   D. Incorrect: Subtracted instead of divided.

   E. Incorrect: Added instead of subtracted.

6. Divide the number of needles by the number of clients. *(Lesson 7)*

   F. **Correct:** 100 ÷ 10 = 10. 100 split into 10 groups is 10 in each group.

   G. Incorrect: Divided incorrectly. 100 ÷ 10 ≠ 50.

   H. Incorrect: Subtracted instead of divided.

   J. Incorrect: 100 is the dividend.

   K. Incorrect: Added instead of divided.

7. Divide the number of crackers by the number of children. *(Lesson 7)*

   A. Incorrect: Divided incorrectly. 35 ÷ 7 ≠ 4.

   B. **Correct:** 35 ÷ 7 = 5. 35 split into 7 groups is 5 in each group.

   C. Incorrect: 7 is the divisor.

   D. Incorrect: Subtracted instead of divided.

   E. Incorrect: 35 is the dividend.

8. Divide the number of pencils by the number of students. Find the remainder. *(Lesson 7)*

   F. **Correct:** 144 ÷ 5 = 28 R4. The remainder is 4.

   G. Incorrect: 5 is the divisor.

   H. Incorrect: The remainder cannot be larger than the divisor.

   J. Incorrect: This is the quotient.

   K. Incorrect: 144 is the dividend.

9. Choose the unit of measurement that goes with small lengths. *(Lesson 8)*

   A. Incorrect: Miles measure long distances.

   B. Incorrect: Ounces measure volume or weight.

   C. Incorrect: Gallons measure volume.

   D. Incorrect: Pounds measure weight.

   E. **Correct:** Inches measure small lengths.

10. Choose the unit of measurement that goes with volume. *(Lesson 8)*

    F. Incorrect: Inches measure small lengths or distance.

    G. Incorrect: Pounds measure weight.

    H. **Correct:** Fluid ounces measure volume.

    J. Incorrect: Degrees measure temperature.

    K. Incorrect: Feet measure medium lengths.

11. Find the correct number of degrees measured on the thermometer. *(Lesson 8)*

    A. Incorrect: The thermometer measures higher than 89°F.

    B. Incorrect: The thermometer measures higher than 90°F.

    C. Incorrect: The thermometer measures higher than 95°F.

    D. **Correct:** The thermometer measures 100°F.

    E. Incorrect: The thermometer measures lower than 105°F.

12. Find the correct number of pounds measured on the scale. *(Lesson 8)*

    F. Incorrect: The weight shown is greater than 20 pounds.

    G. Incorrect: The weight shown is greater than 35 pounds.

    H. **Correct:** The weight shown is 40 pounds.

    J. Incorrect: The weight shown is less than 45 pounds.

    K. Incorrect: The weight shown is less than 50 pounds.

13. Find a fraction showing the parts sold as the numerator and the total amount of apples as the denominator. *(Lesson 9)*

    A. **Correct:** 5 out of 11 crates have sold: $\frac{5}{11}$.

    B. Incorrect: This fraction shows the amount of apples left.

    C. Incorrect: $\frac{5}{11}$ does not equal $\frac{1}{2}$.

    D. Incorrect: 5 is the numerator.

    E. Incorrect: 11 is the denominator.

14. Find the fraction equal in value to $\frac{9}{12}$ *(Lesson 9)*

    F. Incorrect: $\frac{1}{4}$ is equal in value to $\frac{3}{12}$.

    G. Incorrect: $\frac{1}{3}$ is equal in value to $\frac{4}{12}$.

    H. Incorrect: $\frac{1}{2}$ is equal in value to $\frac{6}{12}$.

    J. **Correct:** $\frac{3}{4}$ is equal in value to $\frac{9}{12}$. Divide both the numerator and the denominator by 3.

    K. Incorrect: $\frac{5}{6}$ is equal in value to $\frac{10}{12}$.

15. Find the fraction showing the number of slices left as the numerator and the total number of slices as the denominator. *(Lesson 9)*

    A. **Correct:** 3 out of 8 slices remain: $\frac{3}{8}$.

    B. Incorrect: This fraction shows the number of slices sold.

    C. Incorrect: $\frac{1}{2}$ is $\frac{4}{8}$. More than 4 slices have sold.

    D. Incorrect: 8 is the denominator.

    E. Incorrect: 8 is the denominator.

16. Find the fraction equal in value to $\frac{2}{3}$. *(Lesson 9)*

    F. Incorrect: $\frac{1}{2}$ is lower in value than $\frac{2}{3}$.

    G. Incorrect: $\frac{3}{5}$ is lower in value than $\frac{2}{3}$.

    H. **Correct:** $\frac{6}{9}$ is equal in value to $\frac{2}{3}$. Multiply both the numerator and denominator by 3.

    J. Incorrect: $\frac{8}{10}$ is equal in value to $\frac{4}{5}$.

    K. Incorrect: $\frac{10}{12}$ is equal in value to $\frac{5}{6}$.

17. Choose the correct operation to split a number into equal groups. *(Lesson 10)*

    A. Incorrect. Addition is used to find the total.

    B. Incorrect: Subtraction is used to find the difference.

    C. Incorrect: Multiplication is used to find the total of multiple groups of the same size.

    D. **Correct:** Division is the correct operation to split 1,050 into equal groups.

    E. Incorrect: Rounding is used to estimate.

18. Choose the correct expression to find the difference between the higher amount and the lesser amount. *(Lesson 10)*

    F. Incorrect. Addition is used to find the total.

    G. **Correct:** Subtract $4.50 from $5 to find the correct change.

    H. Incorrect: Multiplication finds the total of multiple groups of $5.

    J. Incorrect: Division splits $5 into equal groups.

    K. Incorrect: Subtract the lesser amount from the higher amount, not the other way around.

19. Choose the correct operation to find the total of multiple groups of the same size. *(Lesson 10)*

   A. Incorrect. Addition finds the total of different numbers.

   B. Incorrect: Subtraction is used to find the difference between numbers.

   C. **Correct:** Multiplying 45×6 shows the total amount of time spent on the phone.

   D. Incorrect: Division splits a number into equal groups.

   E. Incorrect: Comparing is used to compare number values.

20. Choose the correct expression to find the total. *(Lesson 10)*

   F. **Correct:** Add 216 and 6 to find the total.

   G. Incorrect: Subtraction finds the difference between two amounts.

   H. Incorrect: Multiplication finds the total of multiple groups.

   J. Incorrect: Division splits an amount into equal groups.

   K. Incorrect: Division splits an amount into equal groups.

Answer Key ■ ■ ■
Locating Information

Level 1

Lesson 1 (pp. 168–175)
Skill Practice:

1. B	2. F	3. B	4. F

On Your Own:

1. C	3. E	5. D	7. B	9. A
2. F	4. F	6. G	8. G	10. H

Lesson 2 (pp. 176–183)
Skill Practice:

1. D	2. G	3. E	4. H

On Your Own:

1. E	3. E	5. B	7. D	9. A
2. J	4. K	6. K	8. F	10. H

Lesson 3 (pp. 184–191)
Skill Practice:

1. C	2. J	3. D	4. F

On Your Own:

1. C	3. E	5. D	7. A	9. D
2. J	4. H	6. J	8. K	10. J

Lesson 4 (pp.192–199)
Skill Practice:

1. D	2. G	3. C	4. H

On Your Own:

1. A	3. A	5. D	7. A	9. C
2. J	4. F	6. G	8. H	10. F

Lesson 5 (pp. 200–207)
Skill Practice:

1. B	2. J	3. B	4. J

On Your Own:

1. E	3. D	5. C	7. B	9. E
2. J	4. J	6. G	8. F	10. G

Level 1 Performance Assessment (pp. 208–213)
1. Determine what the sign means. *(Lesson 1)*

   A. **Correct:** The sign shows a person washing his or her hands.

   B. Incorrect: The sign does not show the water being turned off.

   C. Incorrect: The sign does not indicate hot water.

   D. Incorrect: The sign shows a specific use for running water.

   E. Incorrect: The sign does not show water being turned on.

2. Determine what the traffic sign means. *(Lesson 1)*

    F. Incorrect: The sign does not show a right turn.

    G. Incorrect: The sign does not show an arrow pointing one way.

    H. **Correct:** The sign shows a 180 degree turn, or a U-turn, crossed out.

    J. Incorrect: The turn is crossed out to mean "not allowed."

    K. Incorrect: The sign does not include a red light.

3. Determine what the symbol means. *(Lesson 1)*

    A. **Correct:** The symbol indicates power. The button turns on the computer.

    B. Incorrect: The symbol is on the computer, not the printer.

    C. Incorrect: The symbol does not indicate turning up the volume.

    D. Incorrect: The symbol does not indicate turning down the volume.

    E. Incorrect: The symbol does not indicate opening the display menu.

4. Read the table title to determine the main idea of the whole table. *(Lesson 2)*

    F. Incorrect: Money spent on clothing is a detail in the table.

    G. Incorrect: Money spent on reading materials is a detail in the table.

    H. Incorrect: Money spent on small appliances is a detail in the table.

    J. Incorrect: Money spent by one specific age group is a detail in the table.

    K. **Correct:** The main idea of the table is how much different age groups spend on specific categories each year.

5. Use the column and row headings to find which category people under 25 spend the most money on. *(Lesson 2)*

    A. Incorrect: People under 25 spend only $49 on small appliances.

    B. **Correct:** People under 25 spend $1,351 on clothing.

    C. Incorrect: People under 25 spend only $380 on pets, toys, hobbies, and playground equipment.

    D. Incorrect: People under 25 spend only $83 on laundry and cleaning supplies.

    E. Incorrect: People under 25 spend only $48 on reading materials.

6. Use the column and row headings to find which country has the second highest population. *(Lesson 2)*

    F. Incorrect: China has the highest population.

    G. **Correct:** India has the second highest population.

    H. Incorrect: The United States has the third highest population.

    J. Incorrect: Indonesia has the fourth highest population.

    K. Incorrect: Brazil has the fifth highest population.

7. Find the polka dots in the map key and read what they symbolize. *(Lesson 3)*

    A. Incorrect: A snowflake indicates flurries.

    B. Incorrect: Diagonal lines indicate rain.

    C. Incorrect: Wavy vertical lines indicate showers.

    D. Incorrect: A line of half-circles indicates a warm front.

    E. **Correct:** Polka dots indicate snow.

8. Find State Road 200 on the map and look at which direction Missoula is from Lincoln. *(Lesson 3)*

    F. Incorrect: Missoula is to the left of Lincoln, so it could not be east.

    G. **Correct:** Missoula is west of Lincoln.

    H. Incorrect: Missoula is below Lincoln, so it could not be north.

    J. Incorrect: Missoula is below Lincoln, so it could not be northwest.

    K. Incorrect: Missoula is below and left of Lincoln, so it could not be southeast.

9. Find Helena on the map and find the road number that passes close by it. *(Lesson 3)*

    A. Incorrect: US Highway 10 is west of Helena.

    B. **Correct:** Interstate 15 passes through Helena.

    C. Incorrect: State Road 43 is southwest of Helena.

    D. Incorrect: State Road 83 is northwest of Helena.

    E. Incorrect: Interstate 90 is west of Helena.

10. Read the label on the horizontal *x*-axis at the bottom of the graph. *(Lesson 4)*

    F. Incorrect: Percent is the label on the *y*-axis.

    G. Incorrect: This is the title.

    H. Correct: The label on the horizontal *x*-axis is Foods.

    J. Incorrect: Hamburger is one unit on the *x*-axis.

    K. Incorrect: 60% is one unit on the *y*-axis.

11. Find the percent of fat in steak on the table. *(Lesson 4)*

    A. Incorrect: Tuna has 5% fat.

    B. Incorrect: Eggs have 12% fat.

    C. Incorrect: Lamb has 20% fat.

    D. Correct: Steak has 35% fat.

    E. Incorrect: Hamburger has 51% fat.

12. Compare the items on the graph to determine which one has the least amount of fat. *(Lesson 4)*

    F. Incorrect: Eggs are the second lowest in fat.

    G. Incorrect: Hamburger has the greatest amount of fat.

    H. Correct: Tuna has only 5% fat.

    J. Incorrect: Lamb has more fat than eggs and tuna.

    K. Incorrect: Steak has the second greatest amount of fat.

13. Look for the title at the top of the graph. *(Lesson 5)*

    A. Incorrect: Year is the *x*-axis label.

    B. Correct: The title of the graph is US Government Spending 1940–2010.

    C. Incorrect: Trillions of Dollars is the *y*-axis label.

    D. Incorrect: Spending is the line label.

    E. Incorrect: This is only part of the title.

14. Locate 1970 on the graph. Find the point where the *x*-axis and *y*-axis meet at 1970. *(Lesson 5)*

    F. Correct: According to the graph, government spending was $1 trillion in 1970.

    G. Incorrect: The *x*-axis and *y*-axis do not meet at $1.5 trillion in 1970.

    H. Incorrect: The *x*-axis and *y*-axis do not meet at $2 trillion in 1970.

    J. Incorrect: The *x*-axis and *y*-axis do not meet at $2.5 trillion in 1970.

    K. Incorrect: The *x*-axis and *y*-axis do not meet at $3 trillion in 1970.

15. Compare the points on the line graph to see where the biggest increase in spending occurred. *(Lesson 5)*

    A. Correct: There was about $1 trillion in increased spending between 1940 and 1945.

    B. Incorrect: There was less than $0.5 trillion in increased spending between 1955 and 1960.

    C. Incorrect: There was almost no increase in spending between 1970 and 1975.

    D. Incorrect: There was little increase in spending between 1980 and 1985.

    E. Incorrect: There was little increase in spending between 1995 and 2000.

Locating Information

Level 2

Lesson 6 (pp. 214–221)
Skill Practice:

1. A	2. G	3. D	4. K

On Your Own:

1. D	3. D	5. A	7. B	9. D
2. J	4. F	6. F	8. H	10. J

Lesson 7 (pp. 222–229)
Skill Practice:

1. A	2. H	3. C	4. J

On Your Own:

1. D	3. E	5. E	7. B	9. E
2. H	4. H	6. F	8. F	10. H

Lesson 8 (pp. 230–237)
Skill Practice:

1. A	2. K	3. E	4. K

On Your Own:

1. B	3. C	5. E	7. E	9. D
2. F	4. J	6. H	8. K	10. H

Lesson 9 (pp. 238–245)
Skill Practice:

1. E	2. F	3. B	4. H

On Your Own:

1. E	3. C	5. A	7. D	9. C
2. G	4. J	6. J	8. J	10. J

Lesson 10 (pp. 246–253)
Skill Practice:

1. E	2. F	3. C	4. J

On Your Own:

1. B	3. E	5. A	7. C	9. E
2. J	4. J	6. K	8. H	10. H

Level 2 Performance Assessment (pp. 254–259)

1. Determine the common information in the segments of the circle. *(Lesson 6)*

    A. Incorrect: The segments do not show the size of the adult population.

    B. **Correct:** Each segment shows a marital status percentage.

    C. Incorrect: Only one segment shows the married percentage.

    D. Incorrect: Only one segment shows the separated percentage.

    E. Incorrect: Only one segment shows the divorced percentage.

2. Find the segment showing the percentage of divorced adults. *(Lesson 6)*

    F. Incorrect: This percentage is for separated adults.

    G. **Correct:** According to the graph, the segment of divorced people is 8%.

    H. Incorrect: This percentage is for single people.

    J. Incorrect: This percentage is for widowed people.

    K. Incorrect: This percentage is for married people.

3. Compare the percents of each segment to find the greatest. *(Lesson 6)*

    A. Incorrect: The percent of divorced adults is only 8%.

    B. Incorrect: The percent of widowed adults is only 13%.

    C. Incorrect: The percent of separated adults is only 4%.

    D. **Correct:** The percent of married adults is 63%.

    E. Incorrect: The percent of single adults is only 12%.

4. Read the chronological order in the time line to see which event happened last. *(Lesson 7)*

    F. Incorrect: The election of Lincoln happened first, in 1860.

    G. Incorrect: The Confederate States were formed early in the war, in 1861.

    H. Incorrect: Secession happened before the war, in 1860.

    J. **Correct:** The 13th Amendment was approved toward the end of the war, in 1865.

    K. Incorrect: Sherman's March to the Sea ended before the 13th Amendment was approved, in 1864.

5. Read the flowchart to see which step comes after checking the items in the sequence. *(Lesson 7)*

    A. Incorrect: Getting the items for the order is first in the sequence.

    B. **Correct:** Protect and pack the order once it has been checked.

    C. Incorrect: The order needs to be packed before it is labeled.

    D. Incorrect: The order needs to be logged before it can be shipped.

    E. Incorrect: The order needs to be addressed before it can be logged.

6. Find Clay on the schedule and read what time his shift begins. *(Lesson 7)*

    F. Incorrect: Clay is not scheduled for 4–5 p.m.

    G. Incorrect: Clay is not scheduled for 5–6 p.m.

    H. **Correct:** The first hour Clay is scheduled for is 6–7 p.m.

    J. Incorrect: Clay should already be at work at 7 p.m.

    K. Incorrect: Clay should already be at work at 8 p.m.

7. Find the word *protein* on the label and read how many grams of protein the cereal contains. *(Lesson 8)*

    A. Incorrect: The cereal contains 0 grams of trans fat, not protein.

    B. Incorrect: The cereal contains 0.1 grams of saturated fat, not protein.

    C. **Correct:** The cereal contains 1 gram of protein.

    D. Incorrect: The cereal contains 2 grams of sugars, not protein.

    E. Incorrect: The cereal contains 25 grams of carbohydrates, not protein.

8. Read the list of annual percentage rates to find out what the rate will be for a balance transfer of $3,500. *(Lesson 8)*

    F. Incorrect: Balance transfers of $4,000 or more get this rate.

    G. **Correct:** Balance transfers of $3,500 or less get this rate.

    H. Incorrect: This rate is for new purchases.

    J. Incorrect: This rate is for cash advances.

    K. Incorrect: This rate is for when you miss a payment.

9. Read the contact information in the ad to see how to apply for the job. *(Lesson 8)*

   A. Incorrect: The ad asks for no phone calls.

   B. Incorrect: The ad asks for no in-person visits or phone calls.

   C. Incorrect: The ad asks for no in-person visits.

   D. Incorrect: The ad asks for no phone calls.

   E. **Correct:** The ad asks for an e-mail or mailed résumé.

10. Read the signature required at the bottom of the form. *(Lesson 9)*

   F. Incorrect: The child should not sign the form.

   G. **Correct:** The child's parent should sign the form.

   H. Incorrect: Contact #1 is just an emergency contact person.

   J. Incorrect: Contact #2 is just an emergency contact person.

   K. Incorrect: The child's doctor does not have to sign the form.

11. Read the line numbers in the Medical Information section to find which one corresponds with allergies. *(Lesson 9)*

   A. Incorrect: Line 8 is the child's doctor information.

   B. Incorrect: Line 9 is information about vaccinations.

   C. **Correct:** Line 10 is where allergies would be listed.

   D. Incorrect: Line 11 lists illnesses, medications, or other conditions.

   E. Incorrect: Line 12 is for any additional information about the child.

12. Read the instructions in Line 9 about attaching a document. *(Lesson 9)*

   F. Incorrect: Contact information is on the form, not attached.

   G. **Correct:** A vaccination record should be attached to the form.

   H. Incorrect: Parent signature is on the form, not attached.

   J. Incorrect: Medical history is not required to be attached.

   K. Incorrect: Doctor information is on the form, not attached.

13. Look at the Quantity column. Find the Apple row and read the number. *(Lesson 10)*

   A. Incorrect: She ordered 1 cherry pie.

   B. Incorrect: She ordered 2 sweet potato pies.

   C. **Correct:** She ordered 3 apple pies.

   D. Incorrect: She ordered 5 pecan pies.

   E. Incorrect: She ordered 6 pumpkin pies.

14. Find the space in the order form right below the total prices for each kind of pie. *(Lesson 10)*

   F. Incorrect: Quantity tells you how many pies are ordered.

   G. Incorrect: Payment information tells you if the order has been paid for.

   H. Incorrect: You put the tax amount in 8% Sales Tax.

   J. Incorrect: Total includes the prices of the pies and tax.

   K. **Correct:** You put the total for the pies before tax in subtotal.

15. Look for the space on the form where a date goes. *(Lesson 10)*

   A. **Correct:** Date Ordered tells you when an order was placed.

   B. Incorrect: Quantity tells you how many pies are ordered.

   C. Incorrect: Name tells you the name of the person ordering.

   D. Incorrect: Phone Number tells you the contact information for the order.

   E. Incorrect: Payment information tells you if the order has been paid for.

Glossary ■ ■ ■

A

abbreviation a shortened form of a word (20)

acronym an abbreviation made from the first letters of several words (20)

addends the numbers that are added (104)

addition combining two or more numbers (104)

advertisement a notice or announcement that promotes a product, service, or event (230)

analog clock a clock that shows time using hands (122)

antonym a word that has the opposite meaning of another word (20)

B

bar graph a graph that uses bars to show information (192)

borrowing taking an amount from another column of a problem; also called *regrouping* (110)

C

calculator a device for solving mathematical problems (157)

cause an action or event that brings about another action or event (58)

circle graph a circle-shaped graph that shows an entire quantity divided into segments (214)

column a vertical section of a chart or table (176)

common workplace words words that are often used in the workplace (74)

comparative adjective a word that contrasts two nouns or pronouns (67)

compare to identify how two or more things are the same (66)

comparison clue a context clue in which a new word is compared to another word or phrase you are probably familiar with (51)

compass rose an item on a map that shows north, south, east, and west (184)

conclusion an idea based on more than one observation or fact combined with common knowledge (83)

context surrounding words or sentences that help you understand the meaning of a new word (28)

context clue surrounding words or sentences that help you guess a word's meaning (28)

contrast to identify how two or more things are different (66)

D

decimal a number with a decimal point (116)

decimal point a small dot (like a period) that separates the whole number from an amount less than 1 (116)

denominator the number on the bottom of a fraction (150)

detail individual fact or feature that supports the main idea of a passage (12)

diagram a drawing that represents information (222)

difference the answer to a subtraction problem (110)

digit any of the Arabic numerals 1–9 and 0 (98)

digital clock a clock that shows time using digits (122)

distance a measure of how far it is between two things or places (144)

dividend the number being divided (138)

divisor the number that divides into the dividend (138)

dollar sign a symbol that represents a dollar amount (116)

E

effect an action or event that happens as a result of a cause (58)

equation a mathematical expression showing two equal quantities (156)

equivalent fractions two or more fractions that represent equal parts of a whole (151)

F

factor a number being multiplied (132)

floor plan a diagram that shows the layout of a room or a building (185)

flowchart a diagram showing a sequence of actions (223)

form a document that asks for information to be filled in (238)

fraction a part of a whole (150)

G

graph a picture display of information (192)

grid a network of lines that cross each other at right angles (201)

H

hour hand the shorter hand on an analog clock (122)

I

inference a guess based on what you read and what you already know (82)

invoice a form that businesses use to bill for goods and services (246)

J

job application a form used to apply for a job (238)

K

key a graphic that shows what segments of a graph represent (214)

L

label a marker that explains what numbers and words represent (200)

length a measure of how long something is (144)

line graph a graph that uses points and lines to represent information (200)

M

main idea the most important idea in a passage or document (4)

map key an item that shows what the symbols on a map mean (184)

minute hand the longer hand on an analog clock (122)

multiple-meaning word a word that has more than one meaning (50)

multiply to perform repeated addition (132)

N

numerator the top number in a fraction (150)

O

order form a form used by consumers and businesses to order goods and services (247)

P

place value a system in which the value of a digit depends on its place in the number (98)

prior knowledge information you already know (82)

product the answer to a multiplication problem (132)

Q

quotient the answer to a division problem (138)

R

regrouping moving a number to another column of a problem; also called *borrowing* or *carrying* (105)

remainder any part left over from a division problem (138)

road map a map that shows roads and highways in a given area (185)

round to make an estimate, ending in zeroes, that is close to an original value (99)

row a horizontal section of a table or a chart (176)

S

scale a diagram that shows distances on the map (184)

schedule a diagram that shows when events occur (223)

segment a section of a circle graph (214)

sequence the order in which things happen; also called *time order* (36)

signal word a word that helps you recognize the connection between cause and effect (58)

street map a map that shows the streets in a city or district (185)

subtract to take one number away from another (110)

sum the total in an addition problem (104)

superlative adjective a word that contrasts three or more nouns or pronouns (67)

supporting evidence details such as statistics, facts, examples, or reasons that support a main idea (13)

symbol something that stands for something else (168)

synonym a word that has the same meaning as another word (20)

T

temperature a measure of how hot or cold something is (144)

time line a diagram that shows information over time (222)

time order the order in which things happen; also called *sequence* (36)

title a heading that describes a document or graphic (176)

topic sentence a sentence that states the main idea of a passage or document (4)

total the entire amount of something (156)

traffic sign a sign that is posted on roads and gives important information (169)

trend a pattern of information (201)

V

volume a measure of how much space something takes up (145)

W

want ad a brief notice that promotes a job opportunity (231)

weight a measure of how heavy something is (145)

whole number a number that 1 divides into with no remainder (98)

workplace sign a sign that is used in the workplace to communicate information (168)

X

x-axis the horizontal line that runs across a graph from left to right (192)

Y

y-axis the vertical line that runs up and down on a graph (192)